Adult
Programs
in the
Library

ALA Editions purchases fund advocacy, awareness, and accreditation programs for library professionals worldwide.

Adult
Programs
in the
Library

SECOND EDITION

Brett W. Lear

ala
editions

An imprint of the American Library Association
Chicago   2013

Brett W. Lear is director of the Martin County Library System in Florida. From 2008 to 2011 he served as the reference, adult services, and programming coordinator for Multnomah County Library (MCL) in Oregon. While at MCL he worked with a team that planned, scheduled, coordinated, and produced more than 2,500 family and adult programs and special events each year. He worked as a library manager with the Jefferson County Public Library in Colorado from 1996 to 2008, where he chaired the Program Steering Committee several times over the years. He has been actively involved in adult programming since accepting his first professional position with the New York Public Library in 1992. From 1995 through 1999 he served on the Reference and User Services Association's (RUSA) Services to Adults Committee. This committee presented a program titled "Adult Programming: When You Have to Do It Yourself" at the 1996 American Library Association (ALA) Annual Conference. While serving on the Services to Adults Committee, he participated in the writing of the RUSA publication *Adult Programming: A Manual for Libraries*. He was a panelist on the program "What Have You Done for Me Lately? Adult Programming in Public Libraries" at the 2002 Public Library Association Conference. He has presented programming workshops in Colorado, Kansas, Iowa, and Florida.

Printed in the United States of America
17 16 15 14 13   5 4 3 2 1

Extensive effort has gone into ensuring the reliability of the information in this book; however, the publisher makes no warranty, express or implied, with respect to the material contained herein.

ISBNs: 978-0-8389-1140-2 (paper); 978-0-8389-9649-2 (PDF). For more information on digital formats, visit the ALA Store at alastore.ala.org and select eEditions.

Library of Congress Cataloging-in-Publication Data
Lear, Brett W.
   Adult programs in the library / Brett W. Lear. — 2nd ed.
     p. cm.
   Includes bibliographical references and index.
   ISBN 978-0-8389-1140-2 (alk. paper)
   1. Adult services in public libraries—United States. 2. Libraries—Cultural programs—United States.
3. Libraries and community—United States. I. Title.
   Z711.92.A32L43 2012
   027.6'2—dc23
                            2012019783

Cover design by Karen Sheets de Gracia. Cover image © hellbilly/Shutterstock, Inc.
Text design in Fanwood and Gotham by Casey Bayer.

♾ This paper meets the requirements of ANSI/NISO Z39.48-1992 (Permanence of Paper).

Still for Grandpa, and for Schreiber, too

Contents

WEB   Additional materials are available online at www.alaeditions.org/webextras.

Preface

I wrote the first edition of this book in 2001, and it went to press in 2002. The World Wide Web was only a little over ten years old. Graphical web browsers had been around for just six years or so. We were only beginning to speak of the forthcoming wave of retiring boomers. Libraries were getting serious about providing a "sense of place" for their patrons. A Starbucks was opening on every corner, and we were becoming more familiar with terms such as *third place* as we observed that the residents in our communities were looking for that special place that was neither work nor home. And we developed programming that introduced our patrons to eBay, helped our boomers transition to empty nesters, and provided a comfortable place to learn something new or experience something beautiful through a workshop or live performance.

In 2013 many libraries are serving more patrons through their websites than they are through the doors of their physical buildings. Our patrons use the Internet to shop, communicate, collaborate, work, and learn. Many boomers are looking for opportunities to become even more engaged with their communities. We have experienced some hard economic times of late, and libraries and other community organizations have turned to each other seeking partnerships.

Libraries have always been exceptional at doing more with less. The recent tough economic times have affected our patrons and our library budgets. Many of us have developed programs to help our patrons make smart choices during these tough times while simultaneously watching our programming budgets shrink due to budget cuts. We have seen our endowments dwindle to nearly nothing. So it's no surprise that when I asked my peers what they would like to see in a revised edition of this book, they told me to show steps that libraries can take to ensure that their programming aligns well with their mission and priorities. They asked for tips on how to say no to potential performers who want to partner with us, but either charge too much or offer something that doesn't fit within our priorities or possess a talent that just won't draw the crowds to fill the room (either physical or virtual). Library staff told me that they wanted tips for evaluating programs and that these evaluations should be outcome-based and measure whether the attendee learned something new or felt more connected to her community because of the program. I've addressed these requests in the chapters that follow.

The technology now exists to help us with the planning, promoting, producing, and evaluating of our programs. This edition has a new chapter dedicated to technology. I've also added or expanded sections that reflect the issues that libraries are facing today: the need for our patrons to feel engaged with their communities and the programming that we can offer to foster this civic engagement; the desire our patrons have to volunteer their time to help us, and our need to take them up on that offer; the creativity and exceptional programs that can come out of partnerships; the niche populations that we want to serve if only we could hit on the right topic, served up in the right format, hosted in the right venue at the right time . . .

Technology, trends, library services, and our patrons have all changed in the last ten years. And yet many things have endured. People still look for opportunities to learn, share, listen, collaborate, and have fun. Whether online or in person, library programs offer these opportunities to our patrons. I wrote much of this revision while working for Multnomah County Library (MCL). (I worked for MCL from 2008 to 2011—hence all the MCL examples contained within this book!) MCL's mission is to "enrich lives by fostering diverse opportunities for all people

to read, learn and connect." By providing information and recreational programs on a variety of topics, libraries play a key role in creating a place where our patrons gather to connect socially and intellectually with others. And that's pretty cool.

Libraries are not just for reading in, but for sociable thinking, exploring, exchanging ideas and falling in love. They were never silent. Technology will not change that, for even in the starchiest heyday of Victorian self-improvement, libraries were intended to be meeting places of the mind, recreational as well as educational.

—Ben Macintyre, "Paradise Is
Paper, Vellum, and Dust"[1]

P.S.

Something that I quickly discovered as I wrote this book was that many of the resources I consulted are no longer in print. I imagine this is because few books that cover library services make the *New York Times* best-sellers list. Unless these books get updated and republished in a revised edition, they tend to go out of print. However, libraries throughout the United States do have these titles in their collections. These libraries were kind enough to allow me to borrow many of these titles via interlibrary loan. I promise you that I looked through a copy of each of the books cited in the Resource Directory.

NOTE

1. Ben Macintyre, "Paradise Is Paper, Vellum, and Dust." *Times Online*, December 18, 2004.

Acknowledgments

Many people helped me during the year that I wrote the first edition of this book. I want to thank all those people once again. I turned to my peers this time too, and I asked for their insights and ideas many, many times during the eighteen months that I spent working on this new edition. Thanks to Amber Fisher, Larry Domingues, and Cindy Phillips of Jefferson County Public Library (CO); Linda Mulford of Arlington Heights Memorial Library (IL); Amita Lonial of Skokie Public Library (IL); Bobbie Wrinkle of McCracken County Public Library (KY); Liz Goodrich of Deschutes Public Library (OR); Laura Raphael of Tulsa City-County Library (OK); Liz Dannenbaum of Middleton Public Library (WI); Cari Dubiel of Twinsburg Public Library (OH); Rachel Smith of St. Louis Public Library (MO); Jennifer Baker of St. Helena Public Library (CA); Uma Hiremath and Madeline Miele Holt of Ames Free Library (MA); Lori M. Crowe of Norfolk Public Library (VA); Mary Hurlbert Stein of East Baton Rouge Parish Library (LA); Rosalind Kutler of Redwood City Public Library (CA); Deborah Dowley Preiser of Oak Park Public Library (IL); Laurel Shelley-Reuss of Laramie County Library System (WY); Leslie Burke of Northwest Reno Library (NV); Kris Chipps of Arapahoe Library District (CO); Carol Ann Carter of Lake Bluff Public Library (IL); Lisa Newman of Salina Public Library (KS); Ryan P. Donovan of New York Public Library (NY); Karen L. Gill of Newport News Public Library System (VA); Barbara Eichman of Broward County Library (FL); Deborah Prozzo of Manross Library (CT); Melissa Bittinger of Hershey Public Library (PA); Afton Seal of Guilford Smith Memorial Library (CT); Kelly Ireland Rembert of Southfield Public Library (MI); Marlena Boggs of Mid-Continent Public Library (MO); Kathy Shields of Palo Alto City Library (CA); Lesley Williams of Evanston Public Library (IL); Linda Holtslander of Loudoun

County Public Library (VA); Kathryn Ames of Athens Regional Library System (GA); Sally Tornow of New Milford Public Library (CT); Barb Wright of High Plains Library District (CO); Mimi Nothacker of St. Tammany Parish Library (LA); Ellen Stross of Plymouth District Library (MI); Maura O'Malley of Lifetime Arts, Inc.; Mary Kay Moran of Loutit District Library (MI); Mary Beth Conlee of Burlington Public Library (WA); Tom Moran of Austin Public Library (TX); Susan Baldwin of The Ferguson Library (CT); Carol Ann Attwood of Patient and Health Education Library, Mayo Clinic (AZ); Beth Keller of Highland Park Public Library (IL); Donna Marie Smith, David A. Kelly, Adam Davis, and Tom Cipullo of Palm Beach County Library System (FL); Sharon Blank of Screven-Jenkins Regional Library System (GA); Teresa Windham of Richland County Public Library (SC); Robyn Truslow of Calvert Library (MD); Rhonda Snelson of Lisle Library District (IL); Michelle Cervantes and Chris Sauder of Round Rock Public Library (TX); Marc Chery and Jeff Davis of San Diego Public Library (CA); Patsy-Ann Street of Christchurch City Libraries (New Zealand); Don Gardner of Salinas Public Library (CA); Nancy Martinez of Lodi Public Library (CA); Mary J. Soucie of Three Rivers Library District (IL); Yvonne Oliger of Brown County Public Library (IN); Dorothy Stoltz of Carroll County Public Library (MD); Elizabeth Dickinson and Amanda McClaine of Cary Memorial Library (MA); Melissa Panio-Petersen and Melissa Tikalsky of Orland Park Public Library (IL); and Elizabeth S. Neill and Jessica Wilson.

Many staff members at Multnomah County (Oregon) Library—Terrilyn Chun, Cindy Strasfeld, Jeremy Graybill, Jane Salisbury, Sara Ryan, Vicki Cornwell, Kim Anderson, Stephanie Miller, Alison Kastner, Martha Flotten, and Don Bradley—patiently answered all of my various questions and sent valuable documents and perspectives my way. Thank you all!

I want to thank Marlene Chamberlain for approaching me all those years ago and offering me such a wonderful opportunity. And special thanks to Stephanie Zvirin of ALA Editions for contacting me and asking me to write this new edition.

And the biggest thanks—THANKS!—goes to Marjorie for all of the editing, proofreading, bibliography writing, and so much more. I'll do the dishes for the next year at least.

Introduction

WHO INVENTED THE PROGRAM?

I figured that a good place to start a book on programming is at the beginning. That seems to be where most books begin, so here goes. The first examples of library programming in the United States and England began appearing in the late 1800s. Like now, back in the 1890s the average library patron seemed to favor fiction over nonfiction. Some librarians of the day thought this was because the public needed a bit more guidance. A form of readers' advisory was born. Librarians would ask the public to stop reading and listen to lectures on what they should be reading and reminders of the proper uses and potential abuses of fiction books. The lecture series was born.

Thankfully, librarians moved on from captive-audience lectures to exhibits and displays. The librarian Charles A. Cutter believed that exhibits would bring people to the library who might not otherwise come. Photography was still a relatively new medium in 1900 America, and Charles was certain that photography displays would attract an audience. By the early 1900s, libraries had also learned that they could tie a display to the books in the library. For example, Native American rugs could be placed on display along with a table full of books about Native Americans.[1] Another step forward.

It turns out that the idea of the library as a social or entertainment center has roots in the past, too. By the early 1800s, societies were offering balls and concerts with the intent of enlightening people to the wonders of art. Social settlements sprang up during this period, offering workshops in the arts and sciences to the working poor. Clubs, such as men's clubs, appeared in the latter part of the nineteenth century and offered concerts, lectures, and games such as billiards. As American and English libraries came of age during this time, many of them began offering games, lectures, visits to poor neighborhoods, and festivals for ethnic groups.[2]

WHAT IS PROGRAMMING?

As you can see, we can trace the inception of library programming back to the nineteenth century. Many of the types of programs (lectures, workshops, and concerts) we host in our libraries today were being held in libraries more than a hundred years ago. Let's now shift our gaze from the past to the present. What types of programs are being produced in libraries today? Why do libraries sponsor programs? Perhaps we should first attempt to define what we mean by "programming."

When I began writing this book I realized that I would have to change my life. For the next year I knew that I'd be very, very busy. I'd say to people, "I'm writing this book on adult programming and I'm going to have to really knuckle down . . ." Fellow library staff had a pretty good idea of what I was up to. But my friends outside the library didn't really get what I was writing *about*. Adult *programming*? Perhaps they thought I was writing about programmers of adult computer software. Sometimes I'd say I was writing a book on adult *programs*. I received the same blank stare. Perhaps they thought I was creating a book on how to create a newsletter for adults—sort of like the program they sell you at the horse races, but different. Their confusion led to my confusion. What is a *library program*? The term itself isn't very attractive. It doesn't grab your attention. If someone walked up to someone who'd never been in a library before and said to that individual, "Hey, guess what? The library down the street is really big into library programs," what would the response be? I suspect the person would offer a quizzical look and say something like, "Hmm. Really." Why don't we call library programs *library events*, or *library classes*, or *library*

spectaculars? We do use some of these terms. But we frequently use the words *program* and *programming*.

As I wrote the second edition of this book, the words that we use in our profession were becoming critical to how the public perceived us. Valerie J. Gross of Howard County (Maryland) Library wrote a great article for *Public Libraries* called "Transforming Our Image Through Words That Work: Perception Is Everything."[3] She makes a good case that the words we use to describe the work we do influence how people perceive us and the image of libraries. Howard County Library uses terms such as *classes*, *seminars*, and *workshops* rather than *programs*. Many libraries *present events* rather than *hold programs*. Rather than using the word *performer* or *programmer*, words such as *instructor*, *teacher*, and *facilitator* are working their way into public libraries. I find that I use the word *event* when I speak to a neighbor or friend who doesn't work in libraries; I just assume that this will be a more meaningful word for him or her. Although I *will* use the terms *program* and *programming* and *performer* in this book, words do matter, and you should use whatever terminology you feel will resonate most strongly with your patrons.

So let's agree that the word *program* for us encompasses lectures, classes, panel discussions, workshops, and more. But what does that word *really* mean? How do we define a library program?

"IF YOU DON'T KNOW THE ANSWER, LOOK IT UP"

I checked my (old!) 1965 edition of *Webster's Seventh New Collegiate Dictionary* and it said that the word *program* means "a public notice." That seemed relevant. When I organize a program, part of the process involves giving public notice, generating publicity. The dictionary also said that a program is a "brief outline of the order to be pursued or the subjects embraced."[4] That's part of programming, too. I might ask a performer to submit an outline to me of her program, specifying what topics she will cover. This outline is then brought before a program committee, and if the concept is approved, the outline helps the marketing office in generating publicity. The dictionary then told me that a program is "the performance of a program." It also defines a program as a plan or procedure. This definition reminded me of a programming policy and the various internal documents that libraries develop over the years to address such things as authors selling their books after a program or the use of live animals in programs. A program is, according to *Webster's*, a proposed project or scheme. This must be the planning part of programming. Someone on staff gets an idea for a program and he becomes the program's coordinator, working out the details of who will perform the program, what topics will be covered, which branches will offer the program, and so forth. *Webster's* says a program is a comprehensive schedule, and that's also true. Our libraries' program committees spend a great deal of time with scheduling. We try to tie programs into monthly celebrations, such as Cinco de Mayo. We try to book only a certain number of programs each month, to ensure that each program will get adequate coverage in our newsletters and the local newspapers. We track who has booked our meeting rooms and when. The dictionary also defines *program* as a "printed bill, card, or booklet giving a program." That sounds like a newsletter!

But programming is more than the sum of its parts. Programming can be a central ingredient of your library's mission. In 1979 the Public Library Association (PLA) produced *The Public Library Mission Statement and Its Imperatives for Service*. Information is defined as "not only the sum total of recorded human experiences—factual, imaginative, scientific, and humanistic—but also the unrecorded experience which is available only from human resources to which library users may be referred."[5] This definition places people and books on equal footing as information resources. Programming can become an extension of your library's collection and resources. Through programming, you can fulfill your mission of meeting the informational, educational, and recreational needs of your patrons. By combining PLA's definition of *information* with a typical mission statement, we can create a good definition of programming. Let's try it: "Programming is a process by which the informational, educational, and recreational needs of your patrons are met by bringing patrons into contact with the human resources best able to meet those needs." It's a bit long-winded, but it establishes programming as an essential library service that fits snugly within your library's mission.

TO PROGRAM OR NOT TO PROGRAM?

If programming is so complicated, why do it? This is a good question. Many libraries justifiably feel that it's all they can do to keep their information desks adequately staffed while also attending to the various off-desk tasks that need to be completed each day. The actual direct cost of a program can be very minimal. It's fairly easy to find a knowledgeable speaker who will appear at your library free of charge. The staff member planning the program can usually coordinate the program and negotiate the arrangements with the performer in a short amount of time. For example, I've gotten an idea for a program, located a performer, and selected dates and locations—all in less than two hours. It would seem as if the program's total costs (if the performer does not charge a fee) would be the two hours I invested in planning the program. It's not quite that simple.

- A staff member—probably you—begins coordinating the program by contacting the performer and submitting the forms needed for publicity, meeting rooms, and extra equipment (chairs, computer equipment, etc.).
- A program committee may exist to approve the idea, performer, and cost and to ensure that the program is consistent with the library's mission.

- Other staff in other branches may be notified of the program to see if they would like to host the program in their branches as well.
- Meeting rooms may have to be booked in various branches. Some libraries will have an administrative assistant who organizes the meeting room reservations from a central location.
- Someone in administration or the programming office (if you are lucky enough to have one!) drafts and mails a contract to the performer.
- The people in your public relations or marketing office write news releases and distribute them to the local media. They also write the content for the newsletter and flyers.
- Your graphics staff create the flyers and include the program description in the library newsletter.
- Your marketing staff mail some of these flyers and newsletters to organizations and individuals within the community.
- Some of your building services staff may need to bring extra chairs and equipment to your meeting room and help you set them up.
- As the program approaches, the coordinating staff member confirms with the performer, pulls together materials (related books, videos, bibliographies, etc.) to display during the program, introduces the performer, watches the program and writes an evaluation, compiles the patrons' evaluations, and, later, writes a thank-you note to the performer.
- Building services staff remove the equipment and chairs.

The indirect costs of a program can be significant. You want to produce high-quality, well-attended programs, but do you have the resources necessary to pull off? Should you offer adult programs at your library?

The answer is yes if (1) you've worked programming into your library's mission and (2) you've either confirmed that you have the staff and other resources necessary to complete the tasks just listed, or you've found ways to eliminate many of these tasks and still produce quality programs that draw an audience. If you answered yes to both these questions, then you are ready to proceed. Here are some reasons to say yes to programming:

- Programs can promote your collection. Have a performer give a talk on the Holocaust and create a display of books and videos to accentuate the performance.
- Programs can be the best way to present certain types of information. For example, a presentation on the ten best business-related Internet sites ensures that the information is current. Or experiencing a live musical performance can be much more meaningful than listening to a song downloaded from iTunes.
- Programs can get people into your library who might not otherwise visit. Free English as a New Language classes would be a good way to attract some of your non-English-speaking community members into the library.
- If your library is in a community that doesn't have much access to the theater or to nationally known authors or orchestras, then the library may be the perfect community center to host these artists and events.
- Programs are ideal for those who can't afford or choose not to pay for certain types of information. Just as someone may choose to use your library instead of buying the e-book online, some people will choose to attend a program on selecting a home computer instead of paying for a similar workshop at a community college.
- Programming can establish goodwill between your library and other local agencies. For example, many agencies have information

to share with the community, but they don't have the facilities. You can invite these groups into your library and publicize their lecture or workshop as a library program.

- Programming increases your library's visibility in the community through news releases, flyers, Facebook and Twitter announcements, and the positive word-of-mouth of satisfied patrons.

- And, like most things, programming gets easier the more you do it. The process becomes streamlined and second nature, performers start coming to you asking for permission to perform, patrons get excited and begin offering suggestions, and the staff can directly see the benefits of their time and effort.

Perhaps your library is not currently offering adult programs, but you intend to change that. Some people will read this (or parts of this) book because they are just beginning to offer programming in their library or organization. It is my hope that this book will help.

GETTING ADMINISTRATION ON BOARD

Perhaps your director or administration or both aren't outright opposed to the idea of adult programming, but they just aren't nearly as enthusiastic as you are at the prospect of bringing in someone to do some artsy thing for ninety minutes at $100 an hour. Although most libraries offer some type of adult programs, many do not see programming as central to their mission. Approximately half of the libraries that offer adult programming feel it is central to their mission; the other half say it isn't.[6] Your patrons might feel a bit more passionately about library programs. According to the ALA report *The State of America's Libraries, 2011,* "Eighty-four percent of adults consider it very or somewhat important that the library serves as a community center, is a source of cultural programs and activities (83 percent, up four percentage points

from a year earlier) and provides computer access, training and support (83 percent, up seven percentage points)."[7]

If your library has not yet embraced programming for adults, there are a few strategies you can pursue to help get folks on board. Administrators are managers, and managers are usually convinced to go in new directions through proposals and studies. If you are in a position of some influence, such as a library manager, perhaps you can present a proposal to a director or a coordinator of adult services. If you work for a system that is largely decentralized, perhaps you only need to get your branch manager involved. If you don't have a good feel for your library's hierarchy and culture, work with your supervisor or your mentor or a knowledgeable peer and learn how things get done in your library system. Eventually, programming will get a yes.

We librarians are a creative bunch, so I know you have plenty of ideas. And you finally have the go-ahead to make these ideas *happen*. But—you guessed it—I'm going to advise you to take a breath and read on before you call the local raptors society to give a talk on the American bald eagle. There's more you need to know.

NOTES

1. D. W. Davies, *Public Libraries as Culture and Social Centers: The Origin of the Concept* (Metuchen, NJ: Scarecrow Press, 1974), 64–65.

2. Ibid., 97, 100, 104–5.

3. Valerie J. Gross, "Transforming Our Image Through Words That Work: Perception Is Everything," *Public Libraries* 48, no. 5 (September–October 2009): 24–32.

4. *Webster's Seventh New Collegiate Dictionary* (Springfield, MA: G&C Merriam Company, 1965), 680.

5. *The Public Library Mission Statement and Its Imperatives for Service* (Chicago: American Library Association, 1979), 5.

6. Debra Wilcox Johnson, *Cultural Programs for Adults in Public Libraries: A Survey Report* (Chicago: American Library Association, 1999), v.

7. *The State of America's Libraries: A Report from the American Library Association* (Chicago: American Library Association, 2011), 18.

PART I

Building a Framework
for Success

Tying Programming to Your Library's Mission

When an institution first considers offering adult programs, the following questions will arise, in one form or another: What are we trying to do here? Will programs be offered as a way to get people into our building? Will they closely reflect our library's collection? Will they be used to fill a cultural or informational gap in our community? Is programming really a service that aligns with our mission?

As libraries continue to face difficult financial times, many of our libraries have had to look very closely at the services that we deliver and how we deliver them. We have become extremely strategic in how we deliver services. Mission statements have been rewritten. Priorities have been fine-tuned to optimize diminishing resources. As door counts and online visits have increased during these tough times, a few trends have emerged that may actually result in some increased staffing capacities. One such trend is the dwindling number of ready reference questions that library staff answer day-to-day. Many of our patrons now find answers to basic questions such as, "How long is the Mississippi River?" by turning to Google first. Yes, we still answer these questions, but almost every public library has seen its ready reference statistics drop in the past decade. Rather than chase after a train that has already left the station (by trying to entice our patrons to come to us for answers that they readily now find themselves), we might be wiser to look at ways in which we can better align our library services with the current needs of our communities.

The mission statement is a place to start. Mission statements and value statements now contain words such as *connect* and *synergy*. For example, one of the core values of New York Public Library is to "bring people together to spark creative synergies and learn from each other." We see priorities that describe the importance of civic engagement and services to immigrants. As libraries revise and perhaps streamline their mission statements and priorities, each of us should take the opportunity to explore the role that programming can play in carrying out the mission of our library. A Google search of "trends in libraries" will result in as many mentions of "connecting people with people" as "connecting people with materials." Although we may have fewer patrons turning to us with their ready reference questions, we do have patrons asking for our help with learning English, asking whether we offer help with developing a new set of job skills, and asking for opportunities to connect and share ideas with and learn from other residents in our communities. And a library program can be one of the best approaches to meeting these needs of our patrons. A library program called "Talk Time" that brings speakers of various languages together to practice their English can be a very effective way for patrons to improve their English while also connecting them to others in the community who may share similar life situations. If civic engagement is one of your stated priorities, then programs such as the Great Decisions series (www.fpa.org) beautifully align with that priority. Sometimes the best way to meet the informational or recreational need of a patron is to connect him or her with another person who has the right knowledge and talent. And library programming does just that.

So how do you ensure that any programs that you offer align with your mission and priorities? Developing a programming policy is a good place to start. Frequently, the first sentence of your programming policy and the first sentence of your mission statement will be nearly identical. For example, the mission of the Martin County (Florida) Library System is to: "Enhance the lifelong learning of our diverse community through education, recreation, cultural immersion and intellectual stimulation." This statement is very similar to the opening sentence of Merrimack (New Hampshire) Public Library's programming policy. Their policy states: "The Merrimack Public Library will present programs that offer information, education, and recreation to the citizens of Merrimack."

Both the mission statement and the programming policy just quoted contain the word *recreation*. Your mission statement and your programming policy are your guides. Be sure they say what you want and intend to do. If you include the word *recreation* in your policy, then the types of programs you can offer become very broad indeed. Libraries with such broad policies can offer programs such as singles mixers, consisting of music, dancing, and light refreshments. Such a function would probably be well attended, and it might bring people into the library for the first time. If your library would be reluctant to offer purely recreational programming, then you might want to omit this word from your mission statement and programming policy, or you might want to add a sentence defining what you mean by *recreational*.

Some mission statements say that the library provides informational and cultural materials and services. The programming policy can then be written to state that the library provides informational and cultural programs. You may also want to mention in your programming policy that the programs offered are consistent with materials that your library collects. This assertion then gives your library quite a bit of flexibility, even if the word *recreational* is not included in the policy. Think of a programming topic. Now go to your library's catalog and do a search on that topic. You will probably have to be really creative to think of a programming topic that is not addressed in a book in your print and electronic collections. If you decide to pursue programming that is informational and cultural—but not recreational—in content, then your library might choose to offer a program on how to start a singles club or how to locate singles clubs in your community. But, hosting a singles dance party will probably not fit within your mission.

Now that you've decided on the type (recreational, informational, cultural, etc.) of programming you will offer, you are ready to get into the finer details. Here are some other questions you might want to address in your policy:

Will you produce programs on topics that are already covered by other agencies? For example, will you ask a local doctor to present a lecture on high blood pressure, or will you invite the American Heart Association into your library to present a program on that topic?

Will you charge an admission fee to your programs? Will you charge a materials fee at some of your programs? For example, if you get someone to offer a workshop on calligraphy and each patron needs paper and pens for the workshop, will your library purchase the materials, and will you then pass this expense on to the patron?

Who selects the performers—someone in your adult services or programming office, a centralized committee, individuals in the branches, the library director, your Friends group?

Can for-profit groups and individuals present programs or will you limit performers to those people who are members of nonprofit organizations and associations? If you permit for-profit groups, will these groups be allowed to promote their products or services during the program? Can they at least mention their products or services and offer their business cards to patrons?

Can performers sell products during or after the program? If not, do you want to make an exception for authors selling their books?

How will you ensure that the content of a program is accurate? Will you evaluate the performer's PowerPoint slides and handouts before the program? Will you ask for and check references? Will you interview other agencies that have hosted the performer?

Figure 1.1 is an example of a programming policy that addresses some of the preceding questions and issues.

Your programming policy will be the compass that keeps you on the right path. If you want to offer programs that will supplement or enhance your library's collection, say this in your policy. Sometimes, the best way to convey information is through human interaction. For example, the best way to convey information on learning English might be through literacy classes and ENL (English as a New Language) classes. If your library intends to offer these programs even though the collection does not contain ENL materials, don't craft your programming policy to state that your programs will be limited to topics that are represented in your materials collection. Other topics for programs might include a class on how to use your library's web page or a workshop instructing people on how to fill out their census form. These topics are not going to be covered in books within the library. If you want to offer these programs, state in your policy that you offer programming to provide information that is best transmitted by human interaction.

Last, consider adding a line to your programming policy that states where the buck stops regarding decision making and programming. Some policies will state that this authority resides with the director, but if responsibility resides with you or the library manager or a programming coordinator, then state in the policy which position has final decision-making authority. The line within the policy can be as simple as this: "The Library Director/ Programming Coordinator/Library Manager has final approval over which programs are produced within the library."

The American Library Association (ALA) created a document called "Library-Initiated Programs as a Resource: An Interpretation of the *Library Bill of Rights*."[1] This document fits library programming within the context of the *Library Bill of Rights*.[2] It also serves as a good model when drafting a program-

FIGURE 1.1 | **PROGRAMMING POLICY**

Adult Programming Statement of Policy for Library-Initiated Programs

A library program is an event that promotes the use of library materials, facilities, or services and/or offers the community an informational, entertaining or cultural experience. Programs are planned for the interest and enlightenment of all the people of the community.

MCPL [McCracken County Public Library] strives to offer a variety of programs that support the mission of the library and reflect the broad range of community interests. These programs will often be presented in cooperation with other agencies and institutions as well as other public and private resources.

Selection of library program topics, speakers, presentations, and resource materials will be made by library staff on the basis of the interests and needs of library users and the community.

Programs will not be allowed to serve as a platform for generating income for any sponsoring group or individual, except funds to support the library. Library programs must be noncommercial in nature. Although a businessperson or other professional expert may present a program, no solicitation of business is permitted.

The sale of products at an adult library program is not allowed. There are two exceptions:

1. Writers, performers, and artists may sell their own works at the library following library programs.
2. The Friends of the Library may sell items at library programs they sponsor.

Library sponsorship of a program does not constitute an endorsement of the content of the program or the views expressed by the participants.

Attendance at library sponsored programs is open to the public and shall not be restricted because of gender, race, background or beliefs. *Article V of the Library Bill of Rights*

McCracken County Public Library
555 Washington Street
Paducah, KY 42003

Source: McCracken County (Kentucky) Public Library

---

ming policy. The document is available online and is included in figure 1.2.

This next point may be obvious, but once you have drafted a programming policy, you will want it to become an official document within your organization. It should be as official as your mission statement and collection development policy. This may mean that the director or even your library board will need to sign off on the policy. If you are the director, you are well on your way. But if you are a member of a subcommittee that is drafting this document as an initial step in offering adult programming, be sure to use your supervisor to help you steer the policy through the proper channels.

It is sometimes a good idea to ask around and get an idea of what seems possible before you even begin writing. If possible, speak with those people who have a good feel for how your administration thinks.

FIGURE 1.2 | **LIBRARY-INITIATED PROGRAMS AS A RESOURCE**

An Interpretation of the *Library Bill of Rights*

Library-initiated programs support the mission of the library by providing users with additional opportunities for information, education, and recreation. Article I of the *Library Bill of Rights* states: "Books and other library resources should be provided for the interest, information, and enlightenment of all people of the community the library serves."

Library-initiated programs take advantage of library staff expertise, collections, services and facilities to increase access to information and information resources. Library-initiated programs introduce users and potential users to the resources of the library and to the library's primary function as a facilitator of information access. The library may participate in cooperative or joint programs with other agencies, organizations, institutions, or individuals as part of its own effort to address information needs and to facilitate information access in the community the library serves.

Library-initiated programs on site and in other locations include, but are not limited to, speeches, community forums, discussion groups, demonstrations, displays, and live or media presentations.

Libraries serving multilingual or multicultural communities should make efforts to accommodate the information needs of those for whom English is a second language. Library-initiated programs that cross language and cultural barriers introduce otherwise underserved populations to the resources of the library and provide access to information.

Library-initiated programs "should not be proscribed or removed [or canceled] because of partisan or doctrinal disapproval" of the contents of the program or the views expressed by the participants, as stated in Article II of the *Library Bill of Rights*.

Library sponsorship of a program does not constitute an endorsement of the content of the program or the views expressed by the participants, any more than the purchase of material for the library collection constitutes an endorsement of the contents of the material or the views of its creator.

Library-initiated programs are a library resource, and, as such, are developed in accordance with written guidelines, as approved and adopted by the library's policy-making body. These guidelines should include an endorsement of the *Library Bill of Rights* and set forth the library's commitment to free and open access to information and ideas for all users.

Library staff select topics, speakers and resource materials for library-initiated programs based on the interests and information needs of the community. Topics, speakers and resource materials are not excluded from library-initiated programs because of possible controversy. Concerns, questions or complaints about library-initiated programs are handled according to the same written policy and procedures that govern reconsiderations of other library resources.

Library-initiated programs are offered free of charge and are open to all. Article V of the *Library Bill of Rights* states: "A person's right to use a library should not be denied or abridged because of origin, age, background, or views."

The "right to use a library" encompasses all the resources the library offers, including the right to attend library-initiated programs. Libraries do not deny or abridge access to library resources, including library-initiated programs, based on an individual's economic background or ability to pay.

Adopted January 27, 1982, by the ALA Council; amended June 26, 1990; July 12, 2000. [ISBN 8389-6528-8]

Source: American Library Association, "Library-Initiated Programs as a Resource: An Interpretation of the *Library Bill of Rights*" (Chicago: American Library Association, 2000), www.ala.org/ala/issuesadvocacy/intfreedom/librarybill/interpretations/libraryinitiated.cfm.

Even if administration asked you to frame the policy, it doesn't hurt to ask them what they have in mind before you begin. Communication along the way can increase the chances of getting your initial draft approved without major changes. This saves time, which means you will be that much closer to offering programs to your patrons. You can always propose to expand or alter the policy at a later time.

Once your approved programming policy is in place, you have established *what* your programming focus will be. Now you are ready to begin sketching *how* you will translate your policy into programming.

NOTES

1. American Library Association, "Library-Initiated Programs as a Resource: An Interpretation of the *Library Bill of Rights*" (Chicago: American Library Association, 2000).

2. American Library Association, *Library Bill of Rights* (Chicago: American Library Association, 1996).

Developing Guidelines and Procedures

All right. You've written a programming policy and now you're ready to go get your performer. Not so fast. Before you plan your program, you will want to have some procedures and documents in place first. As you begin to think of ideas and develop them, you will quickly discover that some "what ifs" emerge. Some examples of "what ifs" are:

- What if the author I scheduled wants to sell his book after the program?
- What if the cook giving the "Healthy Eating During the Holidays" program wants to prepare something and feed it to the audience?
- What if the representative from the zoo suggests bringing a twelve-foot python and a hawk to a children's nature program?

Figures 2.1 and 2.2 represent policies—for food and live animals—written by Jefferson County (Colorado) Public Library.

You'll find that your written programming policies will expand over time. Putting these policies in writing will save staff time because staff will know from the start what is acceptable and not acceptable within your library. You will also be doing your performers a service because you will be applying the same guidelines and policies to each of them. You won't say no to one author who wants to sell his books after a reading and then say yes to another author six months later.

While we're knee-deep in policies, this might be a good time to make sure that your library has some type of patron behavior policy. Figure 2.3 offers an example of such a policy. These guidelines will come in handy on the very rare occasion when a patron acts out during a program. For example, I worked at a library that held a series of classes that assisted patrons with English-language

FIGURE 2.1 | **USE OF FOOD IN THE LIBRARY**

Jefferson County Public Library
Food at Public Programs Guidelines

Anything the Library may offer or sponsor in regard to food is under guidelines established and enforced by the Jefferson County Health Department. Library programs fall under the Jefferson County Health Department's "occasional events" guidelines. We do not need to contact a health inspector to approve our use of food, as long as we adhere to the following guidelines:

1. Food to be served must be purchased from inspected, approved sources.
2. Everyone handling food must wash his/her hands.
3. If perishable food is distributed at the library, the food must be transported and stored properly (must remain hot, if necessary, or cold if necessary).

The Library limits the instances in which it serves food as refreshments at its programs. Simple food items such as water, juice, coffee, tea, and milk and cookies may be offered at programs such as book discussion groups and children's and YA family nights and poetry readings. Staff is expected to obtain the food through a FN request and clean up afterward.

Food may be used in programs if it is integral to the subject of the program. Be sensitive to the possibility that food may create a mess and plan to protect carpeting and furniture. Library staff is responsible for cleaning up after programs.

Practical examples include:

It is okay to:

- distribute individually wrapped candy at Halloween.
- serve a cake from King Soopers (because King Soopers is an inspected, approved source).
- conduct food programs with children, such as churning butter, as long as the food is purchased from an approved source (grocery store as opposed to our personal garden or goat in the backyard) and everyone washes his/her hands.

It is not okay to:

- serve the public food that has been prepared in our own homes (since we are not inspected, approved sources).

Document Review Dates

Document Name	Food at Public Programs Guidelines
Document Basis:	
Effective Date:	February 2002
Review/Revision Date:	January 2008
Next Operational Review Date:	January 2012
Reviewed By:	Public Services Management Team (PSMT)
JCPL Operational Category:	Customer Service and Staff & Organization Development
Approved By:	Director of Library Programs and Services
Replaces:	Food at Public Programs Guidelines, rev. July 2005

Source: Jefferson County (Colorado) Public Library

FIGURE 2.2 | **USE OF ANIMALS IN LIBRARY PROGRAMS**

Jefferson County Public Library
Use of Animals in Library Programs Instructions

The Program Coordinator should contact the Director of Administrative Services before contract negotiations begin for scheduling a program that includes animals. Information to be shared includes:

- A brief description of the event
- The date(s) of the program
- The location(s)
- The animal(s)
- The organization/agency sponsoring the animal(s) and handler(s)
- A description of the animal handler (i.e., "a certified trainer from the Rocky Mountain Raptor Society")

This step is especially critical when a program includes predatory or poisonous animals.

While the Library's insurance covers all activities usually associated with a public library, adjustments may need to be made. The Director of Administrative Services will work with the Library's insurance carrier to provide the insurance coverage the program requires. Whenever there is a question in the mind of the insurance underwriter about whether a program meets the requirements for coverage or if the Director of Administrative Services cannot justify the insurance cost or potential liability, the Director of Administrative Services will confer with the program chair and/or the Deputy County Librarian for resolution.

Document Review Dates

Document Name	Use of Animals in Library Programs Instructions
Document Basis:	
Effective Date:	July 1998
Review/Revision Date:	November 2007
Next Operational Review Date:	November 2011
Reviewed By:	Public Services Management Team (PSMT)
JCPL Operational Category:	Customer Service and Staff & Organization Development
Approved By:	Deputy County Librarian
Replaces:	Use of Animals in Library Programs Instructions, rev. May 2002

Source: Jefferson County (Colorado) Public Library

learning. A patron informed us that she would show up at these classes to express her disapproval of the concept of teaching English to adults. And she did show up. When her behavior began to disrupt the class, the instructor called in a supervisor, who explained the library's behavior policy to the patron and directed her to leave. The patron felt that showing up and disrupting a program fell under freedom of speech. The supervisor explained that the policy specified that some behaviors, including speech, may interfere with others' use of their library, and that, during such occasions, those behaviors must stop or the patron must leave.

Before we go much farther with drafting various documents, let's pause and reach some consensus on why we are doing this. Let's not write these policies because we want to be able to tell staff and performers what they can or cannot do. It may seem as if that's the intent of these documents. Your goal is to provide quality programs to your patrons in a manner that is consistent with the mission and priorities of your library. Good policies can help you meet this goal. Just be sure that they are as simple as possible. The policies and procedures you develop are paving your way to organized, successful programming.

Let's assume that you or your library or both are new to adult programming. You have a written programming policy in place, and you've written a few other policies that address issues that will come up right away, such as authors selling their books and performers preparing food. You are now getting closer to actually putting on a program. It's probably time to ensure that you have the necessary staffing and budget in place.

USING VOLUNTEERS

The extent to which you use volunteers may be influenced by your budget realities or by your library's position on and commitment to engaging with volunteers in your community. Regardless, since you are

now at the point where you are developing programming guidelines and procedures, it's a good time to think through how you will use volunteers within your programming efforts. Following are some ways volunteers might be of assistance.

Volunteers as Performers

Most of us will partner with volunteers as performers at some point. Depending on our budgets, some of us will turn to volunteers almost exclusively! If you are not paying your performer, and she is not a paid library staff person, then she is a volunteer. Many of us get our volunteers through contacting universities or colleges and asking whether they have faculty able to speak about a certain topic. Museums, associations, and coalitions in our communities are often very willing to partner with us and send volunteers our way. Sometimes members of our communities will come to us and offer to share their expertise in yoga or poetry writing with our patrons.

As we develop relationships with these volunteers, we should look for opportunities to create ongoing programs. For instance, if the yoga program is a success, you might consider asking your volunteer to come back once a year to present a program on yoga. You could ask her to tweak the content a bit each year in order to keep the program fresh for return attendees. By offering ongoing calendar slots to some of your volunteers, you will take some of the pressure off yourself in having to come up with all new ideas and performers each year. You will also free up some time to put back into planning those events that *will* be new in the coming year.

Volunteers as Instructors

Throughout this book I usually use the word *performer* to identify the person who provides the content of the program. Whether they sing or lecture or teach, I call them *performers* in this book. But in this section I'd like to split hairs a bit and mention using volunteers as per-

FIGURE 2.3 | **PATRON BEHAVIOR POLICY**

Redwood City Public Library
Patron Behavior Policy

The function of the library is to provide information services and educational, informational, and recreational materials to the public.

Patron activities or behaviors which interfere with these basic functions are considered grounds for remedial action by library staff as are any illegal activities. When necessary, such action may include requesting such patrons to leave the library and/or calling the police.

The library staff is directed to:

1. Define behaviors which interfere with the designated functions of the library.
2. Define and exclude from remedial actions those behaviors which may by eccentric but do not interfere with proper library functions.
3. Create procedures for dealing with those behaviors which interfere with legitimate patron use or staff service to patrons.
4. Train staff in use of these procedures.

Library Board of Trustees
Redwood City Public Library
Adopted: August 14, 1984
Last reviewed: June 11, 2007

Source: Redwood City (California) Public Library

formers who teach our patrons how to perform a certain task. Let's call this type of performer an *instructor*. An example of an instructor is someone who leads a hands-on workshop on how to find free, high-quality Android and Apple applications on the Web for your mobile device. A group of volunteers who are good at instruction can be a wonderful resource for your library and patrons. You will now be able to turn to people whose talent you trust, and you can offer to collaborate with them to create new workshops that address emerging information needs in your community. I offer further details on how to create this type of volunteer-based workshop in chapter 10.

Assistance in Planning and during the Program

Volunteers can also be a great help in ensuring that a program runs smoothly. They can help you set up the room. For large events, particularly those held off-site, they can assist patrons in finding the correct room and welcome them to their seats. They can also help overcome language barriers. If you know that a significant percentage of your community speaks Spanish, for example, a Spanish-speaking volunteer could quietly circulate and explain verbal content of the program to your Spanish-speaking patrons.

Generating Publicity

You might be lucky enough to have a volunteer who is skilled in writing press releases or who has a talent for graphic design. Volunteers are often very connected within the community, and the buzz that they can generate by merely talking up the program among their friends cannot be overestimated.

Offering Technical Expertise

Sometimes our volunteers possess skills that we just don't have! Want to videotape that lecture and put it on the Web so that your patrons can access it from home? Chances are someone in the community can help you with that. This is probably the most sophisticated way in which to engage your volunteers. If you can get to the point where your volunteers are planning and coordinating programs, you not only are greatly supplementing your staffing capacity for programming, you are also providing a very rewarding volunteer experience for members of your community. Just remember that it will take a good deal of staff time to familiarize volunteers with your library's programming priorities, policies, and procedures, and it will take some ongoing, high-level coordination to ensure that the volunteers have the consistent communication and support that they need in order to sustain their successful programming efforts. You might want to create a training workshop for volunteers that will convey the nuts-and-bolts of your library's programming policies and procedures. Some type of programming toolkit—either online or in print, or both—will also be helpful. This toolkit should contain and clarify programming procedures and direct volunteers to the various forms—program request forms, equipment request forms, contracts, and the like—that are mentioned throughout this book.

Recruiting Volunteers

How will you recruit and coordinate your volunteers? You may know of a group of people in your community who have a specific interest, such as storytelling. See if they would like to help you produce an annual storytelling event. They will know the storytellers in your community and beyond, and they can help publicize this event to the folks in your community. Another approach is to call on an existing group—such as your library's Friends group. An adult advisory council or adult programming advisory group could also be established to assist with your adult programming efforts. Members can help with the logistics of the program—setting up the room, handing out and collecting evaluations, and so forth. This is probably the most rewarding and sophisticated form of volunteerism—creating an opportunity that allows the volunteers to take a leadership role in the work that they are doing for your organization.

If you are still building up your volunteer base, the good news is that there are places in your community that you can turn to for help. Agencies exist in your community—such as the Retired Senior Volunteer Program (RSVP)—whose primary purpose is to provide meaningful volunteer opportunities for their members. Give these agencies a call. Also, online services such as Idealist (www.idealist.org) allow you to post volunteer opportunities that are available at your library.

Always be sure to work closely with your volunteer services folks or whichever library unit coordinates your volunteer efforts. (Perhaps that buck stops with you!) They may have time sheets and other documentation that they will want you to use to track the hours that your volunteers donate to the library.

CREATING YOUR BUDGET

Now let's turn from volunteers to money. Perhaps you don't have any money to dedicate to programming, but you've still created your policies. This probably means that you are prepared to persevere and pursue programs that are free. Either you will have library staff present the programs or you will work with agencies and individuals who are willing to perform without a fee. Remember, these programs will still require staff time and facilities, as well as publicity costs. If you choose to pursue only free programs, then you may want to include this preference in your programming policy. Be sure to state that you are seeking no-cost programs when you speak with organizations and potential performers. This disclosure will save both your staff and potential performers a good deal of time during the initial negotiations.

If you are fortunate enough to have funds for programming, it is a good idea to create a budget line with a specific sum of money. Try to get a "programming" line added to your operating budget and place a certain dollar amount in this budget at the beginning of the year. Once you have created a budget line, you'll have to decide how to divide the money among the types of programming: children's, adult, young adult (YA), and so on.

After you've placed money into a programming budget line, you'll need to decide how this money can be spent. Will this money only pay for performers' fees? What if you are hiring a local poet to give a poetry reading, and you'd like to serve cheese and crackers during the reading? How do you pay for these snacks? Perhaps the poet's appearance was planned to coincide with the conclusion of a poetry contest. You'd like the poet to announce the winners and hand out books of poems as prizes. Will the programming budget pay for the books? Some libraries just take the money from the cash register, ring it up to petty cash, and go purchase snacks or prizes. Other libraries might pay the performer from the programming budget, charge the books to a supply budget, and pay for the food from money awarded to the library by its library foundation. It's a good idea to establish a consistent procedure. Libraries that are publicly funded might want to be especially careful with their budgeting practices. Will it look funny to taxpayers or board members if they see "$200 for candy and soft drinks" charged to your supply budget?

As programming becomes fully integrated into your library's overall mission, you will notice that this service will become part of your library's budgeting and strategic planning processes. As your programming offerings expand, your budget will gradually (ideally) expand as well. As this happens, it's a good idea to begin thinking in terms of yearly output or outcome measures in order to push your library toward excellence in programming and to focus on results that can then be used to demonstrate the value of programming within your community and therefore make a strong case for continued funding. Here are some sample output measures from Multnomah County Library (MCL):

Output: Number of financial literacy programs
offered

Outcome: Attendees who say library programs
connect them to their community

Outcome: Attendees who say they learned
something new at a library program

Outcome: Attendees of library programs who
rate them as good or excellent

For much more detailed information on budgeting
and funding, please turn to chapter 5.

CREATING A COMMITTEE

This programming stuff is beginning to sound like
a lot of work. And it is. This doesn't mean that it is
drudgery. But it *is* work. You'll write policies, create
budgets, contact performers, write contracts, create
publicity, and evaluate performers. You'll probably
want to share the workload. Even if you are one person in a one-library system, you can still use others to
help you. Through e-mail, you can communicate with
teachers, museums, and others in your community, all
at once. You can find out which performers they've
hired recently and which programs were successes.
You can then begin collaborating on cosponsoring
events. This outreach can also be done, granted a little
more slowly, over the telephone.

This is also the point where you want to decide
just *how* you will do your programming. If yours is
a single-building library system, then you will book
the programs for your library. But if your system has
multiple branches, you can go about your programming in at least two very different ways. You can
seek out performers and book them at a branch level
without collaborating with other libraries within the
system. You will still probably submit requests and
other forms to some central person or office, but you
will only be submitting a request for your branch.
Another approach is to work collaboratively with
other branches when booking programs. Following

this model, you would contact other branches when
you have identified a topic and located a performer
to see if any of those branches would like to host the
program as well. The first model definitely gives
you plenty of freedom. The second model, however,
spreads the work throughout the system and offers
patrons some choices as to where they can attend the
program.

Regardless of which model you choose, you have
some work ahead of you. But if you have others who
can share the workload, and if you are going to be
working with other departments, such as the accounting office or the marketing office, then you might want
to form a programming committee. Although a committee can seem like an additional layer of bureau-
cracy, in reality it can save you time and generate
some creative ideas. Who would be on this committee and what would they do? Let me answer this by
describing an hour in the life of a hypothetical committee in a typical public library. (Let's assume that
this committee exists within a library system that col-
laborates among branches when booking programs.)

A PROGRAMMING COMMITTEE MEETING

Your meeting begins at 9 a.m. on a Thursday. You
work for a ten-branch public library system. You begin
the meeting by discussing the programming that is
occurring in the library system this month. It's an
average month. Eighty storytimes for children are
scheduled. This month the library has also scheduled
two series of family programs and one adult series. A
"series" is defined as a program that occurs at more
than one library location. The two family series are a
wildlife watching series, where kids can learn tips on
how to spot wildlife such as birds and rabbits, and a
series on Doc Susie. The Doc Susie program involves
a performance artist who dresses up as the pioneering
doctor and tells stories of her life. The wildlife program will be held in five branches, and the Doc Susie
program will be held in three branches. You expect

both programs to attract people of all ages. For adults you have a series of programs on flowers: one program will cover growing roses, another will cover identifying wildflowers, and yet another will cover the history of the rose as a decorative flower. Seven branches have chosen to hold one of the three programs in the flowers series. In addition to all this activity, your library system will host a series of AARP (American Association of Retired Persons) tax assistance sessions in seven of your branches. *And,* thirty-five patron education classes—for both adults and children—are scheduled throughout the library, ranging from a basic Internet instruction class for parents and their kids to classes on how to download digital content to handheld devices.

Before we proceed with the meeting, let's pause and take a look at the members of this committee. There are five members. One person is an adult services librarian from one of the branches. The committee also has someone from youth services. A third member is a specialist in young adult services. Your fourth member is a representative from marketing and communications. This is the office that generates the publicity for your library. Some libraries call this office the public relations or public information office. This office may also be the "voice" of your library, making statements to the local press and paying visits to local businesses and organizations to improve your library's visibility within the community. Office staff also write press releases, create the library newsletter, and send electronic and paper mailings to patrons, local schools, and local businesses and organizations. The fifth member represents your library foundation, a nonprofit organization that supports library services through fund-raising events and grant writing.

The five members of this committee were chosen very deliberately. The adult, children's, and young adult specialists are members of the committee for obvious reasons. They work closely with your patrons. They see what materials adults, children, and young adults are using, and they hear their questions. They will have a good feel for what programs will and won't

fly for various age groups. And, they can communicate with their peers throughout the library (and perhaps throughout the profession, if they actively communicate with colleagues in other library systems).

The member from your marketing office (or your communications office or graphics office) will be an important asset. This person will know what local or national events are occurring, such as local arts or music festivals, and he or she can help you tie programming ideas into such events. For example, the best time to do a program on bicycling might be during National Bike Month in May. This member will also be able to tell the committee when it is overextending itself. Your library can adequately promote only a certain number of programs online and in the local newspapers and other media. In addition, the marketing person will have a good feel for how your patrons may react to certain programs or presenters. Will hiring an investment broker from Best Bank to give a talk on stocks offend the brokers from the other banks around town? Your marketing office might be able to provide some insight. In fact, these folks often bring a comprehensive understanding of the community and offer insights and perspectives that your team hasn't yet considered.

The representative from your library foundation—and let's just assume you have such a foundation—is invaluable. Your library foundation will, it is hoped, have funds at its disposal and, if it is affiliated with your Friends group, might have volunteers as well. By including the library foundation on your committee, ideally you will find that the foundation will offer to pay for and produce (with the help of the Friends' volunteers) certain programs. The foundation will benefit because you will credit it in the program's publicity. Add a "Presented by The Alakazam Library Foundation" byline to the flyers and press releases. Library foundations also frequently fund events such as gala openings for new library buildings. The brainstorming that takes place in your programming committee meetings can help foundations locate performers for such events.

Now that all your members are here and you've discussed this month's programming calendar, it's time to proceed with the meeting. You might be wondering why you are here. The primary function of this committee is to act as a clearinghouse for programming in the library. You look at the agenda for today's meeting and see that the only business is the discussion and approval of programs. The best way to visualize how this committee functions is to look at how programming ideas and information travel through your library system.

Anyone in the library can submit a program idea. This idea goes to the chair of the program committee—you. Ideas also trickle in through patron suggestions on the program evaluation forms. (Please see chapter 13 for detailed information on evaluating programs.) Each branch also has one or two "programming representatives," preferably someone from youth services and someone from adult services. These representatives are expected to be very active in recommending topics and performers. Depending on the size of your library, this group of programming representatives could be fairly large. Ideally, they will be able to communicate with the program committee and among themselves via e-mail.

The first items you discuss are the programming ideas. These are rough ideas and suggestions that come to the chair through staff and patrons. You will also receive proposals from members of your community who want to speak at the library. Patron suggestions are often as simple as "have a program on travel in Europe." The committee encourages staff to try to flesh out ideas before they send them to the committee. When possible, the committee asks staff to include the following information when submitting an idea:

- The topic of the program
- The name of a performer who might be able to present a program on that topic
- The content of the program
- The length of the program
- The cost of the program

- The months of the year that the performer is available
- Whether or not the performer is available to appear at other branches throughout the library system
- Whether the performer has appeared at other libraries or made other local appearances

The committee then discusses the idea. The committee first decides whether the proposed program ties into the library's mission. If someone suggests "a night of disco dancing," does this mesh with your program policy and mission statement? You look carefully at the performer and how the individual presents him- or herself. Does the Vietnam War historian present himself in his cover letter to the library as "Bart of Bart's Vietnam War Emporium"? You might choose to go with Bart, but you will probably want to speak with him first about the amount of publicity he can give his shop during his lecture. You might also want to call Bart's references.

Your public marketing representative will help you decide in which month to place the program. If the library is gearing up to massively publicize the children's and young adult summer reading program in June and July, then it might be too much to try to publicize two adult program series in June. Or, the marketing office might have insight into the current concerns of your patrons. For example, this office fields many of the calls that the library receives from the public. If marketing staff have received twenty-five calls in one month from patrons who want you to install Internet filters on your adult computers, then the marketing person might tell you that now isn't the best time to present a workshop titled "Erotica and E-publishing."

Committee members like the first idea they discuss and decide to proceed: a programming representative in one of the branches has proposed that the library hire a local author who has written a book on natural hot springs. You see that the performer is asking $200 per appearance. You check the programming budget and see that the money is there to fund the program.

You then check the programming spreadsheet calendar, where you track all the pending programs, and see that November seems relatively clear. November makes sense: your library is in Colorado, November is the beginning of the ski season, and people like to relax in a hot spring after a full day of skiing. You all agree that you would like to offer this program in at least three branches. You, as chair, ask someone on the committee to present this approved concept to the branch representatives.

At this point the committee is looking for one of the programming representatives in the branches to coordinate the hot springs program. A committee member e-mails a message to the programming representatives asking for a volunteer. Hopefully one of the representatives will step forward and offer to coordinate the program. This coordinator will then call the performer, get days and times that she or he can appear at the library, verify whether the individual is willing to appear at more than one branch, and settle on the length of the program and the appearance fee. The coordinator should also ask the performer to e-mail, fax, or mail an outline of what will be covered during the program. This outline ensures that the performer will present what you are expecting him or her to present. Also, ask the performer to include a brief (two- or three-sentence) biographical sketch. This background information will help your graphics or marketing office create flyers and press releases. If you plan on paying the performer by check, the coordinator will also need a Social Security number.

The coordinator will then solicit other branches to see if they would also like to offer this program. Coordination and communication are effective ways to make quality programs available to multiple locations This means that each branch doesn't have to think up its own ideas and seek its own performers.

Here's how the hot springs concept will be offered to the branches. The coordinator will present the idea to the branch programming representatives. The quickest way to do this is via e-mail, although it can also be done via fax or interoffice memo. The coordinator sends this message to the programming representatives:

> Hello. Attached you will find copies of a letter and a brochure that Brooke Springs sent the Program Committee describing the hot springs lecture she offers. Ms. Springs has published two books on Western hot springs, both of which appear in our collection. The lecture would be 90 minutes long. She would charge $200 per appearance. The workshops would take place in November. She is available on Saturdays, weekday afternoons, and evenings after 6 p.m. She would like to be scheduled no more than two evenings during this series. She will need a screen for her workshop; let me know if you need a screen and I will submit an AV request for you.
>
> Ms. Springs is permitted to sell her books after her program.
>
> Please respond to me by Monday, February 28, if you would like to host this program.
>
> Thank you.
>
> Donna Smith
> Green Lawn Branch

The library representatives then check their branch calendars and consult with their library managers and let the program coordinator know if they are willing and able to host the program. When the coordinator has heard back from all the representatives, he calls the performer and verifies the selected days and times. Then the coordinator begins submitting the necessary paperwork.

PAPERWORK

Two types of forms are fairly common in libraries: a program request worksheet (figure 2.4) and a graphics request (figures 2.5 and 2.6). The program request

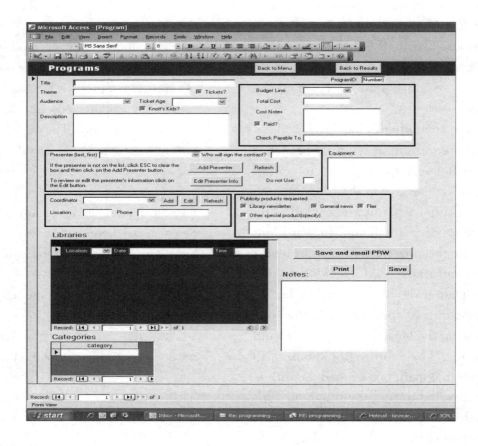

Source: Jefferson County (Colorado) Public Library

FIGURE 2.4 | **PROGRAM REQUEST WORKSHEET**

goes to a program committee (to remain consistent with our preceding program committee meeting scenario) or to a systemwide coordinator, such as the head of adult services. This sheet lists the performer's information needed by the accounting office to draft a check. It also verifies the locations where the performer will appear, and it contains information about the program itself, such as the program's title and the type of publicity requested. Accompanying information on the performer, such as the biographical sketch, should be included with this request to help create the flyers, Facebook postings, and press releases. The graphics request specifies the type of publicity requested and the numbers of flyers and other items for distribution. (Figure 2.5 is an example of a hard copy graphics request and figure 2.6 is an electronic graphics request. You'll most likely want to choose between print or electronic—no need to use both!)

CARING FOR YOUR COMMITTEE

As you can see, a programming committee can be an effective way to plan and produce your programs. This group must work effectively and collaboratively in order to complete the myriad tasks involved in pro-

FIGURE 2.5 | **GRAPHIC ARTS REQUEST (PRINT)**

GRAPHIC ARTS
Job Request

SEND COMPLETED FORM TO: Director of Public Information

Approved by Unit Head _____ Date _____

Director of Public Information _____ Date _____

Senior Management Team member _____ Date _____

Required information

FORMS ONLY
Check one:
☐ **Revise**
——Hold for
next printing
☐ **New**
☐ **Reprint**
☐ **Discontinue***

*Attach copy of form

Distribute completed job to:

Location	Quantity
AR	
BL	
BK	
CF	
CL	
DN	
ED	
EV	
GN	
LSC	
LK	
PIO	
SL	
VI	
WR	
XT	
Supply	
Other ____	

IMPORTANT: Every piece of printed material to be ordered through Central Supplies will be assigned a number. This includes forms, bibliographies, bookmarks, undated brochures. The logo, JCPL, the number, month and year of latest revision will appear on each piece.

Dated publications such as the newsletter and fliers do not require a form number.

Title _____ Form No._____ Quantity_____

PIO quantity _____ ☐ fold ☐ add web page _____

Submitted by_____ Branch ____ Phone # _____

Send proof to_____ Date submitted _____ Date needed _____

REMEMBER: Make a photo copy of your original text.
Proofread carefully
Return proof as soon as possible (call in OK or changes if deadline is near).

SPECIAL INSTRUCTIONS

☐ Staple ☐ Holepunch ☐ Fold ☐ Velobind ☐ Laminate ☐ Collate ☐ Pad

☐ Signs (attach description or use Notes below) ☐ Other _____

Notes (include any suggestions about size, color, etc.):

_____
_____
_____
_____
_____
_____

To be completed by Graphic Arts Department only

Date job in_____ Date completed _____

Press size_____ Finished size_____ Sides_____

Paper weight_____ Paper color_____ Ink color_____

Other_____
_____
_____

Keep white copy (Unit File)   Submit: yellow & pink copy - Director, Public Information

JCPL 215 3/2000

Source: Jefferson County (Colorado) Public Library

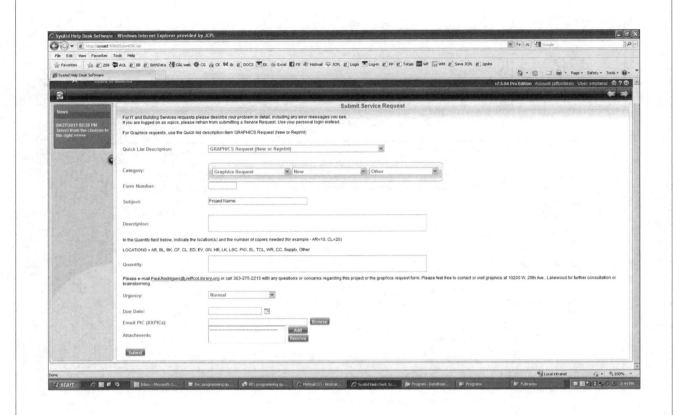

FIGURE 2.6 | **GRAPHIC ARTS REQUEST (ELECTRONIC)**

Source: Jefferson County (Colorado) Public Library

gramming. Nurture this group and give members the training and tools needed to be successful. First, any new members should complete the staff training that is detailed later in this chapter. The committee will spend the majority of any meeting deciding which topics or performers to pursue, and this means that some topics will *not* be pursued. Some members will feel strongly about certain topics or performers that others feel strongly simply won't work. In addition, the chair of the group will certainly benefit from a facilitation skills class. All members of the committee will benefit from becoming familiar with tools and techniques—consensus building, voting, brainstorm-

ing, SWOT analysis, Six Thinking Hats,[1] and so on— that offer guidance in discussion and decision-making techniques. At the very least, any high-functioning group must understand that general discussion is not decision making! Otherwise, you will talk about all those great ideas and possibilities until you've run out of meeting time. Please see figure 2.7 for an example of a programming committee charge. Last, it's crucial to maintain a committee membership that represents a wide perspective of both internal (staff, including administrators) and external (taxpayers, including elected officials) stakeholders and understands which issues and topics need to be handled carefully in order to anticipate and address questions or concerns that might come from library administration or segments of your community.

The process of establishing a committee may seem overly complicated, but it actually does save time by creating a program clearinghouse for the entire library system. Programming is a multidepartmental endeavor. A single program can include librarians, performers, graphic artists, building services staff, and many others. And, in order to get everything done, you must plan ahead.

PLANNING AHEAD

One phrase you will hear over and over again is "plan ahead." A large part of programming involves planning. Space for the program needs to be reserved ahead of time. Time must be set aside for writing whatever publicity you send to the local media. It takes time to create and print and distribute your flyers. Figure 2.8 is a checklist created by the East Baton Rouge (Louisiana) Parish Library. I include it to illustrate the amount of time and the number of people that can be involved in producing a single program. A library with thirteen branches developed this checklist. The workload is dispersed across several departments. A single-branch library might not have the various departments included in this checklist, but it will still have to perform many of the tasks. Someone will have to check the library's calendar to see that the program can be accommodated; someone will need to set up the room; someone will need to create and distribute the publicity; someone will have to set up any necessary equipment; someone will have to distribute, collect, and compile the evaluations; and so on.

The checklist provides a time line for the coordinator of the program. The idea phase should precede the event by about four months. Although four months sounds terribly far in advance, it is fairly common for programming. The people responsible for creating

FIGURE 2.7 | **PROGRAMMING COMMITTEE CHARGE**

Programming Team

The Programming Team provides overall guidance for the library's public programs plan and is responsible for decision-making, implementation and evaluation. Team members represent a cross section of work groups and locations and provide input, advice and staff support for public programs. The group meets six times during the year plus is responsible for communicating regularly on an ongoing basis as needed.

Source: Multnomah County (Oregon) Library

library publicity (marketing offices, graphics departments, etc.) generally want the information at least three months in advance to give them time to create flyers, newsletters, and news releases. It's also very likely that your program is just one of many publicity projects in the works. Plan ahead.

While we're in the mode of planning ahead, let's do a few more things. Let's start with a calendar-like projection of the coming year. What types of programs would you like to offer next year? If you have a budget, how would you like it to be distributed among these programs? When creating this calendar, you aren't worrying about who the performers will be. You are only identifying topics. Then you are guesstimating the costs, based on the number of locations that will host each program. You can either create a systemwide calendar or a branch-specific calendar. The month for each program will require some thought. You can work at this from either end: either you have a topic in mind and you then try to find the best month in which to hold the event, or you have a vacant month and you try to think of an event to host during that month. For example, looking at figure 2.9,

FIGURE 2.8 | **PROGRAMMING CHECKLIST**

Days in advance/ due date	Task—not all tasks are appropriate for all programs, of course!	Responsibility of	Contact or send to
3 months–1 year	Have an idea Look at pop culture, trends and fads, timely news events. See what's checking out from your collection—OR what ISN'T checking out and plan accordingly. Can this program link with other programs?	You	
3 months–1 year	Locate a speaker/performer Get several ways to contact. Make sure other staff members can access this information if needed.	You	
3 months–1 year	Secure program approval from branch manager	You	
3 months–1 year	Secure program approval from division coordinator If speaker requires an honorarium, Division Coordinator must approve this AND it must be a budgeted item.	Branch Manager	
3 months–1 year	Discuss whether program is suitable for collaboration with community partners or potential cosponsors If collaboration is appropriate—does the other group require COA or MOU? Will they share their mailing list? Do they need credit on printed pieces as well as press information? Do we have their logo?	Div Coordinator	
6 months–1 year	Discuss whether suitable for grant Ask Grants Librarian for help. Who will write and submit the grant? Prefer if the Friends group does it—then paperwork to pay speaker is much simpler than if City submits it.	Div Coordinator	
6 months–1 year	Write and submit grant Timing is important—most grants take quite a while to get back to you with a yes or a no.	You and Div Coordinator	Admin approves; City Grants Committee approves
3 months–1 year	Discuss whether suitable for replication in branches throughout the system Bring to programming committee for your target age group; if others are interested in replication, they are also potential volunteers for your event.	Div Coordinator	
3 months–1 year	Reserve meeting room Do not book anything into Children's Spaces without permission of CR. Indicate starting time as opposed to time you actually need the room for setup.	You	
3 months–1 year	Unreserve any dates you do not need	You	

Days in advance/ due date	Task—not all tasks are appropriate for all programs, of course!	Responsibility of	Contact or send to
3 months–1 year	Prepare speaker/performer's contract DO THIS ASAP; contracts are only needed if we are going to pay an honorarium; remember we do not pay travel so instruct speaker to include in fee.	Div Coordinator	Library Business Office; Parish Attorney's office; Purchasing Dept.
3 months–1 year	Order check Do this as soon as possible once the contract is received.	Div Coordinator	Business Office
3–6 months is norm, longer lead time for major events	Flesh out program details with presenter/speaker; arrange for photo or pictures, book jacket, biography, etc. Make sure other staff members can access this information if needed. Get from details, photos, art, etc. from Performer/ Speaker, publisher, website (do not use Syndetics Book Jacket!).	You	
3–6 months is norm, longer lead time for major events	Select date for program Might need to have several dates tentatively booked until Speaker commits. Consider ongoing or competing activities. Discuss waiting list and size of audience. If potential is for large crowd, ask speaker if would consider a second unadvertised event a bit after the first.	You	
3–6 months	Enter into online calendar	Your dept designee	
3–6 months	Submit program info sheet; if more than one branch is offering the same program, it is better to coordinate this form. Use the form on Staff web; please add much more than the basic Who/ What/ When/ Where/ How or Why—PR will need interesting information, facts, quotes to sell your program.	You	PR
3 months	Reserve AV Be sure you reserve ALL the pieces you need . . . and make sure mics are working!!!	You	AV
2 months	Order books from publisher or bookstore Contact publisher or local bookstore; be sure you know whose name needs to be on the check as patrons pay for their books.	Div Coordinator	
1–2 months	Create flyer or postcard. Remember that there are library PR templates available, as well as additional clipart choices through clipart.com. Don't reinvent the wheel. Be sure flyer or postcard includes Library's name, name and address of branch, day of week, date, time, website, and "free." Use grant or partner logos if appropriate.	You or PR	Contact PR concerning downloads from clipart .com

cont.

FIGURE 2.8 (cont.)

Days in advance/ due date	Task—not all tasks are appropriate for all programs, of course!	Responsibility of	Contact or send to
1–2 months	Print flyer or postcard Discuss color vs. black and white with PR and your Division Coordinator; if you are sending the job out to a vendor, know that it requires 5 days to print.	PR	PR sends printing jobs to official printer
varies	Press release The more information you can provide, the better.	PR	
6–8 weeks	Send press release to monthlies Special events warrant a personal call to editor.	PR	
6 weeks	Send info for library's monthly newsletter Depending on event, will want to run it several months in the Library's monthly newsletter.	PR	
1–2 months	Enter into commercial or nonprofit online events sites	PR	
1–2 months	Arrange TV or radio appearances, feature stories in print Discuss whether speaker can appear on Library's own TV show or if can appear on broadcast TV or radio; depends on dates, availability, remote capabilities, etc. For out-of-town speakers, we can often arrange telephone interviews for radio. You might also try for a video podcast to add to Facebook or use on the Library's monthly TV show.	You, Div Coordinator, and PR	PR
1–2 months	Order supplies Discuss with your Division Coordinator; must be in budget.	You or Branch Manager	Business Office
1–2 months	If a craft program, make a sample Make several—use to practice as well as market the program. If you make it early enough, take a picture for use in marketing the program.	You	
1–2 months	Annotated bibliography, playlists, etc. If appropriate, add such info to online posts on the website, LibGuides, Facebook, etc., as well as print.	You or designee	
1–2 months	Bookmark, if appropriate	You or designee	
1 month	Create a special mailing list? Is there a special mailing list for a target market? Ask your partners.	You or Div Coordinator	
1 month	Prepare sign-up registration sheets If speaker agrees to a second program, keep a list of people on the waiting list and invite them closer to the time.	You	
varies depending on importance	Rotating feature on library website If event is to be featured on the Library website home page or Facebook, PR and Webmaster will collaborate.	PR	Webmaster

Days in advance/ due date	Task—not all tasks are appropriate for all programs, of course!	Responsibility of	Contact or send to
varies	Freshen RSS feed, Twitter, blog, and Facebook Vary it—update as event draws closer.	PR	PR or Webmaster
1 month	Send announcements to targeted groups via flyer or e-mail announcements Apologize in advance for cross-posting.	You or Div Coordinator	
1 month	Send info to people on the special mailing list, if appropriate	You or Div Coordinator	
1 month	Prepare speaker's travel guide; send directions to the library and/ or hotel	You or designee	PR
1 month	Reconfirm with performer/speaker You will also follow up 3 days prior.	You	
1 month	Arrange for speaker's guardian angels, schedule, meals, etc.	You or Div Coordinator	
1 month	Ensure sufficient staff or volunteers for program Be sure staff can operate AV, etc. Get prior approval for possible compensatory time for staff from Admin.	You or Div Coordinator	
1 month	Prepare registration sign-up sheets Be sure to label properly.	You or designee	
2 weeks–1 month	Design e-flyer Send to PR to turn into a PDF for easier e-mailing; add grant or partner logos if appropriate.	You	PR
2 weeks–1 month	Announce on library hold notices and overdues Used sparingly—only for major events.	Comp Div	Admin approves
2 weeks–1 month	Arrange to get sufficient change for book sales with the Business Office For author events featuring book sales, etc.	You or Div Coordinator	Business Office
2 weeks–1 month	Post on social media Primarily Facebook—if possible, add photos.	PR	
2 weeks	Send PSAs	PR	
2 weeks	Send press release to weeklies	PR	
1 week	Send notice to media/photographers Remind them the day of or before.	PR	
1 week	Send press release to dailies	PR	
3 days prior	Reconfirm with performer/speaker Last chance to get details right.	You	
1 or 2 days before	Call registrants to remind them of program As people cancel, work the waiting list. If speaker has agreed to a second program, call your waiting list.	You or designee	

cont.

FIGURE 2.8 (cont.)

Days in advance/ due date	Task—not all tasks are appropriate for all programs, of course!	Responsibility of	Contact or send to
1 or 2 days before	Prepare sign-in sheets Be sure to label properly.	You or designee	
1 or 2 days before	Prepare evaluations Decide how in-depth these need to be with Div Coordinator.	You and Div Coordinator	
1 or 2 days before	Make name tags or table tents	You or designee	
1 or 2 days before	Make signs directing patrons to program	You or designee	
1 or 2 days before	Get speaker's check from Business Office Make sure that you give the check to whomever will be working at the program as host—it does no one any good at the wrong branch!	You or Div Coordinator	Business Office
1 or 2 days before	Get change from Business Office	You or Div Coordinator	Business Office
Day before or day of event	Pick up out-of-town speakers from airport Feed and house speaker . . . Try to not have speaker arrive the day of the program—air schedules are very unreliable these days.	You or designee	
Day before or day of event	Set up room Select from standard room layouts; special instructions for room setup require special attention from you.	You or designee	
Day before or day of event	Post on social media—especially Twitter Update Facebook and send Tweet.	PR	
Day before or day of event	Prepare introduction for speaker Last chance to get details right.	You or designee	
Day before or day of event	Pull related books and AV for program Get handouts or other materials ready. Pull books and AV related to the topic for display and check out.	You or designee	
Day of event	Set up AV LABEL the cords!!!!! Get back-up batteries, etc.	You or designee	AV
Day of event	E-mail photographers to remind of event This relationship with media develops over time . . .	PR	
Day of event	Water and special supplies for speaker Do you need water cups or pitcher? If autographing—does the speaker need a special pen?	You or designee	
Day of event	Program Introduce the speaker. Are there handouts? Bookmarks? Related materials?	You or designee	
Day of event	Take photos Take photos to document event . . . be sure and get signed photo release forms.	PR or designee	

Days in advance/ due date	Task—not all tasks are appropriate for all programs, of course!	Responsibility of	Contact or send to
Day of event	Evaluations Are these necessary for grant? Print evaluations at the end of the program or lead to online survey after?	You or designee	
Day of event	Library commercial at beginning and/or end of program Make the commercial relevant to the program. Remember to thank the Board, the Friends, volunteers, etc.	You or designee	
Day of event	Give speaker his/her check and return him/her to hotel Ask speaker if he or she wants want photos by e-mail, copies of program, etc.	You or designee	
Day of event	Clean up RETURN the AV equipment WITH all cords—even the extension cords.	You or designee	
Day of or after	Deliver speaker to airport Wait until speaker is safely in flight to leave—in case flight is canceled.	You or designee	
Day of or after	Return all supplies	You or designee	
Day of or after	Return leftover books to vendor Sometimes Library keeps leftovers for prizes, etc. Check with Division Coordinator and Collection Development.	You or designee	
Day of or after	Submit any book sale proceeds to Business Office Designate whether it was for Library sales or via the Friends group.	You or designee	
Day of or after	Post on social media Especially the photos	PR	
Day of or after	Thank speaker Prefer to send a handwritten thank you; send to Main Library for stamps and mail-out.	You or designee	
Within 1 week	Reconcile book bills with book sale receipts If you wait too long to do this, you will be SORRY!	You or designee	Business Office
Within 1 week	Thank other staff members, volunteers	You or designee	
Within 1 week	Thank partners or cosponsors Send them copies of printed pieces, etc.	You or designee	
Within 1 week	Thank funders; complete any necessary reports Send them copies of printed pieces, etc.; save copies for files, board reports, etc.	You or Div Coordinator	
Within 2 weeks	Evaluation by staff If you wait too long, you just won't get around to it.	You or designee	
At will	Replicate (and/or revise) the program	You and Div Coordinator	

Source: East Baton Rouge (Louisiana) Parish Library

FIGURE 2.9 | **PROGRAMMING CALENDAR, EXAMPLE A**

Adult Programming in 20XX

This table details how the Program Committee proposes to spend $5,000 on adult programming in 20XX.

Type of program	Description	Estimated cost per location	Cost of five locations	Projected month of program	Total cost
Travel in Europe	Speaker will explain how to book cheap flights, how to find inexpensive lodging, and how to eat, entertain yourself, and shop on a tight budget.	$75	$375	January	$375
Nonfiction Workshop	Speaker will discuss the art of writing nonfiction, as well as the craft of writing a book proposal and the process of finding an agent.	$100	$500	February	$500
Roses and Colorado Wildflowers	Speaker will offer programs on Colorado wildflowers, romantic roses, and general rose culture in Colorado.	$30	$150	March	$150
Quilts	Speaker will cover the history of quilts, collecting quilts, tips on making quilts.	$50	$250	April	$250
Bird Watching Program	Speaker will instruct attendees on types of birds from Colorado and where to go to watch them.	$75	$375	May	$375
Glen Hanket: Underwear by the Roadside	Author shows slides of his twelve-month tour of U.S. spent picking up roadside litter.	$100	$500	June	$500
ESL Class	Hire teachers from an ESL organization to give an ESL course to 15–20 patrons.	$2,000	$0	July	$2,000

Type of program	Description	Estimated cost per location	Cost of five locations	Projected month of program	Total cost
Colorado History	Local author and/or historian will offer a talk on Colorado History. (We are pursuing a program on historic Colorado barns.)	$75	$375	August	$375
Motorcycling in the Rockies	Speaker will talk about the equipment needed to cycle in the Rockies. Will also point out the best highways in Colorado for cycling.	$75	$375	September	$375
Adult Book Talk on Biographies	Hire a local professor to talk about the best biographies of recent years.	$75	$375	October	$375
Investing	Kathy Buys will give a program on investing. JCPL owns two of her books: *Invest with Confidence* and *Investment Basics for Women*.	$225	$1,125	November	$1,125
Winter Sports Other Than Skiing	Bring in a sports writer or owner of a local sporting goods store to give a talk on winter sports for the nonskier	$75	$375	December	$375 Annual Total: $6,775

you might already know that you want to host a wildflower program next year. People plant their flowers in late winter, and they begin thinking of taking nature walks during this time as well. So, how about March? If your December calendar is still vacant, perhaps you could find someone to give a talk on the winter sports possibilities in your state.

Creating such a calendar can keep you focused. It doesn't have to be etched in stone; changes can be made. But it will definitely help you set goals and project your spending. This calendar is a kind of strategic plan. A plan can only help you if you intend to ask a group—such as your Friends group or library foundation—for money. Potential funders are impressed by proposals that show them what you intend to do, when you will do it, and how much it will cost. They may have suggestions, but this feedback only verifies that you have gotten their attention and interest. Figure 2.9 is an example of a basic calendar that ensures that you have one adult program planned for each month of the year. Figure 2.10 is a calendar that sketches out a year for a library (MCL) that produces a *lot* of programs.

While we're busy creating calendars and such, I'll mention another piece of record keeping that can be very helpful. How do you intend to track the programs that you have booked? If you use a program request worksheet (similar to the one included in figure 2.4), then you will probably have an electronic or paper copy of that request somewhere. That works fairly well if yours is a one-branch system or if your branch is the only location hosting the program. However, if yours is a multibranch system and several locations have agreed to produce the program, then all the branches that booked the program will want some way to track their requests. Will each branch submit its own request for the same program, or will one person coordinate the program series for everyone with one request? If you choose the latter, then you will have a single request for multiple branches. This results in less paperwork, but how will all the branches keep track of the programs they've requested? One way is to create a central calendar or database that tracks the programs occurring within the library system. The program committee chair might maintain this database. It will track which branches requested which programs, the name of the performer, the title of the program, and the dates and times. You might also want to track housekeeping details such as whether meeting rooms have been booked and the program coordinator's name. Figure 2.11 is a sample database from McCracken County (Kentucky) Public Library.

> Do I contradict myself? Very well, then I contradict myself, I am large, I contain multitudes.
> —Walt Whitman, "Song of Myself"

Now let me backpedal a little bit and contradict myself. Ideally you will build into your programming processes some capability to offer that unexpected program or two that falls into your lap and is just too good to pass up. The agent or publisher of a fairly well-known author might call you and offer an appearance at your library on short notice and at no cost. Or a breaking news item might continue to develop and evolve to the point that it compels you to quickly coordinate a panel discussion on that topic while it remains newsworthy. Whatever the reason, it's ideal if you have a fast-track process in place that allows you to offer the occasional program within a tight time frame. For example, you might realize that a last-minute program is possible if you forgo print publicity and rely on publicizing it via your website and Facebook and Twitter accounts. You might also realize that those programs that are offered to you at no cost can be produced fairly quickly since they don't require contracts or checks. So your guidelines for fast-track programs could specify that in order for programs to be produced quickly, they must be free to the library and not require graphic design resources. With some thought and flexibility, you will find ways to create the capacity that allows you to add that too-good-to-pass-up program that comes along just when you thought you had everything so nicely planned.

Another way to build in flexibility and speed might be to create a recurring, monthly series that allows you to plug topics into the mix as they emerge. For example, you could create a series called Conversations and Community and publicize this event as an ongoing discussion around issues that are important to your community. Then you or the facilitator of the series would monitor local news and remain informed of community concerns in order to plan each month's conversation around issues that are currently trending. You could then announce the specific topics of conversation a day or two in advance of the event by posting that information on Facebook and Twitter.

So what's the right balance between planning and flexibility? Planning has its advantages. We know that good publicity gets the word out and increases attendance; contracts clarify expectations between the library and your performers. But flexibility and speed allow you to say yes to programming opportunities that materialize unexpectedly. For most of us,

FIGURE 2.10 | **PROGRAMMING CALENDAR, EXAMPLE B**

Ideas	July 2011	August 2011	September 2011	October 2011	November 2011	December 2011
	Summer Reading	Summer Reading	*Hispanic Heritage Month (9/15–10/15)	*wordstock *Hispanic Heritage Month (9/15–10/15) *Teen Read Month *Zinesters Talking—NPO, WOD, HWD, CEN *Mid-Autumn Festival	*Native American Heritage Month *National Caregiver Month *Tapestry of Tales Prostate Cancer Awareness at CEN	Pride and Passion

Civic Engagement

*Writer's Resource Fair	Pageturners Teen Council East County issues/divide program HGT current issues group	Pageturners Teen Council East County issues/divide program HGT current issues group This Zine Will Rock You at CEN	*Cafe Banned *International Literacy Day Pageturners Teen Council East County issues/divide program HGT current issues group Conversation Projects Feasting on Forbidden Fruits	Pageturners *Books Into Action Teen Council East County issues/divide program HGT current issues group Conversation Projects	Teen Council East County issues/divide program HGT current issues group *Louisa May Alcott Programming/Book Group Pageturners	*A national issues program (America Speaks, Great Decisions, National Issues Forum) Pageturners Teen Council—Social East County issues/divide program HGT current issues group

Resources for Immigrants

	Citizenship classes Talk Time Intercambio ELL labs Vietnamese computer classes/labs/other TL labs ESL languages at ROC Storytimes in TL Chinese Knitting	Citizenship classes Talk Time Intercambio ELL labs Vietnamese computer classes/labs/other TL labs ESL languages at ROC Storytimes in TL	Citizenship classes Talk Time Intercambio ELL labs Vietnamese computer classes/labs/other TL labs ESL languages at ROC Storytimes in TL Chinese Knitting	Citizenship classes Talk Time Intercambio ELL labs Vietnamese computer classes/labs/other TL labs ESL languages at ROC Storytimes in TL Chinese Knitting	Citizenship classes Talk Time Intercambio ELL labs Vietnamese computer classes/labs/other TL labs ESL languages at ROC Storytimes in TL Chinese Knitting	*Russian Programming Citizenship classes Talk Time Intercambio ELL labs Vietnamese computer classes/labs/other TL labs ESL languages at ROC Storytimes in TL Chinese Knitting

Resources in These Economic Times

*Surviving Change *Computer classes Office productivity (Word, etc.) job labs GED ELL tax labs TL classes *Tax help	*Computer classes Office productivity (Word, etc.) job labs GED ELL TL classes *FINRA, financial literacy programs	*Computer classes Office productivity (Word, etc.) job labs GED ELL TL classes	*Fun and free entertainment and recreation programs (concerts, crafts) FINRA, financial literacy programs Opera Previews/Workshop	*Fun and free entertainment and recreation programs (concerts, crafts) FINRA, financial literacy programs Opera Previews/Workshop	*Fun and free entertainment and recreation programs (concerts, crafts) Holiday Budgeting Homemade gifts	*Fun and free entertainment and recreation programs (concerts, crafts) Holiday Budgeting

cont.

FIGURE 2.10 (cont.)

Resources in These Economic Times (cont.)

*Medicare programs *Writers Resource Fair *Writers workshops/ Attic *International Literacy Day *FINRA, financial literacy programs *Smart Choices programs *Timely programs: Where are the jobs now that things are picking up? *Fun and free entertainment and recreation programs (concerts, crafts)	*Fun and free entertainment and recreation programs (concerts, crafts)	*Fun and free entertainment and recreation programs (concerts, crafts) FINRA, financial literacy programs

Early Literacy/Success in School

*Preschool fair at HLS *Storytimes including bilingual and other *Math fun/Go figure program boxes *Month of the Young Child programs *Summer Reading themed/related programs *Teen Lounges *Dia de los Ninos *Teen service events *Ongoing family and children's programs *Children's book fair at NPO	*Ongoing family and children's programs Summer Reading SR Volunteer Opps for Teens	*Ongoing family and children's programs Summer Reading SR Volunteer Opps for Teens	*Ongoing family and children's programs	*Ongoing family and children's programs Matt de la Pena

Other

*TLF grant funded programming (children's programming, Native American programming, humanities programming) *Special programs *Exhibit-related programming	backpacking/hiking	

Source: Multnomah County (Oregon) Library

FIGURE 2.11 | **PROGRAM DATABASE**

FIGURE 2.11 | **PROGRAM DATABASE**

	Date	Title	Presenter	Sponsor	Attending	Contact
2	7/9/2009	Rebel in the White House-Emillie To	Betsy Smith	KHC & Friends	51	Betsy Smith
2	08/06/09	African-Americans in the Civil War	Susan Hawkins	MCPL	46	Susan Hawkins
2	9/17/09	The Houses of Alben Barkley	Steve Gabany	MCPL	32	Steve Gabany
2	10/22/09	More Ky Ghosts	Lynwwod Montell	MCPL & KHC	31	Lynwwod Montell
2	11/12/09	Myths & Misconceptions About Padu	John Robertson	MCPL & Friends	70	John Robertson
2	12/10/09	Ky Politics :Bombast , Burgoo	Berry Craig	MCPL & KHC	22	Berry Craig
2	1/14/10	Recycling : Adding Quality to Your Liv	Merle Paschedag	MCPL & Friends	15	Merle Paschedag
2	3/11/10	Wildflower Myths & Realities	Dr. Thomas Barnes	KHC & Friends	49	Dr. Thomas Barnes
2	4/22/10	Taking Care of Family Quilts	Judy Schwender	Nat. Quilt Museu	26	Judy Schwender
2	5/13/10	Kentuckians are Storytellers	Georgia Green Stamper	KHC & Friends	18	Georgia Green Stamper
2	6/10/10	In Search of Adolph Rupp	Dr. Duane Bolin	MCPL	18	Dr. Duane Bolin
2	7/08/10	Investigating Local Cemeteries	Tommy Thompson	MCPL	50	Tommy Thompson
2	8/19/10	Railroading in Paducah Then & Now	Bob Johnston	MCPL & Friends	41	Bob Johnston
2	9/16/10	Got Milk ? Dairies from Paducah's Pa	B.J. Summers	MCPL	26	Bobby Summers
2	10/22/10	Ghosts, Spirits & Angels :True Tales	Thomas Freese	MCPL	70	Thomas Freese
2	12/2/10	Rosemary Clooney -Sentimental Jour	Bet Stewart	KHC & Friends	51	Bet Stewart
2	1/20/11	canceled due to weather			0	
2	2/17/11	The Underground Railroad in Ky	Stephen Brown	MCPL & KHC	40	Stephen A Brown
2	3/17/11	Culinary Tourism	Albert Schmid	MCPL & KHC	33	Albert Schmid
2	4/28/11	Preaching to the Choir /Quilt Progran	Judy Schwender	MCPL & Quilt Mus	7	Judy Schwender
2	5/12/11	Commemorating the Civil War with F	Nikos Pappas	MCPL & KHC	37	Nikos Pappas
2	6/23/11	In Search of Baptist History	J. Duane Bolin	MCPL	20	Dr. J. Duane Bolin
2	7/08/11	D-Day to Berlin -Freedom is Not Free	Michael Freeland	MCPL & Friends	39	Michael Freeland
2	8/04/11	African American Genealogy -Tracing	Stefan Jagoe	MCPL & Friends	19	Stefan Jagoe
2	9/15/11	The Ohio River & Its First Steamboat	Kadie Engstrom	MCPL	25	Kadie Engstrom
2	10/20/11	A Strange Brew	Thomas Freese	MCPL	60	Thomas Freese
2	11/17/11	Postcards From Paducah's Past	B. j. Summers	MCPL	49	B.J. Summers
2	12/08/11	Paducah Year in Review 2011	Steve Hecklinger	MCPL & Friends	15	Steve Hecklinger
2	1/05/12	Identity Theft	Dean Patterson/John Si	MCPL	35	State Trooper Dean Patter
2	2/9/12	Lift Ev'r Voice & Sing	Daryl Harris	MCPL & KHC	46	Daryl Harris
2	3/15/12	Mary Settles, The Last Shaker @ Plea	Janet Scott	MCPL & KHC	50	Janet Scott

program planning is just one of the things that we do during our busy workdays. We certainly want to be nimble and flexible in order to offer the programs that seem too good or too newsworthy to pass up. And we also need to plan in advance to ensure that we have set aside the time and completed the steps needed to create successful programs. The best mix is to work some flexibility into your overall game plan.

POLICIES VERSUS PRACTICE

As you continue to offer programs, you will encounter more and more questions that need answers. If your organization stresses documentation, you will want to answer these questions by creating new policies. Or you might just want to answer these questions through staff training. Or you might do both. Alright already, you say, what are these questions? We will address many of these in later chapters, but questions you will eventually face as a program coordinator include the following:

- What do I do if the performer wants to alter his contract?
- What do I do if the media, the performer, or a patron wants to videotape or take photographs?
- How much am I willing to pay a performer? Many performers are professionals. They do amazing work, and they charge amazing prices. It isn't hard to find a performer who is willing to charge $175 or more an hour.
- How many branches can offer the same program during the same month? When does the library begin to compete against itself?
- How do I conduct crowd control? If I know a program will be hugely popular, do I hand out tickets as people arrive? Do I take reservations over the phone?

Some of these questions can be addressed as written policies. Others are better answered through training. For example, many libraries have a ticket policy, but I imagine few have a "how many locations are too much?" policy. Through training, you can teach program coordinators to judge how many locations should host a particular program. Through practice, you will begin to notice which topics and performers draw large crowds regardless of the number of locations that host the event. Over time, you can create a programming manual that addresses various programming issues. Consider including an FAQ section and posting the manual electronically as a web page for staff reference.

TEACH YOUR STAFF HOW TO PRODUCE GOOD PROGRAMS

Adults can learn from reading, but we have better retention if we can actively participate in the training process and practice what we learn. If you can find a programming mentor or if you can become a mentor, you will learn more and you will enjoy learning. Let someone talk and walk you through the process, from start to finish—from the initial idea, through the production, and into the evaluation process. Be sure that training involves producing an actual program. Knowing that the result is a real performance will increase your desire to learn and participate.

Another training format is the training workshop. This workshop can cover all the dry things, such as paperwork and evaluation forms, and it can accentuate the better parts, such as choosing a topic and selecting a performer. Ending the workshop with a performance is a nice touch. Before the performance, one of the workshop presenters can explain how the performer was located and how long it took to organize the program, and then it's show time! A workshop might run ninety minutes with thirty minutes reserved for the performance. Topics covered in the workshop can be assigned to people from various departments. For example, someone from your marketing or graphics office can present the piece on publicity.

Here is a possible workshop outline:

I. Introduction (including a brief mention of how programming ties into the library's mission)
II. Types of programming
    A. Adult programming
    B. YA programming
    C. Children's programming
III. Getting started
    A. Getting to know your community
    B. Selecting a topic
    C. Planning the program's content: includes identifying a performer, choosing the right format, deciding on the performer's fee, etc.
IV. Understanding how publicity works (including deadlines for when to submit publicity)
V. Filling out the paperwork (either online or on paper)
VI. Producing a live program

Homework: each person in attendance will coordinate a program during the next year.

We've covered quite a bit in this chapter: programming policy, budgets, ways to engage volunteers, forming programming committees. We've created some tools that will help us in the planning process, such as calendars and databases that track our pending programs. And we've trained our staff in these policies and techniques. Most of the staff that received this training are probably public services staff—relevant reference, adult, and children's librarians, circulation staff, and the like. They will be coordinating the programs. But before we put our training into practice, let's be sure that we have included administrative services in our plans.

NOTE

1. Edward De Bono, *Six Thinking Hats* (Boston: Little, Brown, 1985).

Administrative Necessities

For those of us who don't work in administrative services, it's easy to list at least one thing that the people in this department do: they write our paychecks. What else happens there? We're pretty sure that administrators somehow control the budget. But what relation could administrative services have to programming?

Depending on your library's hierarchy, administrative services may also be responsible for your insurance, the performers' contracts, and the facilities and equipment you will need to host your program. Because the people in your administrative offices perform their duties so proficiently, it can be easy to overlook what they do. If you happen to perform these duties within your library, then you are very aware of how crucial they are.

We will look closely at budgeting in chapter 5. In this chapter we will look at three other administrative necessities: insurance, contracts, and facilities and payments.

INSURANCE

Here's the main point to address: be sure that your library's liability insurance policy includes programming as a "covered activity." Be prepared to talk with and negotiate with your insurance provider to get this activity included. Your policy's premium may go up as a result of adding programming as an activity. If your insurance provider balks at the idea of adding programming, stand firm. You are the customer. Let the provider know that library programming is an ingredient within your overall library mission. Give the representative a copy of your library's mission statement and programming policy. Be sure to be up front and honest about the types of programs you expect to offer. If you plan on cosponsoring a sky diving class and other extreme sporting events, tell your insurance provider. You don't want the company to be caught completely off guard if it is ever confronted by a claim from a program gone wrong. If you are planning a program that might have an element of danger to the audience, such as a wild animal exhibition, call the person in administrative services who handles your insurance policy and explain the program. That individual may then call the insurance agent and explain the program to him or her. The result might be that the insurance company boosts the coverage on the policy for the time period in which this program will occur. Just please stay in close communication with the person in your library who handles your insurance and legal issues.

You will also want your performers to sign an indemnity clause that states that the performer holds the library harmless from all claims and damages arising from the performer's actions. Run this clause past an attorney before you begin using it. Many performers have their own liability insurance. If this is the case, ask the performer to include the library as an additional insured on the policy. Always ask for proof of this insurance. Figure 3.1 is a policy for a performer, John the Juggler. In the bottom left-hand corner labeled "certificate holder," you can see that John has included the library as an additional insured.

CONTRACTS

You will want to provide a written agreement—a contract—to the performer. The most important thing about a contract is making sure that you have one. A sample contract is included in chapter 8. Have an attorney look over your contract before you put it into use. Let your attorney also look at your programming policy. This will help the attorney see what you are trying to accomplish with your contract. Ideally, you will develop a fill-in-the-blank contract that can be used with all your programs. It is important that you have the administrative processes in place that allow you to meet the terms of the contract. Be sure that the check is drafted in time. And give the performer a phone number for a contact person that she or he can call with contract questions. Performers frequently ask if they can tweak the contract slightly. You will want to make sure that your contact people know how to answer these questions or know to whom they can refer these questions.

MEMORANDUMS OF UNDERSTANDING (MOUS)

Memorandums of understanding (MOUs)—sometimes called "letters of understanding"—are useful documents to create when you are forging partnerships. If you work for a county library and you are partnering with the county health department to produce a series of programs on diet and exercise, then an MOU will be helpful in documenting what role each department will play. Your administrative services staff should be able to assist you in developing MOUs. They will most likely also want to keep a copy of your MOU on file in their offices. Figure 3.2 is a sample MOU between Multnomah County Library (MCL) and Life by Design NW.

FACILITIES AND EQUIPMENT

The administrative departments within your library probably transport equipment from one location to another. They may also set up the rooms. They may clean the rooms, or they may contract with outside companies that do the cleaning. Regardless of which department does the work, it needs to be done before the program begins. In order for this to happen, you will need a process in place that allows the program coordinator to effectively communicate with the people who do the preceding tasks. Maybe you

FIGURE 3.1 | **PERFORMER INSURANCE POLICY**

ACORD™ CERTIFICATE OF LIABILITY INSURANCE

DATE (MM/DD/YY)
11/22/1999

PRODUCER (415)957-0600 FAX (415)957-0577	THIS CERTIFICATE IS ISSUED AS A MATTER OF INFORMATION ONLY AND CONFERS NO RIGHTS UPON THE CERTIFICATE HOLDER. THIS CERTIFICATE DOES NOT AMEND, EXTEND OR ALTER THE COVERAGE AFFORDED BY THE POLICIES BELOW.
Maroevich O'Shea & Coghlan 425 Market Street 10th Floor San Francisco, CA 94105	**COMPANIES AFFORDING COVERAGE**
Attn: Ext:	COMPANY A Royal Insurance Company of America
INSURED	COMPANY B Republic Indemnity
John the Juggler, Inc.	COMPANY C
	COMPANY D

COVERAGES

THIS IS TO CERTIFY THAT THE POLICIES OF INSURANCE LISTED BELOW HAVE BEEN ISSUED TO THE INSURED NAMED ABOVE FOR THE POLICY PERIOD INDICATED, NOTWITHSTANDING ANY REQUIREMENT, TERM OR CONDITION OF ANY CONTRACT OR OTHER DOCUMENT WITH RESPECT TO WHICH THIS CERTIFICATE MAY BE ISSUED OR MAY PERTAIN, THE INSURANCE AFFORDED BY THE POLICIES DESCRIBED HEREIN IS SUBJECT TO ALL THE TERMS, EXCLUSIONS AND CONDITIONS OF SUCH POLICIES. LIMITS SHOWN MAY HAVE BEEN REDUCED BY PAID CLAIMS.

CO LTR	TYPE OF INSURANCE	POLICY NUMBER	POLICY EFFECTIVE DATE (MM/DD/YY)	POLICY EXPIRATION DATE (MM/DD/YY)	LIMITS	
A	GENERAL LIABILITY COMMERCIAL GENERAL LIABILITY CLAIMS MADE [X] OCCUR OWNER'S & CONTRACTOR'S PROT	PSP045676	11/20/1999	11/20/2000	GENERAL AGGREGATE PRODUCTS - COMP/OP AGG PERSONAL & ADV INJURY EACH OCCURRENCE FIRE DAMAGE (Any one fire) MED EXP (Any one person)	$ 2,000,000 $ 1,000,000 $ 1,000,000 $ 1,000,000 $ 300,000 $ 5,000
A	AUTOMOBILE LIABILITY ANY AUTO ALL OWNED AUTOS [X] SCHEDULED AUTOS [X] HIRED AUTOS [X] NON-OWNED AUTOS	PST244513	11/20/1999	11/20/2000	COMBINED SINGLE LIMIT BODILY INJURY (Per person) BODILY INJURY (Per accident) PROPERTY DAMAGE	$ 1,000,000 $ $ $
	GARAGE LIABILITY ANY AUTO				AUTO ONLY - EA ACCIDENT OTHER THAN AUTO ONLY: EACH ACCIDENT AGGREGATE	$ $ $
A	EXCESS LIABILITY [X] UMBRELLA FORM OTHER THAN UMBRELLA FORM	PLA433286	11/20/1999	11/20/2000	EACH OCCURRENCE AGGREGATE	$ 5,000,000 $ 5,000,000 $
B	WORKERS COMPENSATION AND EMPLOYERS' LIABILITY THE PROPRIETOR/ PARTNERS/EXECUTIVE [INCL] OFFICERS ARE: [EXCL]	13459203	10/01/1999	10/01/2000	[X] WC STATU-TORY LIMITS / OTH-ER EL EACH ACCIDENT EL DISEASE - POLICY LIMIT EL DISEASE - EA EMPLOYEE	$ 1,000,000 $ 1,000,000 $ 1,000,000
	OTHER					

DESCRIPTION OF OPERATIONS/LOCATIONS/VEHICLES/SPECIAL ITEMS
Issued as Evidence of Insurance

CERTIFICATE HOLDER	CANCELLATION
Jefferson County Public Library 10200 West 20th Avenue Lakewood, CO 80215	SHOULD ANY OF THE ABOVE DESCRIBED POLICIES BE CANCELLED BEFORE THE EXPIRATION DATE THEREOF, THE ISSUING COMPANY WILL ENDEAVOR TO MAIL __30__ DAYS WRITTEN NOTICE TO THE CERTIFICATE HOLDER NAMED TO THE LEFT, BUT FAILURE TO MAIL SUCH NOTICE SHALL IMPOSE NO OBLIGATION OR LIABILITY OF ANY KIND UPON THE COMPANY, ITS AGENTS OR REPRESENTATIVES. AUTHORIZED REPRESENTATIVE

ACORD 25-S (1/95) ©ACORD CORPORATION 1988

FIGURE 3.2 | **MEMORANDUM OF UNDERSTANDING**

[Name]
Multnomah County Library
801 SW 19th Avenue
Portland, OR 97205
Re: Life by Design NW Letter Agreement

This letter constitutes a Grant Agreement from Portland Community College ("PCC"), designated administrator of grant funds awarded to the Portland Community College Foundation (collectively, the "Grantor") to Multnomah County Library (the "Grantee") for Grantee to implement aspects of the PCC program, Life by Design NW. Administration of the program will be through the Life by Design Program Director (the "Program Director"), an employee of PCC. The mission of Life by Design NW is to support people as they age in discovering their passion and purpose and engage their wisdom and skills to strengthen the community and achieve personal fulfillment. The objective is to develop and implement a comprehensive program for employers and the public to reach and engage adults over 50 years of age in life planning and community involvement.

Life by Design NW is a grant-funded program of the Grantor. This Agreement is subject to the Grant requirements of the various nonprofit entities funding the project, including Atlantic Philanthropies, Meyer Memorial Trust, and The Collins Foundation.

Funding Arrangements

Each partner or subgrantee organization will be required to submit requests for funds in accordance with the policies and procedures of PCC, the terms and conditions of this Agreement, and the requests by the Program Director.

Disbursement of funds is contingent upon fulfillment of goals, objectives, and reporting requirements as specified by the Program Director and this Agreement.

Disclosure and Use of Information

It is expected that all information obtained as a result of this grant will be shared with PCC by the Grantee or subgrantee.

Reporting Accountability to Funding Agencies

Grantor is responsible for providing interim and final reports to funding Foundations on a schedule prescribed in the grant awards (see below) as a contingency for receiving awarded funds. Due dates for submission to the Program Director of data and information necessary for completing the reports are listed next to the report dates. Grantees and subgrantees receiving funding for specified activities to meet the goals and objectives of the program will be responsible for submitting reporting forms to the Program Director by the report schedule due dates listed below. Disbursement of funds will be contingent upon each Grantee meeting reporting requirements as specified by the Program Director and Grantor. Reports will be submitted electronically and by first class mail to the addresses below:

Program Director
Life By Design NW Program
Portland Community College
PO Box 19000
Portland, OR 97280

The Atlantic Philanthropies

Data to Program Director	Type	Report Schedule Due Date
July 1, 2008	Progress Report	August 15, 2008
January 1, 2009	Progress Report	February 15, 2009
July 1, 2009	Pre-final Report	August 15, 2009
October 1, 2009	Final Report	November 30, 2009

Meyer Memorial Trust

Data to Program Director	Type	Report Schedule Due Date
May 1, 2008	Progress Report	June 15, 2008
November 1, 2008	Progress Report	December 15, 2008
May 1, 2009	Pre-final Report	June 15, 2009
November 1, 2009	Final Report	December 15, 2009

The Collins Foundation

Data to Program Director	Type	Report Schedule Due Date
October 1, 2008	Progress Report	November 15, 2008
October 1, 2009	Final Report	November 15, 2009

The Program Director will distribute reporting forms for each grant. Grantees and subgrantees will be required to send completed forms by the respective due dates. Reporting information may include, but will not be limited to:

1. Goals and objectives, work plans, activities taken place, statistics for participation, and any other evaluation results obtained.

cont.

FIGURE 3.2 (cont.)

2. How results/activities have met or contributed to meeting goals and objectives, and any reasons for variation between intention and experiences.

3. Anticipated or unanticipated events that affected the project; any modifications.

4. Measurable effect on organization (attracted more funding, increased collaboration with organizations, increased volunteers, etc.).

5. Measurable effect on populations served.

6. Political, regulatory, and socioeconomic operating environment.

7. Lessons Learned: successes and failures, problems encountered and your responses, lessons learned.

8. Financial Review: back-up receipts and accounting for expenditures to date, line item comparison between current and original budget and explanation of any changes, overall financial status report on expended and unexpended funds.

9. Submission of annual reports.

10. In-kind resources.

11. Any other information required by the Program Director or Grantor.

Evaluation

Each Grantee or subgrantee receiving funds for the purposes of these grants will be required to collect participant data, track participation (pro-active as well as upon completion), administer evaluations, and provide evaluation results on specific due dates as determined by the Program Director. These must be submitted as directed by the Program Director to the designated representative of the evaluation team at the Institute on Aging, Portland State University.

General

Each Grantee or subgrantee will help develop and implement participant feedback mechanisms, including participant-initiated suggestions, compliments, complaints, and related communications, and include this feedback in progress reports to the Program Director and Grantor.

Each Grantee or subgrantee will be required to support the development of the comprehensive website by providing related content information in their respective fields and agencies, including events and activities for a real-time calendar of events, assessment tools, online resources, links to related organizations and resources, and other information as may be requested by the Program Director or Grantor.

Each Grantee or subgrantee will be required to participate in the overall marketing and outreach activities designed to support the successful implementation and sustainability of the program as requested by the Program Director or Grantor, to include but not be limited to: development of collateral items, media toolkit, photos and other multi-media presentations, public service announcements, etc. Any press releases or other public relations materials and/or activities must be submitted in advance to the Program Director for review and approval. Grantee or subgrantee may only use the names of the funding agencies (The Atlantic Philanthropies, Meyer Memorial Trust, or The Collins Foundation) with Grantor's prior approval. Requests for such approval must be submitted at least one month in advance.

Copies of any RFP's, marketing materials, and/or the use of the Life by Design NW or funding agencies' logos, and any other significant bodies of work developed by a Grantee or their subgrantee must be submitted to the Life by Design NW Program Director at least one month in advance of publication for review and/or approval.

Each Grantee or subgrantee will be required to develop integrated systems for participants to flow between other Grantees, develop internal continuous quality improvement feedback systems, and create referral systems to non-partner outside organizations.

Staff

Any staff secured for the purposes of fulfilling this grant may be used for the sole purpose of this grant and not to supplement or substitute the organization's normal and customary staffing.

Financial Arrangements

Any adjustments of over 10 percent in a line item should be shared with the Program Director. Financial summaries of funds expended for the purposes of this program must be submitted quarterly or upon request.

Amendments

The terms of this Agreement may only be amended with the mutual written consent of the parties.

Subject to the foregoing reporting obligations and their performance to the satisfaction of Grantor, the Grantor will pay the Grantee organization $0,000.00 in return for the following tasks designed to further the initiative:

- Use of seven computer labs at county libraries for online assessment by the public.
- Volunteer Services Program: Connect LBD participants with volunteer opportunities (Friends of Library/The Library Foundation).
- Offer 4 programs/month across 17 locations on life-planning and older adult programming.
- Offer PR via library website, news release, and bookmark/brochure for Library and LBD Events.
- Link LBD website to library-created resources.
- Assist in content development of LBD website.

- Provide lists of electronic resources for local, national and international organizations.
- .5 FTE Program Director.
- Admin support.
- Provide technical assistance to program development.
- Manage budget allocations for supplies, printing, travel and other expenses.
- Reporting as required.
- Support mission, goals and other activities and objectives of the organization.
- Responsibilities as outlined in MOU for Life by Design NW Leadership Council Members.

cont.

FIGURE 3.2 (cont.)

General terms and conditions of this Agreement are as provided in Appendix A, attached hereto and incorporated into this Agreement by this reference, and agreed to by signature below.

MULTNOMAH COUNTY LIBRARY

By: _____

    Signature   Date

_____

    Title

PORTLAND COMMUNITY COLLEGE

By: _____

    District Vice President   Date

    Administration and Finance

Appendix A: General Terms and Conditions

Time is of the essence in the performance of this Agreement. The Agreement may be terminated: (1) by written agreement with the consent of both parties; (2) by Grantor for any reason on 30 days' written notice to Grantee; (3) by Grantee for any reason on 30 days' written notice to Grantor, subject to the conditions below; or (4) by either party within 15 days of written notice of breach of the Agreement by the other, provided the allegedly breaching party is allowed to cure that breach within those 15 days. Grantee's termination of the Agreement under provision (3) above is subject to Grantee carrying out its program responsibilities and maintaining fiscal accountability, including transfer of information and work related to its participation in the program, a termination date at the completion of a logical phase of work, and meeting its commitments up to the effective date of its withdrawal. Any failure to meet these obligations will constitute a breach of the Agreement.

Grantee shall submit requests for distribution of funds by invoice to the Grantor with their progress reports as services are performed. Payment shall be made within 30 days of receipt of invoice. In the event of termination, payment shall be as follows: (1) If termination is by mutual agreement or at the discretion of the Grantor, the Grantor will pay for work performed in accordance with the Agreement prior to the termination date, without liability on the part of the Grantor for direct, indirect, or consequential damages, and without the Grantor waiving any claims it may have against Grantee; (2) if termination is by Grantee with 30 days' written notice, Grantor will pay for work performed, providing Grantee terminated subject to the requirements of discretionary termination above; and (3) if termination is due to breach, the Grantor will pay Grantee for work performed in accordance with the Agreement prior to the termination date, less any setoff to which the Grantor is entitled.

Grantee agrees it is operating as an independent contractor in performing its obligations under this Agreement. No third parties are entitled to enforce the terms of this Agreement. The Grantor may undertake or award other contracts for additional or related work, and Grantee will fully cooperate with such other entities and with any Grantor employees concerned with such additional or related work.

Grantee will not commit or permit any act that will interfere with the performance of work by any other contractor or by Grantor employees.

Grantee shall maintain all fiscal records directly relating to this Agreement in accordance with generally accepted accounting principles. In addition, Grantee shall maintain any other records pertinent to this Agreement in such a manner as to clearly document Grantee's performance. Grantee shall retain and keep accessible all such documentation for a minimum of 3 years, or such longer period as may be required by applicable law, following final payment and termination of this Agreement, or until the conclusion of any audit, controversy, or litigation arising out of or related to this Agreement, whichever is the later date. Grantee agrees that the Grantor and its authorized representatives shall have access to the books, documents, papers, and records of Grantee which are directly pertinent to the specific contract for the purpose of making audit, examination, excerpts, and transcripts.

All work products created by Grantee as part of Grantee's performance of this Agreement, including background data, documentation, and staff work shall be the exclusive property of the Grantor. If any such work products contain intellectual property of Grantee that is or could be protected by federal copyright, patent, or trademark laws, Grantee hereby grants the Grantor a perpetual, royalty-free, fully paid-up, non-exclusive, and irrevocable license to copy, reproduce, deliver, publish, perform, dispose of, use, re-use, in whole or in part, and to authorize others to do so, all such work products. Any work products created by Grantee as part of Grantee's performance of this Agreement may be used by Grantee in providing services to its own non-profit clients, but may not be copied, reproduced, delivered, published, performed, disposed of, or used or re-used, in whole or in part, for any other purpose. If this Agreement is terminated by either party or by default, the Grantor, in addition to any other rights provided by this Agreement, may require Grantee to transfer and deliver such partially completed work products, reports, or other documentation that Grantee has specifically developed or specifically acquired for the performance of this Agreement.

The provisions of this Agreement will be construed in accordance with the laws of the State of Oregon. Any legal action arising under this Agreement must be brought in Multnomah County Circuit Court, or, if a federal forum is required, in the United States District Court for the State of Oregon. If any provision of this Agreement is declared by a court of competent jurisdiction to be illegal or in conflict with any law, the validity of the remaining provisions shall not be affected, and the rights and obligations of the parties shall be construed and enforced as if the Agreement did not contain the offending provision. The rule of construction that an Agreement is construed against the drafter shall not apply to any dispute over the application of this Agreement.

Source: Multnomah County (Oregon) Library

FIGURE 3.3 | **EQUIPMENT REQUEST (PRINT)**

REQUEST FOR BUILDING MAINTENANCE/SERVICES

Unit _LK_ Unit Head _Brett Lear_ Today's Date _5/11_

Request _Please bring 20 chairs to the LK meeting room on Monday morning, May 15th, and remove them on Tuesday, May 16th._

Contact 1 _Brett_ Contact 2 _John Smith_

For Building Services use.

Priority_____

Work Order #_____ Date_____

Assigned to_____

Est. time to complete_____

Special instructions_____

_____

Other items that need attention_____

_____

Fill in, following completion:

Work hours used (include travel)_____

Materials used_____

_____

_____

Date completed_____

Accepted by_____

JCPL 289 7-94

Submit: white and yellow copy   pink copy - Unit File

will do them all yourself, but if not, you will want to develop some method of communication. This will probably take the form of either online or print-based paperwork. Love it or hate it, paperwork is a good way to make a request and keep a record of what's been requested. If you have an online form that you use when sending requests to the building services staff, this form can probably be used when requesting chairs or other equipment for your program. An example of a print-based equipment request form is included in figure 3.3. Also shown are examples of forms—figure 3.4 and 3.5—that can be used when requesting equipment such as a computer projector for your program. (I've included examples of both print-based and electronic forms.)

CREATING NEW POSITION DESCRIPTIONS

I've written most of this book from the perspective that you, the reader, work in a library that might not have the luxury of hiring one or two or more staff members to plan and produce the programs for your library. I have assumed that frontline staff members will coordinate your programs and that frontline staff will also do much of the publicity—flyers, social media postings, and so forth—and other tasks associated with program planning. The section in chapter 2 that covered committee work was written with the assumption that much of your programming work will occur through a team of staff members who ensure that the

FIGURE 3.4 | **EQUIPMENT REQUEST (ELECTRONIC)**

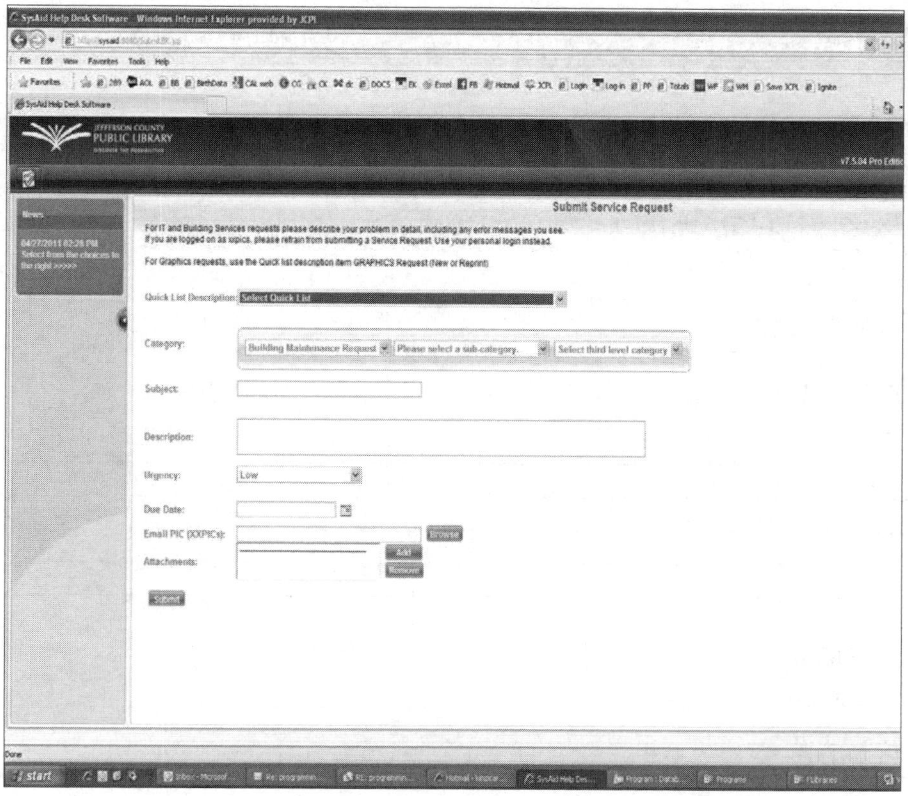

libraries and communities within your service area are well represented by the programs that you plan and produce for them. *But, if* your programs continue to resonate well with your patrons, and *if* budgeting realities offer the opportunity for a new or reclassified position—in other words, if the stars align—then now might be the right time to consider creating a position that is dedicated entirely or partially to program planning. You might decide that having one person spend all her time planning and producing programs is a more efficient and effective way to run your system-wide programming efforts. Or, you might choose to modify a current position to add programming responsibilities. By creating such positions you will begin

moving your library from a decentralized structure of programming where most of the work is done through group efforts and teams to a more centralized form of programming where one or two people handle much of the work of programming—from aligning program topics to the library's community interests to identifying and contracting with performers to evaluating and budgeting. An analogy would be centralized versus decentralized collection development.

In reality, libraries with centralized programming staff (such as MCL) still conduct some work through a programming committee in order to ensure that the programming staff are staying in touch with the needs of the various branch libraries and their patrons. And,

FIGURE 3.5 | **AUDIOVISUAL EQUIPMENT REQUEST**

AUDIOVISUAL EQUIPMENT RESERVATION/CONFIRMATION REPORT

1. PLEASE VERIFY THIS INFORMATION REGARDING THE AV EQUIPMENT YOU HAVE REQUESTED.
2. CALL THE PUBLIC INFORMATION OFFICE (X216) IF YOU SEE ANY MISTAKES OR HAVE ANY QUESTIONS.
3. PLEASE COMPLETE THE BOTTOM OF THIS FORM AFTER USING EQUIPMENT AND RETURN IT WITH THE EQUIPMENT.

Date Needed _____ - _____ - _____   **Time** _____ A.M. _____ P.M.

Equipment Borrowed   From

_____   _____

_____   _____

_____   _____

_____   _____

_____   _____

_____   _____

Borrower's Name _____

What is the Event _____

Event's Location _____

Reserved on this date _____

Equipment must be returned to   **by**

Date _____ - _____ - _____   **Time** _____ A.M. _____ P.M.

PLEASE PROVIDE THE INFORMATION REQUESTED BELOW

Condition of returned equipment (circle one)

  A-OK   Needs Maintenance   Non-functional

Describe any problems you had with this equipment _____

_____

_____

Signature _____   Telephone Extension _____

Submit: **white, yellow** and **pink** copies/PIO
goldenrod copy/Unit

FIGURE 3.6 | **SYSTEMWIDE PROGRAM COORDINATOR**

Multnomah County—Position Description

Section 1. Position Information

Department Name: Library
Division Name: Reference and Adult Services
Working title: Systemwide Programming Coordinator

Section 2. Program Information

Family and Adult Programming plans, coordinates, supports, and executes a wide variety of events and public programs at libraries and other community gathering places, all designed to enrich and transform the lives of children, families, and adults. Programs encourage civic engagement, provide resources in tough economic times, support early literacy and success in school, and provide resources for immigrants to more successfully participate in life in the United States. Examples include book discussions, computer classes, financial literacy labs, and citizenship classes. Programs also fulfill the entertainment and recreational needs of the community and include music, storytelling, and craft programs.

Purpose of Position

This position is responsible for overall coordination of all aspects of the library's system-wide public programming ensuring quality and consistency in accordance with the library's mission and goals and supervises two full time staff positions.

Section 3. Description of Job Duties

% of Time	Essential Job Functions (with the corresponding percentage of time)
40%	FUNCTION 1: Coordinates library's system-wide public programming plan for children, families and adults. Provides leadership for system-wide programming by establishing programming goals, objectives, policies and procedures and overseeing evaluation and long-range planning. Coordinates with library staff in various divisions who are involved in developing public programs to ensure that programs are consistent with mission and goals of the library providing expertise and recommendations as needed. Prepares and monitors department budget for programs, recommending expenditures and overseeing spending. Sets and monitors content, quality and other standards for public programs. Keeps abreast of what other libraries and similar organizations do locally, regionally and nationally. Initiates new programming partnerships on behalf of the library with outside organizations.
15%	FUNCTION 2: Supervises the work of the library's program development technician and program development specialist including giving feedback, setting and approving work plans and work schedules, evaluating and recommending discipline. Supervises work of library volunteers. Coordinates the work of other staff involved in programming as needed.
40%	FUNCTION 3: Independently, or as a member of a team or committee, develops, coordinates and produces programs, projects and events for children, families and adults including Everybody Reads, an annual communitywide reading project. Creates ongoing schedule of Collins Gallery exhibits and related programs.
5%	FUNCTION 4: Provides backup for the Public Relations manager.
100%	

Source: Multnomah County (Oregon) Library

FIGURE 3.7 | **PROGRAMMING SPECIALIST**

Multnomah County—Job Description

Section 1. Position Information

Department Name: Library
Division Name: Reference, Adult Services and Public Programming
Working title: Program Development Specialist

Section 2. Program Information

Multnomah County Library's Family, Teen, and Adult Programming plans and coordinates a wide variety of events and programs at libraries and other community gathering places, all designed to enrich the lives of children, families, teens, and adults. Examples include author talks, exhibits, lectures, film discussions, craft programs, civic discussions, cultural events, educational programs and more. Teens and adults participate in monthly book groups and in Everybody Reads, Multnomah County's community-wide reading project; children boost reading skills in the annual Summer Reading program; families attend craft programs and kid-friendly performances; and Spanish, Russian, Chinese and Vietnamese-speaking residents participate in cultural celebrations and other bilingual programs.

Purpose of Position
This position designs, develops, implements, promotes and evaluates year-round public library programs, projects and special events for children, teens, families and adults that meet the library's mission and goals.

Section 3. Description of Job Duties

% of Time	Essential Job Functions (with the corresponding percentage of time)
40%	FUNCTION 1: DEVELOP PUBLIC PROGRAMS AND EVENTS FOR CHILDREN, TEENS, FAMILIES AND ADULTS. Work with library staff in the development and selection of ongoing library programs to meet the library's mission and goals. Monitor evaluations from library staff, program providers and program participants. Gather and provide feedback, incorporate changes and suggestions, and modify programs as needed. Research potential new program ideas and providers. Use the library's event management system to analyze program evaluation data and compare trends and demographics based on the library's plan. Arrange logistics for events by contracting with equipment rental companies. Monitor what other libraries and organizations in the community are doing and look for ways to partner if possible. Attend system-wide programming committee meetings (6x per year) and other program or special event planning meetings as assigned.
20%	FUNCTION 2: PROVIDE EXCELLENT CUSTOMER SERVICE. Organize program offerings and requests and schedule and confirm events. Effectively communicate the status of projects to both internal and external customers. Reply promptly and thoroughly to queries and requests for information. Solicit and provide feedback for improving the design of programs and events through participation on committees and project teams. Provide advice and knowledge to structure programs incorporating suggestions and input on an ongoing basis.

20%   **FUNCTION 3: MONITOR PROGRAMMING BUDGET.**
Negotiate and monitor fees and contracts of independent performers and program providers. Research and establish community partnerships, funding sources and grant opportunities to obtain additional funding of programs. Develop and maintain tracking system to monitor programming expenses. Assist in budget preparation.

20%   **FUNCTION 4: PROMOTE AND PUBLICIZE PUBLIC PROGRAMS AND EVENTS.**
Write effective and compelling program descriptions. Define focus for program promotion. Synthesize bimonthly program offerings, develop and communicate promotional plan in conjunction with Marketing & Communication and Programming staff. Initiate program publicity and respond to media and public requests for information. Prepare news releases, participate in development of web pages and other press and marketing materials. Use technology and other methods such as social networking to publicize library events and programs.

100%

Source: Multnomah County (Oregon) Library

bringing a group of people together to brainstorm potential programming ideas inevitably leads to some creative and successful events for our patrons. Figures 3.6, 3.7, and 3.8 are abbreviated examples of job descriptions for (1) a system-wide program coordinator (who would coordinate the library's programming efforts and focus on such big-picture areas as community partnerships, grant opportunities, priorities and goal-setting, and budget management), (2) a programming specialist (who would work in collaboration with the program coordinator and do much of the day-to-day work of identifying and booking performers and placing these programs at libraries throughout the system), and (3) a frontline librarian whose position that has been enhanced to include programming work as a primary responsibility. Web extras 3.1, 3.2, and 3.3 show the full-length versions of these job descrip-

tions. Your administrative services staff—whether it's the administrative services director or your head of human resources—will be instrumental in helping you create any new or modified position descriptions that help your library in designing and delivering library programs for your public.

Your administrative services staff are essential to the success of your program. They work within the realms of accountability and stewardship. They tend to our budgets and buildings and enhance our ability to provide quality programming in a responsible manner.

We've spent these first few chapters getting our internal policies and documents in order. Let's now look outward into the community and discover more about who our patrons are and what types of programs they prefer.

FIGURE 3.8 | **PROGRAMMING LIBRARIAN**

Multnomah County—Job Description

Section 1. Position Information

Department Name: Library
Division Name: Central Library
Working title: Central Programming Coordinator Librarian

Section 2. Program Information

Multnomah County Library serves the people of Multnomah County by providing books and other materials to meet their informational, educational, cultural and recreational needs. The Multnomah County Library upholds the principles of intellectual freedom and the public's right to know by providing people of all ages with access and guidance to information and collections that reflect all points of view. Guiding principles include: accountability, certainty of change, excellent work environment, system perspective and cost effectiveness.

Purpose of Position

This position primarily focuses on coordinating programming at Central Library, plus providing direct, professional reference and readers' advisory services to customers of all ages at the Central Library. Duties include planning, coordinating, developing and managing public programs, plus assisting the public at reference desks. This position supports the Program's mission and vision in all of the duties performed, and provides increased ability to spend programming funds wisely.

Section 3. Description of Job Duties

% of Time	Essential Job Functions (with the corresponding percentage of time)
70%	FUNCTION 1: PROGRAM COORDINATION & MANAGEMENT. Works with Library Programming Committee and Central staff to plan public programs throughout the year. Develops opportunities for community partnerships, grants, and other ways to offer the very best programming in a cost-effective manner. Coordinates and assists staff with development, scheduling, publicity, and implementation of programs.
30%	FUNCTION 2: REFERENCE & READERS' ADVISORY SERVICES. Provides direct assistance to library users in reference and readers' advisory. Assists in locating and obtaining materials. Inquiries are received in person, via telephone and electronically. Checks online catalog, databases, print and Internet resources.
100%	

Source: Multnomah County (Oregon) Library

Getting to Know
Your Community

Frankly, I hear the word *demographics* and I groan and then grow limp. I picture myself with a stack of books filled with columns of numbers. Then I picture myself poring through these books, pulling out numbers, and plugging these same numbers into a table I'm creating on my Mac. And, of course, the work is compounded by the fact that I'm far from expert on the particular software program I'm using. So, not only is the work boring, grueling, perhaps even depressing, but it's infuriating as well, as I split cells and add columns and accidentally delete entire rows instead.

Tuggle and Heller's *Grand Schemes and Nitty-Gritty Details: Library PR That Works* does a nice job of winnowing the demographic process. The authors state that you should first identify the community need. You should then be sure that you have evidence of this need. Next you investigate what efforts are being made to meet this need. And last, you decide what, if anything, the library should do to meet this need.[1]

Needs assessment, demographic study, survey, marketing research—whatever you call your process of discovering who your community is and what its needs are, it should be a challenging process that yields useful results.

BEGIN BY ASKING "WHY?"

Before you begin analyzing or creating studies and surveys, ask yourself this question: Why do people attend my library's programs? The answer will help focus your energies when it is time to begin your demographic work. (If you have never offered adult programs at your library, it will be difficult to answer this question.) Some of us have been offering programs for a while, but we've done it in a trial-and-error fashion that's been, surprisingly, more hit than miss. But now you are ready to begin programming in a more systematic way: you'd like to get to know a little bit more about your patrons and what they want. By exploring why your patrons attend programs, you learn about who these people are. For example, you can learn quite a bit about why people attend programs by reading the comments on the program evaluation forms. People will often leave specific comments, such as, "This program gave me an opportunity to share my opinions with others." Another sure-fire approach is to simply observe who walks into your programs. It's okay to talk to people as they exit. Ask them what they thought, and follow up with, "What did (or didn't) you like about it?"

You can learn something about why people attend programs by noting which programs are well attended. Do your patrons flock to programs that enable them to learn about herbal medicine or computers or health care? Do others appreciate your ability to bring big-name authors and artists into their library? Does your evaluation form ask people if they regularly use the library? Do you get the sense that your audiences view your library as a community center and attend programs here rather than attending a local organization that offers similar programs? What age groups seem to attend programs? Does it depend on the subject?

Let us say that you estimate that more than half of your adult audiences attend programs that offer information on issues and topics of interest to them, such as nutritional programs and workshops on buying an e-book reader. Your audiences don't seem as enthusiastic about the recreational and cultural programs—the musical events and poetry readings are poorly attended. Participants say they attend the events at the library because it is convenient for them. And a convenient location is important to them because many are seniors and the library is in their neighborhood, within walking distance. You've not only just learned a lot more about why people attend your programs—you've also learned more about who attends. With this information, you can decide to go in at least

two directions. You might decide to focus on what you are already doing well—serving seniors—and begin investigating further into the community makeup of your senior population. You would do this to learn more about them, which will help you tailor future programs to their wants and needs. Or you can branch off in a different direction. You might decide to investigate the overall makeup of your community, intent on uncovering those populations that are not currently taking advantage of your programming efforts. In which direction do you look?

BEGINNING YOUR SEARCH

Before you begin your studies, be sure you know what you are looking for and why. It's best to begin by asking yourself the following question: Why am I doing this study? Is your library just beginning to offer adult programming? Did you approach your library administrators with a program proposal, and they replied: Do any of our patrons even *want* adult programming? If this question was posed to you, then you will want to conduct a study to learn whether your patrons desire library programming for adults. You might want to focus on the patrons who visit the library. An in-house survey will probably provide you with the answer to your question. Surveys do not need to be long, elaborate, confusing questionnaires; in fact, people are most likely to respond to brief surveys that have clearly written questions and clearly defined options.

Look within Your Library

As you begin to formulate your questions, keep in mind that your library might have already conducted an extensive (though not necessarily confusing) patron-satisfaction survey in recent years. Many libraries conduct surveys, such as the customer satisfaction survey created by Dr. George D'Elia.[2] Sometimes libraries conduct these surveys when they are gearing up for a mill levy campaign as a way to find out what services voters would be willing to support with their tax money.

Large-scale surveys and marketing studies are very labor intensive and expensive. If your library goes down this road, it is probably at the request of your director or library board. A marketing firm has probably been hired. It's not likely that this effort was undertaken to gather programming data, but that doesn't mean that the data won't be invaluable to you. Check with your library manager or marketing office to see what surveys your library has conducted, and ask permission to view the survey and the results. The data will likely contain information on satisfaction levels with particular library services, languages spoken in the community, types of businesses within the community, and the like. If a marketing firm was hired, the data will be massaged into tables, graphs, and bulleted lists, and recommendations will be included in the report. This information quickly gives you ideas for classes and programs for your library.

Your library probably already has other types of information that will be helpful to you. Libraries that have a history of programming will also have some statistics. These might be in a rough format: a binder or a spreadsheet that contains the patron evaluation forms and comments from the programs offered over the last few years. If, upon completing a program, you have to submit an evaluation form to a central office, that office might have a file of past programs that you can look at. Statistics such as these will give you an idea of the popularity of the various topics offered in the past.

Look at State and National Resources

Your library very likely submits reports to your state library. These reports may be available via the Web. You might also have a copy of the reports in your collection. It isn't unusual for these reports to contain information on the number of programs that you

offered in a given year, the attendance, and the attendance per capita. Ask around to determine which organizations your library cooperates with. Does your library complete surveys sent by ALA or the Public Library Association? For example, a publication called the *Statistical Report*[3] compiles statistical data from the Public Library Data Service (PLDS) survey. PLDS receives its funding from the Public Library Association, and the *Statistical Report* contains information on library programs.

The U.S. Census Bureau also conducts a public library survey for the Institute of Museum and Library Services (IMLS) via the Institute of Museum and Library Services Library Statistics Program. Statistics are collected from more than 9,000 public libraries. Data are available at www.imls.gov/research/public_libraries_in_the_united_states_survey.aspx. One feature of this website allows you to compare your library (if you completed the public library survey) to other libraries. The website will even create a graph to illustrate the comparisons. Figure 4.1 was created on the website. This graph compares New York Public Library (the "library of interest") to Brooklyn Public Library and Queens Borough Public Library (the "peer group").

The National Center for Education Statistics (NCES) also collects and analyzes education and library data. In 2002, the NCES published *Programs for Adults in Public Library Outlets*, a report that presents nationally representative data from a survey conducted in 2000 via the center's Fast Response Survey System (FRSS).[4]

DEVELOP A COMMUNITY PROFILE

By now it's becoming clear that quite a bit of information is out there, and it's located in a number of places. But eventually you will want to learn some specific things about your community that won't be included in the sources just mentioned. A good first step is to sit down and sketch out a basic profile of

FIGURE 4.1 | **IMLS LIBRARY COMPARISON GRAPH**

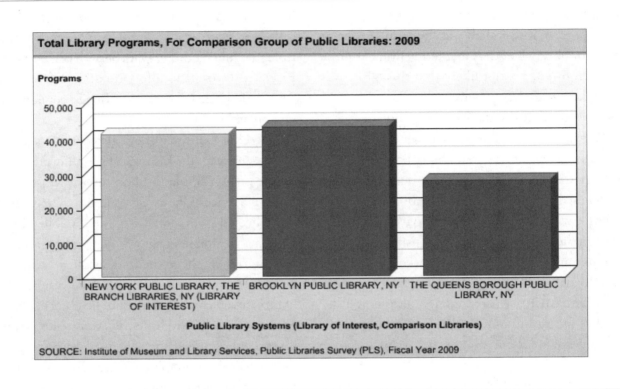

your community. Ask yourself questions that will help you define your community. In their manual *Planning Library Programs*, Peggy O'Donnell and Patsy Read provide a survey (figure 4.2) for conducting a quick community profile.[5] In addition, *Planning for Results: A Public Library Transformation Process—The How-To Manual* contains a chapter called "Scan the Community." The manual also contains an excellent worksheet that you can use when gathering demographic information.[6]

LOOK FOR COMMUNITY PARTNERS

As you are conducting your community scan, be sure to look for organizations that have similar priorities and values. It's rare to get through a day in the library world without someone saying something about "leveraging resources." Partnerships allow you to do just that. As Terrilyn Chun of Multnomah County Library (MCL) notes, "Benefits of a partnership include resource sharing, outreach to new audiences, access to expertise in a different discipline, and the potential for increasing goodwill and support between the organizations and the broader community."[7] As you begin to have conversations with representatives from community organizations, don't forget that your library brings plenty to the table as well. First, our libraries generate a huge amount of foot traffic, which means that we have the potential to draw a large audience to any cosponsored event. And, many of us work for multibranch libraries, which means that a program can be sited at multiple locations and touch people throughout the community. Finally, our patrons are

---

FIGURE 4.2 | **A SURVEY OF YOUR COMMUNITY**

You can develop a profile of your community using the following questions as guidelines. Include any additional information you think is pertinent.

What are the major businesses or industries?
What dominant groups make up the population?
What are the ages and characteristics of the population?
What leisure time activities are available?
What is the general education level of the population?
What economic, social, or political trends are presently affecting people in your town?
What is the town's relation to other communities in the state?
What is the historical background?
What are the present economic conditions?
What are the major cultural and religious influences?

Source: Peggy O'Donnell and Patsy Read, *Planning Library Programs* (Chicago: Public Library Association, 1979), 12.

---

a pretty diverse bunch, and this factor can be very appealing to a partner organization that wants to reach people throughout the community.

So where do you look for those organizations that share many of your library's priorities and values? Community colleges and cultural institutions such as the local symphony can become wonderful partners and provide performers for many of your cultural and educational programs. By partnering with local museums, you open up opportunities for sharing collections and creating exhibits and displays that highlight materials from both organizations. Cafés and other similar partners offer potential spaces for off-site programming. Some local organizations have vast mailing lists and memberships, so, as partners, they can greatly assist in getting the word out to the public to promote any programs that you jointly produce. In addition, a partner organization might be able to assist your library in reaching an audience that you have been trying to grow.

As you begin to form partnerships within your community, you'll want to keep a few things in mind. In addition to writing "Getting the Most (for Both of You!) from Your Museum/Library Partnership," Terrilyn Chun participated on a panel at the 2010 ALA Annual Conference program titled "Programs That Pack the Place: A How-To for Libraries of All Shapes and Sizes." Terrilyn shared these four tips with librarians who are seeking to develop community partnerships: (1) agree on the purpose of the partnership, (2) clearly define the roles and responsibilities of each partner, (3) maintain good and frequent communication, and (4) draft a formal contract or agreement. (Web extra 4.1 shows an example of a letter of agreement between MCL and a local museum.) Partnerships take time to build and effort to maintain. But strong partnerships can create programs that surpass what we can create on our own. The library is just one of several local organizations dedicated to building and nurturing a healthy community. By making contact with the other service agencies in our community, we will inevitably find opportunities to pool resources and create programs that benefit our communities and our residents.

ASK OTHERS FOR HELP

Once you have a better feel for your community, you will know what additional questions to ask. Perhaps you've identified the leisure activities available in your community, but now you want to know which activities are the most popular. If your library hasn't conducted any significant studies, you can ask other agencies and groups for help. Groups that serve most or all of the community frequently conduct demographic studies. School systems, chambers of commerce, radio stations, newspapers, and organizations serving specific populations (such as AARP) all conduct demographic work. Ask them if they will share this information with you.

Other libraries might be able to help. Have other systems with community profiles similar to yours conducted surveys? If you have e-mail access, you could hop onto an electronic discussion group such as PUBLIB and post this question.[8] Describe your community and ask if any libraries with similar communities have conducted surveys. Ask if they will share their results with you. By reviewing the answers given by another library's patrons, you might learn more about your own community.

Another possibility is to seek out published library surveys, such as *Cultural Programs for Adults in Public Libraries*, and see if any of the findings seem applicable to your library and community.[9] For example, the *Cultural Programs* study found that the presence of a strong cultural community influenced the types of programs offered by the libraries within the community. It seems that libraries were able to offer successful cultural programs when the libraries were located within communities whose residents were active in music, poetry, film, and the like. This find-

ing is helpful, because we are often reluctant to offer programs that might compete with agencies that are already providing the service. If your library serves an area that is strong in the arts, it seems that people will attend your programs, even if you are complementing or duplicating events that are currently available in your community.

Another survey to explore is the previously mentioned *Programs for Adults in Public Library Outlets*. The survey found that 56 percent of all public library outlets—buildings that provide library service—provide some sort of computer or Internet instruction; 39 percent offer recreational activities, such as crafts-, travel-, or hobby-related programs; 20 percent offer parenting skills workshops; 18 percent offer financial and investment guidance; and 17 percent offer programs on employment and career planning.[10] About 25 percent of all outlets offer programs targeted specifically toward seniors, and 9 percent of the outlets have developed programs for new immigrants and patrons who speak languages other than English.[11] The study also provides information on the types of programs offered at small, medium-sized, and large outlets/buildings. This survey will give you an idea of what libraries are doing around the country as well as what libraries are doing based on the size of their facilities.

CONDUCT A SURVEY: ASKING YOUR PATRONS WHAT THEY WANT

Although the strategies just described can offer insight into your community, ideally you will be able to pose questions to your own patrons. If your library hasn't conducted a recent survey that addresses programming, you may have to create one. Even if your library has been offering programs for quite some time, it still can't hurt to take another look at your community. And it never hurts to ask your patrons what they want and need, even if they have been asked before.

You can frequently get the answers you need with a brief, postcard-like survey. Actually, a survey in the form of a postage-paid postcard works well. It gives the patron the option of taking the survey home, completing it at another time, and mailing it in to ensure anonymity. Short surveys are a good way to get the answer to yes or no type questions. If you want to ask your adult patrons if they would attend adult programs, try a survey. Before you print the postcards and hand them out to your patrons, however, ask yourself if you just want a yes or a no for an answer. People will almost always say yes if you ask them if they'd like an additional, free service. The survey can be written in a way that makes the patron select a choice, thereby providing you with more useful information. For example, instead of merely asking, "Would you attend adult programs if they were offered at your local library?" you might develop a survey similar to the one in figure 4.3.

More people will stop to fill out a brief survey than will struggle through a five-page monster. How much is enough? Just try to think of what you will and could do with the results. The survey just described is good if you want to know what your patrons in general would like. But if you later decide that you'd like to offer more programs for seniors, then this survey won't help you much. If you added a line that asks the person to check an age range (for example, 17 or under, 18–24, 25–39, 40–54, 55 or older), you could use the results to target programming ideas for a particular age group.

Surveys can be time-consuming. To get a fairly low percentage of error—about 3 percent—on a survey,

---

FIGURE 4.3 | **PROGRAMMING SURVEY**

If we were to begin offering adult programs, which type of program would you be most likely to attend? Please select one of the following:

☐ A monthly book discussion group

☐ A film series covering a theme, such as "Great Silent Classics" or "Film Noir"

☐ A "how to" program, such as "How to Select a Home Computer" or "How to Travel Cheap in Europe"

☐ A speaker sharing his or her knowledge with the audience; for example, a Holocaust survivor recounting her experiences at Auschwitz

☐ Workshops or classes that explain how to use library resources, such as the Internet and downloadable e-books

☐ I do not have an interest in attending library programs for adults

Comments:

_____

_____

_____

_____

you will need to survey about 1,000 people. I'm no statistician, so I grabbed a copy of *E-Z Statistics* by Douglas Downing and Jeff Clark. The authors, in layman's terms, tell me that "a sample of 1,000 does just as well when the population is 200 million as it does when the population is 50,000. You might expect that the sample would become less accurate as the population becomes larger, but it doesn't work that way."[12]

Ideally, you'd hire a marketing firm to construct your survey, determine your sample population, and tabulate the results. In reality, this approach is probably outside your financial capabilities. Instead, try to find a survey that seems to ask the questions you want answered. The book *Library Programs: How to Select, Plan, and Produce Them*, by John S. Robotham and Lydia LaFleur, contains some good examples.[13]

Once your survey is ready, it's time to decide how to distribute it and who your sample will be. Will you conduct the survey via phone? Who will you call? Library patrons with library cards? Registered voters? Calling 1,000 people can be time-consuming and costly. The most cost-effective way to proceed is to keep the survey short and hand it out to folks in some public area. Include a postage-paid envelope or place the survey on the back of a postage-paid postcard. If you're unable to pay the postage on the survey, then be sure to ask people if they can take a few moments to fill out the survey on the spot. Where you distribute the survey determines what population you are surveying. If you survey people in the mall, you are definitely surveying mall users, but you might not be surveying library users. This is fine, particularly if you are trying to discover what additional services—such as programming—might get new patrons into the library. But, if you want to see what new services your library patrons might be interested in, then you should probably hand out the survey inside the library. This method taps into most of your library patrons—but not all of them. Many libraries deliver books to the homebound and to nursing homes. You won't be able to survey these seniors at the library, so you might want to mail the surveys to a contact person at the nursing home and ask him or her to distribute, collect, and return them to you.

In their book on library programs, Robotham and LaFleur include a chapter on publicity. They mention that a library's mailing list can be used to disseminate information. The authors give an example (see figure 4.4) of a stamped, addressed postcard that could be included with the newsletter or program flyers that you send to people on your mailing list.[14] Although its main intent is to update the mailing list, it also asks respondents about their programming preferences.

An online survey is another great way to reach out to a large percentage of your patrons at little cost or no cost. By placing the link to the survey on your home page you'll ensure that the survey is seen by everyone who visits your home page to look up a book in the catalog, check your library's hours, and so forth. I've included a section on online surveys in chapter 10, "Programming and Technology."

WHAT DO YOU DO WITH THIS INFORMATION?

There are at least three things you can do with "new" information. First, you can file it (i.e., ignore it). Second, you can use the information to set new goals. For example, say your survey revealed an increase in the number of low-income families in your community. Your new programming goal for next year could be to offer programs to assist these families. With that goal in mind, you could offer a program on college financial aid that might benefit families wondering whether they can afford to send their children to college. Third, you can use demographic information to write a proposal for something completely new.

An in-house proposal is quite different from a proposal you would submit to a potential funding source, such as the National Endowment for the Humanities. In-house proposals usually take the form of a memo. According to William S. Pfeiffer and Charles Keller, the proposal should have the standard "date," "to," "from," and "subject" lines.[15] Because the purpose of this memo is to persuade library administration to make changes or try something new, it should be sensitive to the political climate of the organization. This means that you should think before you write, and you should share your memo with others before you submit it. If you were to pore over several successful memo proposals that have been submitted within your library over the years, you would probably discover that they contain a similar tone and format. Every library system also has a phrase or concept or something that is anathema to the powers that be. For example, perhaps your library director has spent many hours convincing the library's board members that volunteers are not interchangeable with librarians. You have an idea about how volunteers can assist librarians with data entry projects, such as inputting program evaluations into your program database. Present this idea very carefully and explicitly. You might not want to write, "Volunteers relieving librarians of duties" in the subject line. Instead you could write, "Effective Use of Volunteers in Data Entry Projects." This phrasing shows that your focus is on getting things done without putting librarians out of a job.

Your memo can be up to five pages in length. Write it in a way that grabs and maintains the reader's interest. Use a subject that immediately hints at how the proposal will benefit the library. The opening paragraph should summarize the proposal. Next, include a section that shows why there is a need to go in your suggested direction. You could describe how helpful the database is to the staff, and then explain that the current staffing situation only permits the database to get updated once a month. Data entry is not a primary job of any of your staff. By recruiting volunteers, you could keep the database up to date without infringing on the duties of your staff.

The main body of your proposal will contain the details on how you will recruit and train volunteers and why this proposal is the right thing to do. You can include a bulleted list of benefits that will result

FIGURE 4.4 | **POSTCARD SURVEY**

Dear Library User,

The Klondike Public Library is updating its mailing list. If you wish to continue receiving announcements of programs and other library mail, please fill in the postcard and drop it in the mail box, or bring it with you when you next come to the library.

Name: _____

Address: _____

Organization you represent (if any): _____

_____

Kinds of programs that interest you: _____

_____

_____

Source: John S. Robotham and Lydia LaFleur, *Library Programs: How to Select, Plan, and Produce Them*, 2nd ed. (Metuchen, NJ: Scarecrow, 1981), 275.

from having the volunteers perform this data entry. These points should be as patron-focused as possible. Include points such as these:

- By using volunteers the database will be updated twice a week, rather than once a month.
- An updated database will assist library staff in selecting, producing, and evaluating programs that align with the needs of the patrons in our community.

Proposal writing is a fairly political endeavor, and it doesn't hurt to think politically as you write. If your library is currently conducting a publicity campaign to attract seniors, it might be wise to slip a sentence into the proposal that mentions the number of seniors that attend library programs each month. State that this database will allow you to better analyze which programs are well attended by seniors. In your conclusion, summarize the proposal and emphasize a major benefit. Try to keep the memo itself under five pages. You can always cut statistical tables and other items and add them as attachments or appendixes. Graphics do catch the eye, so a relevant chart or graph as an attachment will accentuate your main points. And remember, before you hit "send," pause, proofread, and ask a coworker to proofread as well.

By now, you have all kinds of ideas, and the community data you gathered tells you who is in your community. In other words, we have our road atlas out, we've planned our trip, and we know where we want to go. Let's make sure our gas tank is full.

NOTES

1. Ann Montgomery Tuggle and Dawn Hansen Heller, *Grand Schemes and Nitty-Gritty Details: Library PR That Works* (Littleton, CO: Libraries Unlimited, 1987), 37.

2. George D'Elia, *The Roles of the Public Library in Society: The Result of a National Survey; Final Report* (Evanston, IL: Urban Libraries Council, 1993), 225.

3. Public Library Association, *Public Library Data Service Statistical Report 2011* (Chicago: Public Library Association, 2011).

4. Laurie Lewis and Elizabeth Farris, *Programs for Adults in Public Library Outlets* (Washington, DC: National Center for Education Statistics, U.S. Dept. of Education, Office of Educational Research and Improvement, 2002), nces.ed.gov/pubs2003/2003010.pdf.

5. Peggy O'Donnell and Patsy Read, *Planning Library Programs* (Chicago: Public Library Association, 1979), 12.

6. Ethel Himmel and William James Wilson with the ReVision Committee of the Public Library Association, *Planning for Results: A Public Library Transformation Process—The How-To Manual* (Chicago: American Library Association, 1998), 37, G-1.

7. Terrilyn Chun, "Getting the Most (for Both of You!) from Your Museum/Library Partnership," *Programming Librarian*, March 28, 2011, www.programminglibrarian.org/library/planning/getting-the-most-for-both-of-you-from-your-museumlibrary-partnership.html.

8. WebJunction, *PUBLIB Electronic Discussion List*, resourcesharing.webjunction.org/publib.

9. Debra Wilcox Johnson, *Cultural Programs for Adults in Public Libraries: A Survey Report* (Chicago: American Library Association, 1999).

10. Lewis and Farris, *Programs for Adults in Public Library Outlets*, iv.

11. Ibid., v.

12. Douglas Downing and Jeff Clark, *E-Z Statistics*, 4th ed. (Hauppauge, NY: Barron's Educational Series, 1997), 270.

13. John S. Robotham and Lydia LaFleur, *Library Programs: How to Select, Plan, and Produce Them*, 2nd ed. (Metuchen, NJ: Scarecrow Press, 1981).

14. Ibid.

15. William S. Pfeiffer and Charles H. Keller Jr., *Proposal Writing: The Art of Friendly and Winning Persuasion* (Upper Saddle River, NJ: Prentice-Hall, 2000), 226–35.

Getting Funded

Libraries can offer terrific programs without any direct dollar costs. Excellent performers can be readily found who will offer their services to libraries for free. Museums, universities, associations, and businesses will all supply performers at no cost. This is particularly fortunate during these uncertain economic times. Some performers will certainly charge a fee, but even many of these professionals can still be hired for $25 to $50 an hour. So until your library really gets its programming effort funded, you probably won't be spending a great deal of money on performers' fees.

IN-KIND EXPENSES

Initially most expenses will come from the in-kind support you provide. In-kind support can include staff, meeting space, publicity, printing, and equipment. And even these expenses can be kept to a minimum. Libraries with budget constraints might limit publicity to a quick paragraph written by a staff member. Some papers will run such an announcement for free. Most papers will at least run the program title, date, time, and location. This publicity might be done in conjunction with creating a flyer on your work computer, posting this flyer throughout the library, and placing a stack at the checkout desk. The total, in-kind expenses would be the staff time involved in planning the program, contacting the performer, and creating the publicity.

Libraries that have the resources to do so, however, will involve other departments and staff as they gain momentum with their programming. A graphics or marketing office will help with flyers and news releases, your building services department will bring additional chairs and tables to your branch, and your

IT people will help you set up the laptop and computer projector and Wi-Fi access so that the social media guru can show your patrons how Facebook and Twitter work in real time. Your in-kind expenses will become your primary programming expenses, and the $25 you are paying the performer will become somewhat irrelevant.

In-kind support does not normally appear in a programming budget, but it does need to be acknowledged in the planning phase. As you begin to offer more programs with better publicity, your program committee will want to look ahead at the in-kind support it will need in the coming months and years. Will your graphics office and your web development unit need additional staffing in order to create the flyers and artwork and web pages needed to adequately promote your various events? Will the library need to hire more staff to plan programs and locate performers? If yes, then these departments will need increases in their budgets to achieve these goals. If such additional funding is not a possibility, this reality will affect how you plan programs. Perhaps you do not have the staff, meeting space, and equipment necessary to produce more than one program a month.

OPERATING FUNDS

Some libraries perpetually operate without creating an adult programming budget. Libraries can get by without an adult programming budget and still offer a very respectable calendar of events. Many adult programs are informational in nature, which is fortunate, because it is fairly easy to find organizations whose mission statements support freely sharing their knowledge and skills with the community. Museums, universities, and associations will send their representatives out into the community—including our libraries—to teach and engage others in conversations. Libraries with limited budgets can also tap into local businesses, which will send experts to present accurate information on topics as varied as the headings in the Yellow Pages. They often do this for free because it is good PR for their businesses.

The performers who do charge are usually those who make their livelihood through their art. The library offers a nice venue for subtle advertising, and some performers may be willing to perform for free in exchange for the publicity exposure. Then again, authors, guitarists, painters, and the like might rely on public readings, concerts, and art instruction opportunities for their weekly paycheck. Your idea for a program is their idea of work. These people might justifiably ask for a small stipend. If your library administration agrees to dedicate a portion of the operating budget to hiring performers, it will want to create a line item for programming. Statistically, about one out of four libraries creates a separate line item in its budget for adult programming.[1]

GIVE PROGRAMMING A HOME WITHIN YOUR BUDGET

Chapter 2 discussed the importance of creating a programming budget. If your library has decided that programming is fundamental to its mission, and if the money is there, then it is imperative that a specified amount of money be placed into a specific programming budget line. This action gives programming a home within your institution. By placing a dollar figure behind programming, you really have etched programming into your basic operating procedures. You will want to work with your budgeting people to determine how to best create this budget. Should it be a single line item for programming, or should the budget specify dollar amounts for children's and adult and YA programming? You will also want to be clear on what the programming budget can pay for. Can supplies such as glue and scissors for a crafts program come out of this budget? Will they instead come from the supplies budget? Can you charge food for an artist's reception to the programming budget? You will find that your organization's policies and priorities determine your programming budget. Your policies will clarify the focus of your programs, and your library's goals and priorities will clarify how programming fits within the overall mission of your library.

If you are just beginning to offer programming within your library, don't be afraid to start out small and simple. The important thing is that you've got your foot in the door.

When it is time to make a request to increase your programming budget, stress the successful history of your programs, and ground the proposal in the idea that programming has accentuated the library's ability to fulfill its mission. You should bullet a few points that illustrate how programming has accomplished this objective, and include hard statistics, such as attendance figures and staff time involved in producing the programs. Positive, anecdotal information from your patrons and staff carries a lot of weight, especially with library board members, and be sure to mention partnerships with other organizations. This shows that you are engaging in resource sharing, which means that you are trying to stretch your dollars. Remember to extend your publicity to include those people and groups that determine or influence your budget. Be sure that board members and community leaders are on your publicity mailing lists. Keep programming and its successes in front of your administrators and policy makers. Try to get a brief programming report integrated into the library board report or annual report. Include statistics and anecdotes in this report, and keep the report very brief to ensure that it gets read. If you coordinate programs for your entire library system or even a single library, include a programming report within the report you submit to your supervisor each month. By making programming a known commodity, you will position it as a strong candidate for continued and possibly increased funding.

SEEKING ADDITIONAL FUNDING

Only about 8 percent of public libraries depend entirely on library operating funds for adult programming. Library Friends groups are the most common outside source of funding for adult programming. In fact, three out of four libraries collaborate with Friends groups. The most common contribution from these Friends groups is money. Other sources of outside funding include humanities councils and art groups or councils.[2] Some libraries have a library foundation instead of a Friends group. (Figure 5.1 is an example of a funding request from Multnomah County Library to the library foundation, and figure 5.2 is a funding request from Jefferson County Public Library to its library foundation.) Whether your library has a Friends group or a library foundation, chances are that the group has nonprofit or not-for-profit status to increase its capacity for fundraising. These groups traditionally exist to support and enhance the services and resources of libraries. Most Friends groups and library foundations are governed by a steering committee. You will probably submit your request for programming support to this committee.

FRIENDLY PROGRAMS

Although you might initially go to your Friends or foundation in search of a check to support programming, in time you might want to encourage these groups to assist with the entire planning process. In chapter 2 we explored the workings of a program steering committee. We placed a library foundation member on this committee. By having a Friends or foundation member on the program steering committee, you have a person who understands how programs are produced. She or he will see programming ideas at their inception. At the very least the Friends or foundation member might see a program that the group

FIGURE 5.1 | **FUNDING PROPOSAL, EXAMPLE A**

The Library Foundation Funding Request

(Please keep requests to 1–2 pages whenever possible.)

Summary

Project Name: Humanities programming	**Contact person responsible for project:**
Total project budget: $15,000	**How many staff positions will TLF funds support?** None
Cash support requested? $15,000	**In-kind requested? What type?** n/a
How many people will be served by project, if applicable? n/a	**How many books/materials to be purchased, if applicable?** n/a

Project Description

Please include goals, measurable outcomes, evaluation plan, branches that will benefit from the project.

The library requests funding to support the following programs:

Louisa May Alcott: The Woman behind Little Women. A viewing, reading and discussion program. November/December 2011. Scholar honoraria, print publicity and related programming. www.ala.org/ala/aboutala/offices/ppo/programming/lma

Pride and Passion: The African American Baseball Experience. Exhibition and related programming Dec. 1, 2011–Jan. 26, 2012. Scholar honoraria, print publicity and opening reception. www .ala.org/ala/aboutala/offices/ppo/programming/pridepassion/prideandpassion.cfm

A Fine Romance: Jewish Songwriters, American Songs, 1910–1965. Exhibition and related programming March 10–April 19, 2012. Scholar honoraria, print publicity and opening reception. www.ala.org/ala/aboutala/offices/ppo/programming/nextbook

Great Decisions. Civic engagement discussion group. Workbooks and other materials for participants. December 2011.

Banned Books Week. In-library displays and programming. September 2011.

Ancient Greeks, Modern Lives. A performance, workshop, lecture and reading program inspiring people to come together to read, see and think about classical literature and how it continues to influence and invigorate American cultural life. Scholar honoraria, print publicity, lectures and other programming. Program dates TBD. ancientgreeksmodernlives.org

Additionally, if the library's grant applications are successful, funding would also support:

Let's Talk About It: Making Sense of the Civil War. Reading and discussion program. Scholar honoraria, print publicity, additional books and related programming. Program dates TBD. www .ala.org/ala/aboutala/offices/ppo/programming/civilwar

Manifold Greatness: Creation and Afterlife of the King James Bible. Scholar honoraria, print publicity, related programming and opening reception. Exhibit and program dates TBD. www.ala.org/ala/aboutala/offices/ppo/programming/kingjamesbible

Programs will be evaluated using the library's standard program evaluation form and criteria.

- At least 98% of respondents will rate the programs either good or excellent.
- At least 50% of respondents will say the program made them feel connected to their community.
- At least 80% of respondents will say they learned something new.

Specify project time line, deadline for funding guarantee and major print deadlines for donor recognition. See individual programs above for project dates; publicity deadlines are typically 8–10 weeks in advance of project time line.

Funding Plans (for requests over $10,000)

Is this request for seed, development or long-term funding for this project? Review the library's funding commitment.

One time funding.

Do you anticipate savings or carryover from the prior or current fiscal year? If yes, please explain.

Yes. There will be approximately $3,000 unspent from the NEH General Endowment Fund and NEH Collins Endowment Fund disbursements for FY 2011.

Please list recognition or corporate sponsorship opportunities and any PR plans.

The Library Foundation Endowment funds would be acknowledged on all print and electronic publicity according to fund requirements.

    The library and the foundation will discuss recognition in May, with the goal of strengthening our process and approach.

Comments

Any additional comments:

_____
_____
_____
_____
_____
_____
_____
_____
_____
_____
_____

Source: Multnomah County (Oregon) Library

FIGURE 5.2 | **FUNDING PROPOSAL, EXAMPLE B**

MEMO

TO: Library Foundation
FROM: Children's Librarians Roundtable (CLRT)
DATE: 1/1/20XX
RE: Children's Programming 20XX Grant Request

CLRT would like to thank the Foundation for the continued support of children's programming at JCPL. Historically, a portion of the library's budget was dedicated to children's programming, with little or no money designated specifically for adult or young adult programming. Because of the Foundation's generous support of children's programming, the library has been able to increase the number and the quality of programs for the adult and YA audience. As adult and YA programming gains momentum at JCPL, the library is committing its resources to building and maintaining programs for this audience.

Since the library will be pursuing approximately $10,000.00 for adult and YA programs, CLRT is looking to the Foundation to supplement the programming budget, enabling children's programs to be fully funded in the upcoming year.

During 20XX, CLRT coordinated 122 programs, attended by 5,340 children system-wide. Our programs ran the gamut and featured dynamic presentations from the Raptor Education Foundation, puppeteers, storytellers, artists and musicians. This summer, children were able to see live eagles and falcons, create treasures from recycled materials, experience a Madagascar cockroach and other insects up close, and be enchanted by storytellers, puppeteers and actors. These highly successful, interactive programs were presented for only 25 cents per child.

We are excited at the possibilities that exist for the Foundation and CLRT to work together in presenting quality programs to the communities we serve. We are confident that we can coordinate a dynamic schedule of programs for children and their families, with the Foundation's support. The attached grant request outlines our specific funding needs.

Jefferson County Library Foundation
Grant Application Form

Name: Children's Programming
Date: January 1, 20XX
Library: JCPL
Department: Children's
Amount Requested: $17,600.00

☐ Designated Funds ☐ Undesignated Funds ☐ Technical Assistance

Purpose of Grant

Specify if the request addresses the needs of staff, library operations, patrons, other. If patron: what segment of the population is affected by the need; Documentation of needs.

The Library currently offers special children's programs for 7–8 months out of the year. Performers in the areas of arts, science and culture are engaged to present programs at each of the library branches. As the evaluations and statistics show, these programs are very popular and serve to establish the library as a focal point in the community for families. Parents and children look to the library to provide high-quality programs that extend the library's physical collection and mission.

The following table illustrates the types and costs of programs offered in 20XX.

20XX Children's Programs

Program	Month	Number of performances	Cost per performance	Total cost
Fun with Science	January	12	$127.50	$1,530.00
Jafrika	February	12	$125.00	$1,500.00
Oh the Animals	April	11	$150.00	$1,650.00
*Puppeteer, Bob Aiken	June/July	12	$185.00	$2,225.00
Merry Andrew Afoot	June/July	11	$70.00	$770.00
Creative Exchange	June/July	10	$87.50	$857.00
*Beetles, Bugs . . .	June/July	12	$75.00 + mileage	$1,170.00
John Orlando	June/July	11	$100.00	$1,100.00
Storyteller, Bett Kopit	June/July	11	$200.00	$2,200.00
Raptor Foundation	June/July	11	$50.00–$100.00	$1,160.00
Dave Sullivan	June/July	11	$65.00	$715.00
David Williams	June/July	11	$150.00	$1,650.00

cont.

FIGURE 5.2 (cont.)

Program	Month	Number of performances	Cost per performance	Total cost
Crystal Clown (bookfair performer)	August	5	$95.00 per hour	$1,485.00
Robert Hansen (bookfair performer)	August	2	$75.00	$150.00
Sugar & Spice (bookfair performer)	August	4 hours	$100.00 per hour	$400.00
Angel Vigil	October	9	$100.00	$900.00
WOW Outreach	November	10	$150.00	$1,350.00
			20XX Total	**$20,812.00**

*Please note, due to construction, the Wheat Ridge Library was not included in the program schedule, with the exception of the asterisked programs.

To maintain the level of programming offered in 20XX, the following budget is estimated.

Proposed 20XX Budget

Estimation based on current schedule of special programs, with no additional performers
14 programs annually for 11 branches at average cost of $150 = $27,600
(includes 2 performances throughout year for CL
and 2 performances in summer months for SL and BL)

ESTIMATED 20XX COST	$27,600
LIBRARY CONTRIBUTION	–$10,000
FOUNDATION REQUEST	$17,600

Methods

Substantiate the strategy or activity which will be used to achieve the desired results. Why is this procedure the best course of action?

- The Children's Librarians Roundtable will research and select performers. The programming representative for CLRT will check references, negotiate prices, schedule and coordinate all performances.
- A Children's program featuring an outside performer will be scheduled for all branches for each month, with the exception of March, May, September, and December.
- A program per week will be scheduled for the 8 weeks of Summer Reading Club for all branches.
- Large branches, such as Columbine, Standley Lake and Belmar Library, will have two scheduled performances of each summer program to accommodate larger crowds.

Evaluation

How will you evaluate the results?
The overall success of Children's Programming will be measured through participant evaluations and gathered statistics.

- Statistics covering the number of program attendees per branch are kept throughout the year and reported monthly to library administration.
- Program evaluations are distributed to participants and their parents during each program. Library staff compiles participant evaluations, completes a staff evaluation and submits all to the Programming Committee.

Department Head (for undesignated funds): _____

(20XX Children's Program Coordinator)

Foundation Director: _____

Source: Jefferson County (Colorado) Public Library

---

would like to cosponsor. This (it is hoped) means that the Friends or the foundation will partially or entirely fund the program in exchange for the group's name being included on any publicity the library creates. Ideally, you will have Friends and foundation members who come to understand all aspects of programming, including contacting the performers and submitting the paperwork. This knowledge can be a great asset to your library, particularly if staffing is one of your budgeting constraints.

Do you have a library foundation (or Friends group) with 501(c)(3) tax-exempt status that contributes money to your programming efforts? If yes, then you should mention the foundation on your program flyers, on your library events web page, on the public service announcements on the radio, and anywhere else someone might see or hear it. When possible, include a line that mentions that the foundation is a 501(c)(3). People look for 501(c)(3) organizations when they want to donate money. People also like to give money to organizations that have a good image. A library foundation will appeal to people.

It's also a good idea to become familiar with online websites where donors can give to the charities of their choice. These websites list just about every 501(c)(3) that files with the Internal Revenue Service. Examples of this type of website include Charity Navigator (charitynavigator.org) and CharityWatch (charitywatch.org). Investigate some of these websites. See if your library foundation is listed. Most of these sites give you 100 percent of the donation. If your library foundation is listed, then you might want to consider placing a link to the charities website on your events web page. Or the library foundation might want to post this link on its web page. People really do use these sites. I've seen $75 and $100 donations trickle in via these charities' websites. Hey, money is money!

LOCAL FUNDS

Before we move on to landing the big fish—the grants—let's talk about what we can do in the local waters. Your library's financial situation and programming policy will guide your fund-raising efforts. For example, let's assume that your programming policy allows authors to sell their books after a reading. You could allow the author to purchase the books herself, bring them to the program, and sign and sell them afterward. Or your Friends group or library foundation could purchase them, and you, the program's coordinator, could sell them to your patrons before the author signing. This would be convenient for both the author and patrons. She doesn't have to carry her books to the library; your patrons get a book signed. But do you sell the books at no profit to the library, or do you raise the price by a dollar or two and generate some money for your Friends or foundation? It could depend on the specificity of your programming policy.

Remember all the money the library spends on in-kind expenses for equipment, staff, and facilities? Other agencies and companies in your community can offer you in-kind support. Approach these groups with an offer that is mutually beneficial. They supply you with meeting space or food, and you publicize them as cosponsors. Don't beg. Make a proposal. It really is beneficial for a local grocery store to get its name on your program flyers and on your events web page. People like libraries, and people like companies that support libraries. Their donation of snacks in exchange for listing them on your promotional materials is a fair trade. It's probably a tax deduction for them to boot. See if you can establish a relationship with local theaters and hotels. A cosponsorship could result in a play being held in a beautiful auditorium or a dance workshop taking place in an elegant ballroom.

After you've gotten the hang of the cosponsorship thing, it's time to approach local companies, individuals, and institutions in an attempt to get them to take on the funding of an entire program series. This undertaking is more appropriate for your Friends group or foundation, if you have them. As we will discuss in chapter 8, local businesses must compete with one another to survive. Think of a way to make the sponsorship open to as many businesses as pos-

sible. If more than one business steps forward, have a plan in place. This plan could be as simple as placing the companies' names in a hat and drawing a winner. Perhaps you could also set a time limit for the sponsorship. Invite new sponsors to compete for the honor every three years. If no one applies, keep the sponsor you have. Whatever your plan, be sure that your current sponsor understands the terms.

GRANTS

The Basics

In *Getting Your Grant*, Peggy Barber and Linda D. Crowe list what they call the Ten Commandments for Successful Grants:

1. Develop a project that enhances the goals and objectives of the library.
2. Involve the staff in every step—developing an idea, funding strategy, the proposal, and its implementation.
3. Be sure the library has the basic resources to support the project.
4. Thoroughly research potential funders.
5. Confirm the interest of a potential funder before writing your proposal.
6. Consider the funder a partner in the project, not a silent source of money.
7. Write a proposal that is clear and concise, demonstrating vision and technical competence.
8. Prepare a budget that is detailed, comprehensive and realistic.
9. Be prepared to publicize the project when funded, during implementation, and when completed.
10. Build and maintain a relationship with the funding organization.[3]

These ten points nicely encapsulate the grant-seeking process. The whole idea of writing a grant, however, can seem completely overwhelming. I remember when everything about grant writing was new to me. This was back in the late 1990s. I had never applied for a grant before in my life, and I had no idea where to begin. In the fall of 1999 I attended the Colorado Association of Community Educators/Colorado Adult Education Professional Association (CACE/CAEPA) Conference in Colorado Springs, Colorado. Jenifer Federico of Denver Public Schools Community Schools Program presented a workshop titled, simply, "Grant Writing." In an hour Jenifer brought me from a fear of grants to an understanding of them.

Through Jenifer I learned that I must do a few things before I begin seeking support for my program. I must first make sure that my program has a direct link to my mission statement. My program should have measurable objectives. If I am seeking funding for an English as a New Language program that teaches adults how to speak English, then I must develop a way to later measure whether the program reached this goal. It is also helpful to form relationships with other agencies in my community, and then develop a program that does not duplicate an effort offered by another agency. Funding agencies are attracted to unique ideas. Ideally, my program will already be in place with a documented history of success. A program that has a proven track record is attractive to funders.

Funding sources include local and national foundations, government agencies, and corporations. Jenifer spoke about the importance of finding out all you can about the potential funder's mission. Funding sources frequently have very specific priorities. Sometimes they limit their funding to a geographic region. Take a look at which programs have recently received funding from this source. Does your program have anything in common with the programs that were funded? Also, take a look at the average amount of funding awarded by this source. Does this source seem to offer much less or much, much more than you need?

Jenifer wrapped up her presentation by talking about the proposal. It is helpful to contact the funding source before you mail your proposal. Call the funder and introduce yourself and your program. You might want to send information about your library and your program. Create a fact sheet about your library. ALA can help you. A page on ALA's website contains quotable facts you can integrate into a fact sheet to capture the reader's attention. For example, did you know that reference librarians in the nation's public and academic libraries answer nearly 5.7 million questions weekly? Standing single file, the line of questioners would stretch from Long Island, New York, to Juneau, Alaska. Facts such as these are available at www.ala.org/offices/sites/ala.org.offices/files/content/ola/quotablefacts/QF.3.8.2010.pdf. Figure 5.3 is a sample fact sheet from Redwood City (California) Public Library that highlights the library, its programming track record, and its event space.

If the funder provides you with an application, fill it out completely. Many funders use a scoring system similar to the rating system libraries use when evaluating job applications. Do not give the funder a reason to mark you down due to an incomplete application. If you are unsure of what the application is asking, call the funder and ask. If the funder asks you to write a proposal from scratch, follow the guidelines if guidelines are provided. Some funding sources will ask that your grant be submitted in a particular format. For example, funders in Massachusetts may ask applicants to use the AGM Common Proposal Form. This means that you would submit your grant in the format developed by the Associated Grant Makers of Massachusetts. (Examples of this form are located at www.agmconnect.org/cpf.) Be sure to ask for a specific amount of money, but also be sure that the amount you ask for is within the funding range. And don't forget the KISS principle—Keep it simple, stupid! Funders will not understand jargon and acronyms. So you'll want to elaborate on what you mean if you say that ALA recognized your library as offering one of the best ENL classes to YAs in the state.

FIGURE 5.3 | **FACT SHEET**

Redwood City Public Library
1044 Middlefield Road
Redwood City, California 94063-1815
www.redwoodcity.org/library

Redwood City Public Library
Public Programs and Events

The Redwood City Public Library lives up to its mission of being "the learning center of our community and the place people turn to for the discovery of ideas, the joy of reading and the power of information." Founded in 1865, the downtown branch of the Redwood City Public Library is a 47,000 square foot facility housed in a beautiful renovated firehouse.

We program aggressively, and include author events, theme or holiday-related programs, cooking demonstrations, live-music, family and film programs, children's events and community-wide celebrations. In March 2007, along with Montalvo Arts Center, the library led *The Big Read* a community-wide reading of *Fahrenheit 451*. The month-long program featured over 40 public events and drew over 1,600 attendees. Author events included renowned science fiction writers Kim Stanley Robinson and Tad Williams. Our upcoming County-Wide *One Book, One Community* event series will feature Michael Chabon.

Recent author events who drew audiences, of over thirty people, include: Sheila and Lisa Himmel (*Hungry: A Mother and a Daughter Fight Anorexia*), Richie Unterberger (*The Unreleased Beatles*), Gail Tsukiyama (*Street of a Thousand Blossoms*), Fred Luskin (*Forgive for Love*) and Logan and Noah Miller (*Either You're in or You're in the Way.*) The library goes all out to tailor our promotions of public events to ensure that each one is enjoyable, unique, and successful.

Venue - Redwood City Public Library - Downtown library

Web site:	www.redwoodcity.org/library
Address:	1044 Middlefield Road,
	Redwood City, CA
Hours:	Monday - Thursday: 10-9, Friday - Saturday: 10-5, Sunday: 12-5
Event space:	The Fireplace Room (Community Room is ideal for lectures & films)
Seating:	Capacity of up to 50
Staffing:	RCPL has dedicated program outreach staff and years of experience with running library and bookstore events
Scheduling:	Typically, events are held weeknights (Tues-Fri at 7:00 p.m.) or Sat. afternoons.
Contact:	Roz Kutler, 650-780-7058, rkutler@redwoodcity.org
Program Partners:	We work with independent booksellers for author events whenever possible.

Promotions

To guarantee high standards for our events, we support each program with the following promotion package:

- Listing in our monthly event calendar flyer (distributed within the library and to Peninsula libraries, community centers, local independent businesses, and community colleges)
- Email distribution to hundreds of community subscribers
- Individual flyers for each event are posted at the library and in local businesses and community centers

Publicity
- Each event is included in our monthly events publicity sent to all local media
- Events are also posted on online calendars including, www.redwoodcity.org/calendar/, www.paloaltoonline.com, www.craigslist.org, and http://events.mercurynews.com/
- For particularly large events, we will contact local book editors at the *Palo Alto Daily News, The Palo Alto Weekly, San Francisco Chronicle* and *San Jose Mercury News* to elicit reviews and mentions of the event.
- The library creates related book displays for author events and other programs

FIRST NATIONAL LIBRARY OF THE YEAR
Member of the Peninsula Library System

Source: Redwood City (California) Public Library

Finally, if your proposal is turned down, give the funder a call and ask what you can do better next time. Many funders will be happy to help you better prepare for the next round of applications.

Resources for Finding Grants

As you begin to look for funding sources, a few standard titles will help you immensely. The *Annual Register of Grant Support: A Directory of Funding Sources*[4] and *The Foundation Directory Online*[5] are both excellent. Your state probably has a directory as well, such as *The Colorado Grants Guide*[6] or *The Oregon Foundation Data Book*.[7] The Foundation Center's website (foundationcenter.org) has many links that will help you find funding sources. The professional literature will frequently carry the RFPs (requests for proposals) of funding sources. Your state library's website is a good source for announcements of grant opportunities for libraries.

It is also a good idea to become familiar with the National Endowment for the Humanities (NEH), your state humanities councils, and ALA. The NEH (www.neh.gov) funds many library projects, such as We the People, Small Grants to Libraries, and Bridging Cultures. ALA receives funding from several sources, including the NEH, for traveling exhibitions, discussion programs, literary programs, and other library cultural programs for adults. Many of these programs are scholar led, such as "From Rosie to Roosevelt: A Film History of Americans in World War II." This program uses documentary films, readings, and discussions to involve library audiences in studying the American experience in World War II. You can find information on these programs through ALA's Programming & Exhibitions website at www .ala.org/programming.

You will also want to look into the Library Services and Technology Act (LSTA). Your state library administers the funds, intended for two broad priorities. The first is for activities using technology for information sharing between libraries and other community services. The second is for programs that make library resources more accessible to urban, rural, or low-income residents and others who have difficulty using library services. Each state has a five-year plan outlining its state programs.

Although much of the money awarded via LSTA grants goes to support the use of technology in libraries, there are many instances of libraries receiving money to do creative programming. For example, Athens-Clarke County (Georgia) Library received $343,100 in LSTA funding in 2010 to partner with an arts center to develop new services and programs for the aging baby boomer population. The partners generated new users through the creative use of new technology to produce live webcasts and a video archive of their programs.

The Grant Proposal

We've already discussed the importance of contacting the funding source ahead of time. Now that you are ready to submit your proposal, be sure you've involved the person who will need to sign off on the grant application before you submit it. This individual may be your director or library board chairperson. A grant may provide the funding that allows you to greatly expand or enhance your programming. With the help of a state department of education grant, you might now be able to offer literacy tutoring to adults three days a week. This is a wonderful thing. Just be sure that your administration and library board have had the chance to discuss the project with you along the way. People feel much less threatened by innovation if they've seen it coming and are prepared for it.

As for the proposal itself, you will either have an application to fill out or you will submit your own proposal. Ask the funding source if you can see examples of successful applications or proposals. There is an excellent chance that the funder will show you examples. (Many of these sources are publicly funded, and the applications they receive become public record.) There are many excellent sources on proposal writing, such as *Proposal Planning and Writing*.[8] The Foundation Center's website (foundationcenter.org) contains a proposal writing course that provides the following proposal outline:

Components of a Proposal

- Executive Summary: umbrella statement of your case and summary of the entire proposal (1 page).
- Statement of Need: why this project is necessary (2 pages).
- Project Description: nuts and bolts of how the project will be implemented (3 pages).
- Budget: financial description of the project plus explanatory notes (1 page).
- Organization Information: history and governing structure of the nonprofit; its primary activities, audiences, and services (1 page).
- Conclusion: summary of the proposal's main points (2 paragraphs).[9]

After you've written and submitted your proposal, your work really begins. In the event that you are not funded, you will get in touch with the funder and find out what you can do to receive funding next time you apply. But let's expect success. When you are funded, write a thank-you letter to your funder. Explain how you plan on publicizing the program, crediting the funder as a sponsor. Send examples of your promotional materials. If the funder has picked up a major, ongoing event, such as an adult summer reading club, ask if a representative would like to become a member of that event's steering committee. The more you involve your funders and give them a chance to see

your program in action, the more dedicated they will become. Also be sure you are clear on what the evaluation and reporting process involves. Begin collecting whatever data you will need, including quotes from the people who've attended and appreciated the program. Show the funder the "Thank yous" from your patrons.

Now that we have generated some money, let's move on to the fun part: finding something to spend it on!

NOTES

1. Debra Wilcox Johnson, *Cultural Programs for Adults in Public Libraries: A Survey Report* (Chicago: American Library Association, 1999), iv.
2. Ibid., iv–v.
3. Peggy Barber and Linda D. Crowe, *Getting Your Grant: A How-to-Do-It Manual for Librarians* (New York: Neal-Schuman, 1993), 2.
4. *Annual Register of Grant Support: A Directory of Funding Sources* (New Providence, NJ: R. R. Bowker, published annually).
5. Foundation Center, *The Foundation Directory Online* (New York: The Foundation Center, updated weekly), fconline.foundationcenter.org.
6. *Colorado Grants Guide* (Denver, CO: Community Resource Center, continuously updated), www.crcamerica.org/grants-guide.
7. *The Oregon Foundation Data Book* (Portland, OR: C&D Publishing, published annually).
8. Jeremy T. Miner and Lynn E. Miner, *Proposal Planning and Writing*, 4th ed. (Westport, CT: Greenwood Press, 2008).
9. Foundation Center, *Proposal Writing Short Course* (New York: The Foundation Center, 2011), foundationcenter.org/getstarted/tutorials/shortcourse/components.html.

6

Selecting a Topic

This is the fun part! Who doesn't like to come up with a bright idea? The sustainable living books have been circulating well . . . let's try a program on the how-tos of composting. The stock market seems to be finally rebounding . . . let's ask an economics professor to give a talk on the history of the New York Stock Exchange. A patron suggests that you should hold a singles mixer at the library on Tuesday evenings. All these ideas might translate into successful library programs. But first you must ask yourself if these programs tie into your library's mission and your library's current priorities. The first two ideas just mentioned seem to qualify as instructional programs. The likely purpose of the third program is to welcome people into your facility. You may want to draw potential new patrons into your building, or you may consider it part of your library's mission to be a community gathering place. Your mission and priorities will help you determine your topic.

You'll also want to have your finger on the pulse of what's happening within your community. Is the unemployment rate still high? Are you offering programs on topics that can assist your patrons during these tough times? Is a controversial bridge being built with taxpayer funding? Have you considered creating a discussion forum around this topic by inviting elected officials to speak about the nuances of the bridge project? Has a certain fashion fad or a certain technology gadget become all the rage in the past few weeks? You'll want to continually scan your community and build in the flexibility to offer both informative and fun topics that tap into current community interests.

The source of your ideas can be influenced by the source of your funding or resources. If your library foundation pays the performers' fees for most or all of your programs, then your foundation may very well request or expect quite a bit of input on programming topics. Ideally, your library will integrate the foundation into your program committee (see chapter 2), which will allow the foundation to contribute equally in the planning process. It is common for a library to turn over its programming efforts either partially or entirely to a Friends group. Two reasons are given most often for using this approach: (1) program planning—from thinking up an idea through producing the performance itself and handling the evaluation—can take a great deal of staff time, and Friends groups can take on many of these responsibilities; and (2) programming can be a lot of fun, and this can be a powerful recruitment tool when your Friends group is looking to increase its membership. If you tell people that they can help plan and produce concerts and plays and other cool things if they join your Friends group, then some people *will* join and eagerly work on developing programs. Again, it is a good idea to get someone from your Friends group on your program committee. This cooperation and collaboration is vital. Library staff need to remain partners in the process, because they will most likely be the people who, at the very least, create the publicity, arrange for the necessary equipment (such as computer projectors and screens), and reserve the meeting space. Library staff are also the folks who will be asked for details on upcoming programs. Therefore staff need to be kept informed about forthcoming programs and the performers, even if staff members were not the ones who planned and funded the programs.

Now let's proceed with choosing a topic.

WHAT ARE THE JONESES DOING?

What are other libraries doing? A study called *Cultural Programs for Adults in Public Libraries* received usable responses from 1,229 medium-sized and large libraries serving populations of 5,000 and more. The survey asked libraries to give participation rates for nine program types. The results are shown here.[1]

Book discussions	61.4%
Author readings/presentations	59.3%
Lecture series	43.8%
Musical performances	41.7%
Dramatic performances	22.9%
Adult Reading Incentive programs	20.1%
Film series	19.8%
Creative writing workshops	18.2%
Dance performances	14.2%

LET THE COLLECTION BE YOUR GUIDE

Which of the program types in the preceding list interest your library users? You most likely know the answer to this question. You know what questions patrons are asking at the information desk. You know which items are always checked out, on hold, or being ordered and reordered. Also, check with your IT or access services staff and ask them if they can generate any data that show circulation trends. Perhaps your library subscribes to an ILS (integrated library system) product such as Encore Reporter that breaks materials use patterns down to a library-specific level. So what *is* circulating well at your library? Books on computers and technology, travel, and cooking always seem to be in demand. Perhaps the technology writer from your local newspaper could give a sixty-minute presentation on things to look for (cell phone carriers, data plans, iPhone vs. Android, etc.) when buying your first smartphone. Monitoring your collection won't tell you what your community as a whole is interested in (some people just don't visit the library), but it will show you the areas of interest to your library patrons.

GET ALL STAFF MEMBERS INVOLVED

Library staff work with your patrons throughout the day. They very likely also live in the community. It's important to let all staff know that they are welcome to generate programming ideas. For example, while patrons are checking their books out, they will talk to circulation staff about what they are reading, what they are doing later in the day, what they like about the library. They will also tell the staff about things they don't like, or they'll suggest additional materials and services. Speaking with the circulation staff provides an accurate snapshot of what patrons are reading, viewing, listening to, and requesting.

TIE PROGRAMS INTO HOLIDAYS, FESTIVALS, AND CELEBRATIONS

When planning programs, especially when planning over the course of a year, you may want to look at what holidays and celebrations occur during the year. For example, a library may want to schedule a program in May to tie into Cinco de Mayo. *Chase's Calendar of Events* is a great resource to use when brainstorming programs.[2] Let's say you want to plan a program in September, but you just can't think of a topic. Open up *Chase's* to the September section and you'll find that September, among other things, is Baby Safety Month. Perhaps you could ask someone from a local organization or association (such as the Injury Free Coalition for Kids) to give a talk on selecting a baby-safe stroller and car seat. *Chase's* is also a good tool to use when you have an idea but are unsure of when to schedule the program. For example, you've decided to produce a program on basic bicycle repair and maintenance, you've located a speaker, but you're just not sure when to have the program. When you check under "bicycle" in *Chase's* index, you see that May is National Bike Month.

OTHER SOURCES OF INSPIRATION

Your state library most likely has information that can help you tie into local and national events. For example, each year the Colorado State Library sent my library a packet of information on National Library Week. The packet included program ideas, outreach activities to elected officials, sample press releases, and clip art for promotional flyers. To find out if your state library offers similar resources, check its website.

Local newspapers are a good source of ideas. Scan the events sections of your local newspapers. You might want to plan programs that will complement an upcoming traveling exhibit at a nearby museum. The classifieds are also a good section to browse. Pay close attention to people who are advertising their services. If someone is advertising her services as a masseuse, perhaps she would be willing to offer a lecture and demonstration at your library in exchange for your allowing her to hand out business cards after the program.

Ideas will come from other sources. If you have a program committee, this group will be a constant source of ideas. Of course you'd like to hear directly from your intended audience, if possible. How do you solicit library patrons and your community for ideas? You could gather community input through a survey (see chapters 4 and 10), an advisory board, or a suggestion box in the library. It also doesn't hurt to speak directly to the audience as you are collecting program evaluation forms. Ask, "What other types of programs would you like to see the library offer?" Programming is a grassroots process. If you are just beginning to offer programming in your library, it may take a while for the audiences to grow in number. But as they do, the participants will become more and more enthusiastic, and you will begin to receive evaluations with comments such as, "Great! Thanks so much for offering this. How about something on writing a will?"

POP OR CLASSICAL?

Chances are that your library's mission statement will give you quite a bit of flexibility in determining which topics you choose. A silent film series or a lecture on Alzheimer's are probably both within bounds. You will probably create a programming calendar that mixes the recreational with the informational. The two really do blur anyway. Often learning begins when you discover a topic that gives you pleasure.

Some programs you will offer because you know the library is a good venue for dispensing the information—the classical programs. You might ask representatives from local agencies to give talks on arthritis, pest control, living trusts, and a variety of other topics. Just as you know that this information should be found in your library in book format, you also believe that this information should be available to patrons in the format of a program. Other programs will aim simply to please—the pop. You'll aim for the Martha Stewart– and James Patterson–type programs—the best sellers. It's great fun planning programs that you know will draw large crowds. Your "how to" programs, such as how-to-buy-a-tablet-computer or how-to-cook-a-feast-in-thirty-minutes can really bring 'em in the doors.

From a program-planning standpoint, you will want to estimate your audience turnout when you select your topic. For example, if you decide to offer a microwave-cooking workshop, ask yourself how many people will attend the program. Just take a guess. How many people will attend a program on applying for a home loan? You will want to ask this question early on. If you foresee that the program will be heavily attended, then you might want to ensure that your publicity mentions that tickets will be required. If you decide that the program may not draw a large crowd, it doesn't mean that you shouldn't offer the program. It just means that you will have to be more diligent with your publicity. You might have to call some local agencies and organizations and talk up your program. You might have to spend some extra time creating buzz about your program via Facebook and Twitter

postings. If you can reach the people who need the information, they will come to your program. For more on publicity techniques, please see chapter 11.

Sometimes a program will form around a desire to meet the needs of a particular group of people. Your idea for a program on arthritis, for example, could originate from an attempt to offer a program for your senior population. Chapter 7 details how you can begin offering programs geared toward a target audience.

Last, I'll mention that there will be times when you will be fortunate enough to have *too many* excellent ideas and topics to choose from. Even after you've reflected on your priorities and your community's needs and done all due diligence, you still might have too many potential programs to fit into your calendar of events. This is where some type of decision-making tool will be helpful (and very welcome). If you are working with a team to select your programs, you could use a simple decision-making tool such as multivoting. Place all the potential programs on a flip chart, give each member of the team three sticky notes, and let each person vote for his or her top three programs by placing a sticky note next to those programs. Count up the votes for each program and then move forward with the top ten or fifteen or twenty programs.

Now that we've selected our topic, let's focus on the program's anticipated audience.

NOTES

1. Debra Wilcox Johnson, *Cultural Programs for Adults in Public Libraries: A Survey Report* (Chicago: American Library Association, 1999), iii.
2. *Chase's Calendar of Events* (Chicago: Contemporary Books, published annually).

Your Target Audience

All programs begin with an idea. There are at least three variations of "the idea." First variation: someone has a topic in mind, such as baseball card collecting, and begins planning a program around that topic. The preceding chapter covered ways in which you can select and pursue a topic. Second variation: some staff person or group decides to target a particular audience type. For example, your library decides to begin a series of summer programs that you hope will draw more 20-somethings into the library. One of the programs in the series will feature a graphic novelist, and another will present an anime artist who will help participants create a short film using a laptop computer. Third variation: you know of a talented performer in the community and you approach him to present a program at your library. This third scenario will be covered in the following chapter. In this chapter we will focus on scenario two: the target audience.

Target audiences will certainly come up at the beginning of the year if you divide your programming budget into categories such as "adult," "YA," and "children." If you outline your programming goals at the beginning of the year (as discussed in chapter 2), then you will probably also discuss intended audiences at this time. This really just amounts to you planning a variety of programs to meet the demands of your entire community. You'll want to include women, men, the young and the elderly, business owners and self-employed artists, the exercise fanatics and those with health concerns. You'll select various topics that you hope will appeal to many of these people. One person might fall within many of these categories. A fit, elderly businesswoman might show up at your program on stroke prevention.

Your programs are, of course, open to everyone, but it can be an exciting challenge to try to offer a program with a particular audience in mind. Perhaps you have noticed, when doing errands during lunch, that Latinos work at many of the local shops and restaurants. You never notice Latinos in the library. Would a particular type of programming bring them in? It might, but what topic would you choose? If you have some knowledge of the Latino population in your neighborhood, then you might be able to select a topic that will appeal to them. If you need a little help, just remember that organizations exist that can assist you. Associations such as REFORMA (The National Association to Promote Library and Information Services to Latinos and the Spanish Speaking) should have local chapters that can offer insight into the interests and needs of your Latino community. Your library collection will have resources that list associations at the state and local levels.

EXPANDING YOUR HORIZONS

When we begin to pursue programming for Latinos, teenagers, our patrons with hearing impairments, and others, we sometimes learn that we are not very knowledgeable about the people we want to serve. We can learn a lot through conversations. For example, after speaking with one of your Latina patrons, you might realize that she identifies more with being a fitness buff and a single mother than she does with being Latina. Spanish speakers are a diverse group who cannot be typified. They will have many of the same interests as your English-speaking patrons. They will enjoy sports, appreciate good cooking, and have concerns about their retirement.

So let's assume that some of your patrons have recently approached you and said they would prefer attending programs in Spanish. You agree that this sounds like a fine idea, but the thing is, no one on staff speaks Spanish. What do you do? You might be tempted to "just do it" and plow ahead. You've already done your demographic work and you know that the Spanish-speaking community exists. Why not just offer some programs? Ask yourself: If I "just do

it" will I be offering a quality program? If you attract a large number of Spanish speakers into your library for a program, and afterward they walk out onto the floor to ask reference questions, borrow books, and get a library card, will you be able to serve them? If the answer is yes, then go for it. If the answer is no, you may want to pursue this audience in a more strategic fashion. To continue using a Spanish-speaking audience as an example, let me present a case study that illustrates how one library began offering services to this audience.

A CASE STUDY

The Jefferson County Public Library (JCPL) is located just west of Denver, Colorado. (If you haven't guessed it already, I'll 'fess up: I worked for JCPL for a long time—thirteen years!) Part of the county stretches into the foothills of the Rocky Mountains. Once an agricultural and mining area, Jefferson County now is a thriving suburban, business, industrial, and residential community with a population of approximately 533,000. In the late '90s, JCPL operated seven full-service branches that were open sixty-three hours a week. The library also had five extension branches whose hours ranged from six to forty-three hours a week. One of the libraries, the Villa Library, was located just a mile west of the City of Denver. (The library has since been relocated to a new facility and renamed.) In the spring of 1997 I was the head of Reference and Adult Services at the Villa Library. Around this time, we began noticing that people whose first language seemed to be Spanish staffed many of the small businesses and restaurants surrounding the library. The library's administration, justifiably, wanted something a bit more concrete than anecdotal evidence gathered through staff visits to the mall. In order to get the entire Villa Library staff involved in this learning process, we invited a representative from the Latin American Research and Service Agency (LARASA) to our staff meeting. The representative explained some of the characteristics of the Latino community in Jefferson County. (LARASA was a nonprofit organization created in 1964 to improve the health, education, and self-sufficiency of Colorado's Latino community. LARASA recently changed its name to CLLARO.) We learned about the population trends, occupations, countries of origin, languages, families, and income levels of the Latino people in the Villa area. The presenter discussed the importance of the extended family. We learned that if we wanted to attract Latino children to the library, we should begin building connections with the moms. And one of the best ways to connect with the moms was to go to them and let them know that they were welcome in the library. "But where do we find the moms?" we asked. "Make an appearance at their churches," the LARASA representative told us.

After the LARASA presentation, we began to put together a demographic report from data collected from such sources as the school district, the census, and local organizations. The study, completed in April 1998, revealed that approximately 9 percent of the people (11,506 residents) in the Villa service area were Latinos. The study also detailed such characteristics as countries of origin, education, and income level. Through the study we learned that the majority of Latinos in Colorado (60 percent) reported that English was their primary language, while 30 percent reported Spanish as their primary language, and 30 percent reported that they were bilingual. This meant that almost 3,500 people in the Villa service area spoke only Spanish.

After viewing the demographic study, library administration gave the go-ahead to begin exploring ways in which the library could serve its Spanish-speaking residents. At this point, although library staff—myself included—were itching to begin buying books and offering other services, we all paused and took a breath. The library decided to lay some groundwork before offering resources and services specifically targeted toward Spanish-speaking Lati-

nos. The pause occurred because the library was not adequately prepared to serve its Latino population. The staff were not prepared, the collection was not in place, and no library publications, such as library card applications, existed in Spanish. Where should we begin? We decided that it was time to offer the staff some additional communication skills.

Communication really is a two-way street. Everyone communicates better when they are in a comfortable situation. In order for library staff to communicate well with patrons, staff must comprehend the patrons' needs and then provide answers or resources to meet those needs. The Villa Library staff just needed training to make this communication possible. With this training, we would feel more confident and open in our interactions with Latino patrons—particularly those who spoke Spanish. And the Spanish-speaking patrons would feel less awkward when asking for assistance if they knew that we were knowledgeable about their language and culture.

(At this point it might not hurt to repeat that I am not suggesting that a great deal of training needs to occur in order for you to communicate with someone who fits under a demographic heading of "Hispanic" or "Over 65." Everyone is an individual, whether they are Hispanic, over 65, male or female, single or divorced, and so on. But, if one of these groups seems to not be using the library, there may be a reason. By learning more about that group and the attributes it shares, we can put ourselves in a better position to serve the group.)

In the summer of 1998 the Villa Library hired an instructor to offer basic Spanish classes to the staff. These classes were ninety-minute sessions, held once a week for six weeks. The staff attended on library time. This six-week series was followed by another six-week series. The second series focused more on library-related words and phrases. We learned how to tell a patron, in Spanish, that his book is due in three weeks. We also learned other library standards, such as, "The library's phone directories for the United States are on CD-ROM"—remember CD-ROMs in the '90s?—and, "Do you know how to use the microfilm/microfiche machine?" All staff members were given a cheat sheet of these phrases in English and Spanish.

With the classes under way, some of the Villa staff made a trip to a distributor of Spanish-language materials and purchased a small number of adult, YA, and children's books. The library also added a few magazines in Spanish and added Spanish to our directional signs within the library so that patrons would become aware of our intent to offer materials and services in Spanish. We also drafted a new section for our collection development policy dealing with the collection of Spanish materials. By this time the staff were excited about the opportunity to offer these new materials and services. In the beginning, the only service we could offer was a few slowly pronounced phrases in Spanish, but the benefits were immediately noticeable. Instead of mutual panic breaking out when a non-English-speaking patron approached an only-English-speaking staff member, both parties relaxed when they realized that between the two of them they spoke just enough English and Spanish to help one another understand the question and then the answer. Instead of being intimidated by the language differences, staff looked forward to the challenge.

After making sure that staff were included in and comfortable with the process, we began concentrating on ways to promote the materials and resources to the Latino community. The Villa Library experimented with a Spanish story hour. We offered library tours to our English as a New Language (ENL) students. We translated our library card application and welcome brochure into Spanish. We began working with local organizations to help us identify the wants and needs of the Latinos in our service area, and we made appearances at the meetings of organizations that served Latinos, such as REFORMA, and promoted our services and materials. We submitted job postings to newspapers and electronic mailing lists aimed at the Latino communities and eventually hired a staff member who was fluent in Spanish. We published our first Spanish/English bilingual article in our library newsletter. We visited other libraries, such as Denver Public Library, that had been offering these services for quite some time, to learn from them.

So, what programs did we begin offering to our Latino patrons? We began a Spanish/English storytime. We began offering programs that focused on Latino culture. For example, we invited a *santero* (a person who carves saints) to give a demonstration on *santos*, which are carved and painted figures of saints. And even though we did not immediately begin offering programs entirely in Spanish, we now had the staff and resources in place to do so. We also learned more about our Latino patrons. We learned that most of them had someone in their family who spoke English. This opened up the possibilities of targeting some programs toward our Latino patrons, while offering the programs in English. We created flyers and other publicity both in Spanish and English. We discovered that musical programs are a good choice for audiences of mixed languages—usually the performers do little talking. We learned that Latinos frequently attend programs as a family and that one of the members usually speaks enough English to fill in any gaps for the family. We also learned that we could ask a staff person who spoke Spanish, perhaps a library page, to walk among the crowd and help those people who did not understand what the performer was saying. We set a goal to offer our first program in Spanish. We knew that there were patrons who preferred to hear their programs in Spanish. We laid a lot of groundwork during this time, which prepared us to move ahead with our programs for Latinos.

PUTTING YOUR EXPERIENCE TO WORK

Once you have learned how to expand your traditional programming into other areas, you will find that the same process can be used again and again. What if, after you have begun offering programs in Spanish, you decide to begin offering intergenerational programming? Many of the steps mentioned in the preceding case study can be applied to intergenerational programming. Rhea Joyce Rubin tells us, "Intergenerational programs combine people of more than one age group in a mutually beneficial, mutually enjoyable activity."[1] An intergenerational program involves more than the young and the elderly being in the same room together. A stamp-collecting workshop that happens to attract both children and seniors is not an intergenerational program. An intergenerational program is a planned event during which different age groups interact. When children begin asking questions about the stamps and the relevance that they have to the older collectors' lives, you have created an intergenerational program.

Children and seniors do have some unique characteristics. For example, seniors are used to being able to make their own decisions, while children are used to being told what to do but appreciate the opportunity to make choices themselves. Identify the agencies in your community that serve seniors, such as the Retired Senior Volunteer Program (RSVP). These agencies can contribute information, supply or recommend senior volunteers who have worked with children, and promote your program to their clients. But before you begin offering intergenerational programs, make sure that your staff have the necessary training. Just as some of your staff might not be prepared to effectively help Spanish-speaking patrons, some of your staff will need to learn more about a particular age range. Some training is probably in order to prepare your staff to work effectively with an audience that could range in age from 6 to 86. For some intergenerational programming ideas, try ALA's Office for Literacy and Outreach Services website at www.ala.org/offices/olos. In addition, ALA's publication *The Whole Person Catalog No. 4* includes a section on discussion programs for special audiences.[2]

As you begin to plan programs for special audiences, the processes described earlier will help guide you through the steps needed to learn more about certain populations and to develop a library staff that

is prepared to assist those patrons. Partnering with organizations that serve specific populations will be crucial as you begin to plan programs for these target audiences. For example, partnering with organizations and entities that serve and even entertain 20-somethings—the university student union, the college radio station, a local music venue—can increase the likelihood of actually getting young adults to show up at your programs. These organizations can serve as bridges that connect you to new audiences, and they can give you insight into the interests of these audiences. This partnering approach works with any population. In addition to your community organizations, members of your staff will emerge as crucial links to segments of your population. Ideally, the staff in your library reflect the characteristics of your community. Or perhaps you are striving to build that diversity into your workforce in the coming years. Multnomah County Library (MCL), for example, has developed a workforce that assists patrons in English and four "target languages"—Spanish, Chinese, Russian, and Vietnamese. One of the many wonderful things about having these folks on board is that the programming staff can go right to them and gather information on potential topics for programs. Programs that allow people to come together for conversation are always popular. MCL has a bilingual Chinese/English knitting circle running at two of its libraries. And the Intercambio programs remain popular where Spanish-speakers and English-speakers come together to learn more about the language and culture of their community neighbors. Another strategy that works well is to hire performers who are bilingual and then publicize certain programs in both English and a second language. By interacting with the audience, the performer can integrate the right mix of each language into the program. It's pretty amazing to watch a program unfold in which a performer transitions between languages. This technique works particularly well with performing arts programs in which the music or physical movements convey as much meaning as do the words.

All these programs and approaches might be just what your patrons want, but if you are new to offering programs targeted toward certain languages and cultures within your community, there is one great place to begin: the cultural celebration. Music and food and crafts that celebrate a culture by acknowledging a certain festival or holiday are sure ingredients of a successful program. MCL offers programming around Lunar New Year, Slavic New Year, and Día de los Muertos, and all these programs are extremely well attended. In fact, in recent years, the library has had to reduce the number of activities that occur during these events because the large crowds were verging on chaos! I wish you the same success (without the chaos).

MEN WANTED

It can be really, really difficult to draw men into our program audiences. Why is that? Well, until the Internet came along in the '90s and libraries began offering public computer access, my observation as a reference librarian was that women entered our buildings more frequently and in greater numbers than did the guys. The Internet age seems to have balanced the scales a bit: a quick scan of the public computers in my library on any given day reveals that people of just about every imaginable demographic are using our computers. According to ALA in *The State of America's Libraries, 2011*, the gals are still using the library more than the guys. Seventy-two percent of the women surveyed had visited a library in the past year versus 58 percent of the men.[3] But when it comes to our programs, what type of male/female mix are we seeing in our audiences? And, more specifically, are we offering programs that appeal to men? Or is it that we are offering topics that *would* appeal to men if only they were aware of what their library has to offer? Do we need to get better at marketing our programs to men?

Since I'm a guy and I don't want to get a pie in my face at the next ALA conference, I'm going to approach this section carefully but with some humor. I've thought a lot about this topic. I know that we get the dads who bring their children into storytimes and children's programs. And we get men who accompany their wives to adult programs. And, sure, there *are* men who already show up at our programs. But I can't count the number of conversations I've had with colleagues over the years on the topic of what a tough draw men can be when it comes to programming. So why is this? One reason may be that many men, like many teens, do not think of the library as the first place to go for a social or even an educational experience. Just as many teens feel the pull of friends and extracurricular activities, such as team sports and naps, so do men gravitate toward places other than the library to get together with people, have fun, and learn something new. Second, many library staff members are women. And many of us also share certain social and political views. These views result in wonderful, welcoming libraries that support bedrock library values such as intellectual freedom. But, and I'm just going to say it, I think at times these same personal values influence the types of programs we offer.

I've produced programs over the years on knitting and couponing and jewelry making. The turnout for these programs is always respectable, and the attendees are usually primarily women. Book discussion groups do better at bringing in the guys. A program on making flies for fly fishing will appeal to even more guys. And on occasion, I've seen programs that just get it exactly right when it comes to appealing to men. For example, ask the World War II veterans in your community to come in and share their stories, and the men in your community will turn out in droves to listen. But libraries can expand their repertoires a bit more.

I've asked peers to think of what their husbands or brothers or sons or male friends do on their days off, and then I ask if we offer programs that align with those activities and interests. If I Google "men's hobbies" or "men's interests," I find websites and articles and lists that mention fishing, coaching, billiards, home brewing, target shooting, collecting, mentoring, parenting, sports . . . We've probably all offered some sort of collecting program at some point, but have we offered a program that gives tips on collecting antique swords or autographed baseballs, or have we just flat-out targeted a program toward guys and called it "Collecting for Guys"? Have we offered a "How to Draft Your Fantasy Football Team" program or a "Getting Started with Home Brewing" program? (If yes, great! And let me know where your library is located; I want to attend!) Have we offered a "Buying the Right Bass Boat" program in the spring as the guys start to dig their fishing gear out of the garage? For the brave, have we offered programs on gun safety or buying-the-target-shooting-handgun-that's-right-for-you? Our collections contain resources on firearms safety and target shooting. Will our programs represent these interests as well? If your library's mission and programming policy encourage bringing people into the library for purely recreational programs, then why not set up the TV in the meeting room and project *Monday Night Football* onto a movie screen and serve pizza and soft drinks?

You will have a good feel for what will and won't fly in your community. But it can't hurt to think creatively and to think beyond what we offer day-to-day. For example, when I was with MCL, I brainstormed with the programming staff and we thought of things that we could do to be sure that we kept the guys in mind when we planned programs. We talked about declaring "The Month of the Guy." We thought we'd approach this a bit tongue-in-cheek and use humor in our marketing, but we would be serious in targeting men and offering some of the topics mentioned earlier. The point is to keep guys in the mix as you build that complex palette of programming and push yourself into considering those programs on interests or hobbies that involve a little bit of risk or speed or dirt or gunk, as well as the guy stuff that involves reading and teaching and loving and sharing. We guys will show our appreciation by showing up at your next program.

Programs for Guys That Worked

Before we conclude this section on programming for guys, let's look at what has worked well in libraries around the United States. (Please be sure to read the Acknowledgments to see all the talented, creative people who contributed fantastic ideas and examples that are included throughout this book.)

Let's start with San Diego (California) Public Library. Program planners have had success in attracting men to a "philosophy talk" series on topics such as existentialism, Socrates, and Sufism. This series draws an equal number of men and women in comparison to most of the library's programs, which draw about 80 percent women. The central library also screened the World Cup and the Tour de France live! Attendance was overwhelmingly male. Programming staff also plan to begin a "schlock-fest" movie series that they anticipate will appeal to young men (and of course anyone else who has an interest in schlock).

Loutit (Michigan) District Library drew a largely male audience with a program on bicycle repair and maintenance. Programmers plan on offering other "hands-on" programs in the future. They've also drawn in baby boomer guys with local history programs on such topics as shipwrecks on Lake Michigan or the Michigan pike (which is a really big fish). Lisle (Illinois) Library District hosted a science program that featured Lee Marek of *Late Show with David Letterman* fame. The program brought in a lot of dads with their kids. Calvert (Maryland) Library held a book discussion series using Patrick O'Brian's novels and invited an instructor from the Naval Academy to lead the series. Lots of men attended the series, and the turnout overall was terrific—twenty to thirty people per discussion. As part of their promotion of the event, staff placed promotional bookmarks in the O'Brian novels and other "guy lit" in the library.

Redwood City (California) Downtown Library offered a "Heist Film Festival" that was popular with men. The library even occasionally includes an R-rated film. Attendance ranged from twelve to forty-five. A local film professor introduced each film, and the library partnered with a local video store that assisted with the event's promotion. One particularly clever aspect of the series is that staff involved patrons in the selection of the films. The programming librarian compiled a long list of heist films and then sent a SurveyMonkey poll to the library's e-mail subscribers asking them to help select films. Here are two film fest tips from Redwood City: (1) popcorn and refreshments are a near must, and (2) be sure to have good equipment because many people now have excellent home entertainment systems and they will expect similar quality at the library.

St. Tammany Parish (Louisiana) Library offers a current affairs program twice a year. A retired CBS news correspondent with a "wonderful resonating voice" hosts the program. The program averages twenty-five to thirty audience members, and about one-third to one-half of those are men. The library's greatest success with the guys was a fishing program. The presenter, an author of fishing books, brought in a collection of rods and reels and lures. One attendee declared that it was the best thing he'd ever seen at the library! The library has also had guy success with history programs on World War II and the Civil War, genealogy, computer classes, and Socrates Café programs (www.philosopher.org/Socrates_Cafe.html). In addition to flyers, news releases, and web page announcements, staff create a PowerPoint presentation that displays information about programs on a large monitor in all the larger library branches.

McCracken County (Kentucky) Public Library holds a cultural program on history-related topics called "Evenings Upstairs." These programs draw anywhere from fifty to one hundred people, and many of them are men. Some programs that have been particularly popular with men include "Origin of Bourbon Whiskey" (sign me up!), "Baseball and Kentucky," "Steamboating and River Lore," "Civil War," "Governors of Kentucky," and "Railroading in Paducah: Then and Now."

What a great array of topics from all over the country! I want to try a few of these programs at my library. I hope you've been inspired as well.

BABY BOOMERS

Depending on where you get your stats, there are between 75 million and 100 million baby boomers in the United States! Given that this (wide-ranging) age group makes up a huge percentage of our population, we do want to be sure that we are offering programming that is relevant and appealing to them. As you begin to plan programs for this group, you will want to be clear on whether you are targeting the specific *generation* of Americans known as the baby boomers or the *age group* of people somewhere between their mid-40s and mid-60s. Since some baby boomers—or "boomers" for short—are already seniors and the rest will (as will we all) get there eventually, it can become confusing to track whether you are targeting a generation or an age group. Perhaps you will choose to do both. MCL, for example, spent time learning more about the people in its communities who are boomers, with the assumption that these folks will carry many of their interests and most of their values with them as they become seniors. At the same time, we must realize that the Gen Xers will soon be our new 50-ish age group. So rather than continually relabel the 50-somethings based on the generational name (boomers, Xers, Millennials, etc.), Multnomah County has started to use the term *mid-lifers* to refer to those people who are somewhere around 50 years of age but do not affiliate at all with being a senior. Confused yet? To add some clarity, I will use the word *boomer* with the understanding that I am referring to a specific generation of Americans (en.wikipedia.org/wiki/Baby_boomer) and to the values and interests that these folks carry with them into extended middle age.

So who are the boomers and what, if any, interests or values do they share as a collective generation?

MCL was one of many libraries with just this question. One common assumption about boomers is that they may continue to work or volunteer or do a combination of both well past what has traditionally been retirement age. To help the library look more closely at this portion of its population, MCL applied for and received a Library Services and Technology Act (LSTA) grant to help identify ways to engage boomers with library services during the "third phase" of their lives. This third phase is defined as a new phase of life that is emerging for the first time in U.S. history—an extended phase between midlife and old age. The following wording is directly from MCL's LSTA grant proposal: "Many Boomers will spend 20 to 25 years in this phase after leaving their primary careers. This phase is marked by a period of reinventing themselves, staying active, and oscillating between work and leisure; in fact, most baby boomers report a desire to continue working in some capacity." (That last piece has proven very true: as the economy faltered in the past few years, many boomers had to continue working and have seen a good percentage of their retirement savings evaporate. A Pew Research Center study in 2010 found that six in ten boomers believed that they would have to postpone retirement.)[4]

What types of information and library resources do boomers need during this third phase? Fortunately, one of the objectives of the LSTA grant stated that MCL would hire a contractor to help identify trends within the boomer population both nationally and locally. What did MCL learn? Boomers are looking for information that will help them plan the transition into retirement. They are looking for meaningful work and service (volunteer) opportunities. They want to continue to learn. They want to remain connected to people within their communities. They may want to achieve some balance and sanity while caring simultaneously for college-age children and aging parents. And they want information that will help them with all of the above. So MCL kept these interests in mind while remembering that this generation is entering an extended middle age that may last twenty to twenty-five years. They are healthier and better educated than any previous generation. So as many of them enter their 60s, they have a lot of smarts and vitality to bring to bear on their interests. What programs can our libraries offer them that appeal to these interests? According to Beth Dempsey in her article "They're Changing Old Age and Library Service with It," the following are just a few of the topics that can be developed into successful boomer programs: planning for your next career, pursuing an active retirement, maintaining health and fitness, tracing your roots, discussing current events, and achieving financial stability after divorce.[5]

As for MCL, it began partnering with a nonprofit organization called Life by Design NW. Life by Design NW (www.lifebydesignnw.org) strives to change "the way people think about life after 50 by empowering adults to discover their passion and purpose as well as give back to the community." Some of the programs that have emerged from this partnership with Life by Design include "Creating Connection and Community," "Helping Your Aging Parent," "Managing Your Digital Identity," and "It's Never Too Early or Too Late to Plan Your Life," which is an introductory life-planning class that helps participants prioritize what's important to them in life and discover ways to find life balance. An aging and spirituality program is also in the works.

Another successful MCL boomer program is the book discussion series Books-to-Action. *The Third Chapter: Passion, Risk, and Adventure in the 25 Years after 50* by Sara Lawrence-Lightfoot is one of the titles that the boomers read and discussed. The heart and soul of Books-to-Action is its volunteerism component: participants are given the opportunity to engage in a community service project following the discussion of the book at one of MCL's neighborhood libraries. The library partners with a group called Hands On Greater Portland (www.handsonportland.org) that identifies and offers community service opportunities reflecting the issues and themes addressed by the author in the book. This volunteer opportunity beautifully ties into many of the participants' desire to share their time, skills, and knowledge with their immediate community.

Here's one thing that MCL has learned about its boomer programs: they have been successful! Attendance ranges from around twenty to sixty. Participants have consistently rated the programs as excellent. The statistics gathered from these boomer programs show that MCL is hitting its target audience: the average participant's age is 54. The evaluation forms used at these boomer programs ask attendees to anonymously share some information about their health, educational background, and employment status. MCL learned that its boomers largely reflect the demographics of boomers nationwide: 65 percent rate their health as very good; more than 70 percent hold bachelor's degrees and beyond; and only 15 percent are retired and intend to stay retired. (Ten percent are retired but want to return to work.) And the vast majority of the participants—73 percent—volunteer somewhere on a regular or occasional basis. So MCL continues to plan creative programs that will appeal to this active, educated, healthy, community-service-oriented population. (For additional information on boomers, be sure to read *Boomers and Beyond: Reconsidering the Roles of Libraries*, edited by Pauline Rothstein and Diantha Dow Schull.)[6]

SENIORS

Some wonderful resources already exist to help you serve the seniors in your community and develop programs that will appeal to them. Take a look at *Serving Seniors: A How-to-Do-It Manual for Librarians* by RoseMary Honnold and Saralyn A. Mesaros[7] and *5-Star Programming and Services for Your 55+ Library Customers* by Barbara T. Mates.[8] The ALA toolkit "Keys to Engaging Older Adults @ your library" also offers some excellent advice on library programming for seniors.[9] And if you want to learn

more about the value that programming can bring to older adults' lives, check out the study conducted by the National Endowment for the Arts and The George Washington University called *The Creativity and Aging Study*.[10]

So who are our seniors? Well, if we let membership in AARP define who our seniors are, then a senior is anyone over 50. Some associate seniors with retirement, which usually occurs at or around 65. *Older adults* is another common term for those approximately 65 and up. But ask a boomer to define an older adult and he or she will tell you that's someone who is over 72![11] So let's agree that seniors are those whose age ranges from around 65 onward. (And this means that the oldest boomers are now also becoming seniors.) So what does a 67-year-old who runs ten miles every day and has no intention of retiring from her faculty position at the local state university have in common with her 92-year-old aunt who lives in an assisted living facility? They might have much or nearly nothing in common. In fact, the challenge of identifying programs that will appeal to seniors is a lot like finding programs that appeal to your adult population in general. (Be sure to take a look at the Library Services to an Aging Population Committee's *Guidelines for Library and Information Services to Older Adults* for some excellent guidance in serving your older patrons.)[12]

As you set out to learn more about the interests of your older patrons, you'll use many of the same methods that you use with your general adult population. You'll want to learn more about their wants and needs. Look for opportunities to learn from and listen to your older patrons. What information can you gather through observing how your current older patrons use your library? Are there times of the day when seniors seem to use the library most frequently? (This information can help you decide the days and times to offer your programs for seniors.) Are there areas of the collection that seem popular with your seniors? (This information will guide you in selecting programming topics.) Talk to seniors that you know and ask them what topics they'd like to see presented through programs. Talk to employees at other agencies in your community that serve seniors and ask if you can speak with their clients—the seniors—as well. Talk up what your library offers and ask them about their interests and ongoing educational pursuits. Consider forming a senior advisory board at your library. Through these methods, you'll certainly learn that your senior population is an incredibly diverse group of people, but themes will likely emerge as well. In *Serving Seniors*, RoseMary Honnold and Saralyn A. Mesaros offer the following insights:

> Most seniors are relatively healthy and active, but even subtle changes in their health can change their needs for information. Most seniors will experience a loss of paid employment, loss of friends, relatives, and spouses, a diminished income, a change in sensory and physical abilities, and role changes, all of which change their needs for shelter, nutrition, and information. The library can provide needed information, education, and recreation for seniors through the stages of aging, and offer opportunities to create new friendships.[13]

As you get to know more about the seniors in your community—and you probably already know quite a bit—you will find that they are an active bunch of people with diverse backgrounds and interests. They are probably already attending many of your adult programs. What you end up defining as a seniors program will likely have more to do with how you set out to market the program than with the topic you choose. You'll certainly want to make contact with the county service agencies that work with seniors, senior centers, churches, and other organizations that are frequented by seniors. For example, MCL has a great relationship with the county's Aging and Disability Services department. The department's staff members have not only assisted the library in learning more about its senior population but also

worked with library staff and shared their expertise in assisting older adults with cognitive impairments. They have also presented educational programs at the library, such as a class that taught attendees the intricacies of the Medicare Part D drug plan. Once you've developed relationships with agencies in your community, make your library literature available at these locations in order to increase the attendance at your programs for seniors. On occasion, consider bringing your program to these locations if the logistics permit it.

Another factor to keep in mind (as we do with all programming) is accessibility. The "Keys to Engaging Older Adults @ your library" toolkit has a good section on accessibility.[14] Ideally, you will have assistive listening devices on hand for your programs targeted toward seniors. Use larger type—12 point and up—on flyers and other print and electronic materials. Jane Salisbury, MCL's supervisor of Library Outreach Services, has this to say about seniors and accessibility:

> Accessibility is important—which translates to a room where presenters can be heard, an hour of the day that works well (daylight is more popular than night!), physical accessibility, and good transportation. When instruction is part of a program, a team approach is great. For example, Cyber Seniors classes always have an assistant roving the room to make sure that people who are slower are caught up, and that people have heard and understood the instructor. Not making assumptions is very important as well. Not all seniors want to read or discuss cozy mysteries, for example. There are many who are more interested in serious fiction or politics. It is really important to keep that in mind. (personal communication)

To ensure that your program is accessible and meaningful to your senior audience, be sure that your performer has some experience working with seniors, particularly if you are offering a program in which seniors will be actively engaged in learning, such as a workshop or class. The National Institute on Aging has produced a great toolkit called "Quick Tips for a Senior Friendly Computer Classroom," available at nihseniorhealth.gov/toolkit/toolkitfiles/pdf/QuickTips.pdf. The toolkit advises trainers of older adults to

Create an environment for learning.

- Put students at ease.
- Tell students what to expect.
- Make it easy to ask for help.

Present information clearly.

- Make sure you are understood.
- Encourage questions.

Help students stay focused.

- Keep focused on the goals.
- Stay on task.
- Keep discussions on track.
- Minimize distractions.

Help students retain information.

- Repeat and reinforce.
- Use written and visual information.
- Provide hands-on practice.
- Schedule classes close together.

Accommodate physical changes.

- Vision.
- Hearing.
- Motor skills.[15]

Taking accessibility into consideration and creating an environment of learning and sharing can be fun! It can also call for some creativity. Years ago at New York Public Library I worked on bringing a discussion group to a senior center. I worked with the activity director beforehand and asked her what types of topics and books the folks might like to discuss. She gave me a few suggestions, and she mentioned that some attendees would have vision and hearing challenges. She also said that some folks would not read something—because of health reasons or attention span or just personal preference—that took more than an hour or so to read. So I decided to discuss one short story with the group each month. In order to make the story easier to read for people with low vision, I used a photocopier to enlarge the print and dropped off copies of the story a week in advance of the discussion. In order to accommodate folks with significant vision issues, I selected only stories that were available in titles offered by the National Library Service for the Blind. I ordered the title and a digital talking book player—although it wasn't digital back then!—for the senior center. The activity director then assisted the people who needed to access the book player to listen to the story before the discussion. And, when the day of the discussion came, I certainly needed to keep the conversation on track and keep folks focused and encourage questions, because . . . they were a feisty group! They were all very smart and very articulate, and it was fun and challenging to maintain the right balance between staying focused on the story and encouraging folks to tell stories about how the story related to events from their past. They also weren't shy about moderating each other: One gentleman kept asking what happened next in the story and a lady finally blurted out, "Dammit, George. Did you even read the story?" He replied, "No! But it sounds good!" I liked that group a lot.

After chatting with the seniors at your library about their preferences, take another look at *Serving Seniors* and *5-Star Programming and Services for Your 55+ Library Customers*—both are packed with great examples, including book discussion groups for seniors; storytelling, music, and craft programs; programs that facilitate reminiscing; film series; and holiday, travel, and food programs. Great examples of library programs for older adults abound. In 2010 the

New York Public Library partnered with an organization called Lifetime Arts to offer a series of programs on "creative aging." These programs covered a variety of creative topics such as singing, drawing, and memoir writing. Learn more about this series at www .nypl.org/blog/2010/08/02/aging-creatively-public -library. MCL has had great success with discussion programs such as a Coffee and Conversation series that offers facilitated conversations around topics such as caring for an aging parent, what to do with your life in retirement, and spirituality. Through the ALA/FINRA "Smart Investing @ your library" grant (smartinvesting.ala.org), MCL has produced a series of financial literacy programs for at-risk seniors on topics such as avoiding online fraud. Knitting groups are always popular, as are music programs and programs such as Cyber Seniors that provides computer instruction to seniors via library-trained volunteers. As for intergenerational programming, Allan Kleiman, a former chair of ALA's Library Service to an Aging Population Committee, has had great success with intergenerational gaming (on Nintendo's Wii) between seniors and teens.[16] For even more programming ideas, take a look at the Library Services to an Aging Population Committee's online publication "21 Ideas for the 21st Century" for additional programming ideas.[17]

BECOMING MORE INCLUSIVE

As you become expert at offering programs for particular audiences, you will acquire the skills that will enable you to make all your programs more inclusive. Once you have learned how to modify your services and collections to respond to community needs, you can produce programs that all members of your community can attend. When programming, there are times when you will target a particular portion of your population. But many of your programs will target a general audience. You will offer a program on a particular topic, such as travel in Europe, and you will hope that anyone who is interested will attend. Ideally, you will provide the environment that makes this possible. For example, we've seen how bilingual publicity and the presence of a bilingual volunteer can make our Spanish-speaking patrons feel welcome at a library program, even if that program is in English.

The way in which you present your programs is very important. Do you structure your programs in a way that make them accessible to most or all of the members of your community? For example, do you give your deaf patrons the opportunity to request an interpreter? Do you inform your performers when an interpreter will be present? A more inclusive program might take additional planning and time. The performer you hired might need to meet before the program with the deaf patron and the interpreter to work out the seating arrangements. You will be surprised at how easily you can integrate everyone into your programs by making a few room modifications and by providing the necessary adaptive technology (such as an assistive listening device for an audience member who is hard of hearing).

A good program will attract an audience, and that audience might include a Spanish-speaker or a deaf patron or a person with a learning disability or all of these. They will have more in common than they have differences. Yet we will want our library to meet everyone's needs during the program and after the program ends. We will want materials relating to the program that are useful for everyone. We will want staff to help the patrons find the materials. We will want facilities that accommodate everyone. These goals require planning. William L. Needham and Gerald Jahoda's 1983 book titled *Improving Library Service to Physically Disabled Persons* includes checklists that libraries can use to determine how well their facilities, resources, and staff (in terms of training) meet the needs of their patrons with physical disabilities.[18] Included in the appendixes is an article Jahoda wrote in 1980 titled "Suggested Goals for Public Library Service to Physically Disabled Persons." The following portion of the article gives insight into the planning that is involved when you begin to expand the accessibility of your library services.

> Goals for public library service to visually, hearing, or mobility handicapped persons are discussed in terms of material, equipment, facilities, services, staffing, including use of volunteers, liaison with organizations of and for handicapped persons, involvement of handicapped persons in the planning and evaluation of library services, publicity, and funding.[19]

When you have learned how to adapt your services and collections to include all members of your community, then you have truly made your library accessible to a general audience.

OUTREACH

In this chapter we have explored how we can identify a particular potential audience, such as seniors, and develop programs, collections, and services that meet their wants and needs. We have also looked at ways that we can make all our programs accessible to all our patrons through planning and through the modification of some of our services and resources. Now that we have this knowledge, we can investigate the possibility of extending our services beyond the library's walls. Outreach has become a basic service for many library systems. Some libraries have a coordinator of outreach services and some even have an office of outreach services. Other libraries must squeeze an outreach program in here and there as staff and time allow. But regardless of the amount of staff you can dedicate to outreach, all libraries begin by asking, "Why should we offer outreach programs?" and "To whom are we going to offer this service?" A common answer to "why" is that it brings your services to the people who want and need them. The answer to "who" narrows the scope of the potential audience. Everyone in your community does not visit your library. Some don't come in because they can't, some stay away because they think your library has nothing for them, and others stay away because they just aren't interested. The first two groups are the people who are most likely to respond to outreach. If the residents of a nursing home can't visit the library, we can bring a program to them. If the Russian-speakers in your neighborhood don't see how the library relates to them, we can ask to speak at their church and announce the materials and services we have for them. Outreach is always a great public relations vehicle. If the local businesspeople in your neighborhood are too busy to visit the library, you can ask to visit them at a chamber of commerce breakfast and give a presentation on the business resources available at the library. Outreach shows the library's goodwill, and some of the people you make the effort to visit will begin visiting you in return.

If you have done some outreach in the past, you know that it's almost impossible to do it alone. Although you are reaching out to people, these people usually congregate in a place. Many of the seniors in need of outreach will be in senior centers or nursing homes. A local church might offer a weekly service in Russian. The demographic work you did back in chapter 4 should help you identify the appropriate church or senior center. These agencies very well may call *you* and ask you to pay them a visit. On the other hand, your demographic work might have told you that certain groups of people just aren't using your library. So you decide to go to them.

This will be the only time you will read these words in this book: It's okay to *not* have a plan at this point. When you get the senior center or church representative on the telephone, introduce yourself and ask if you can pay a visit to a group of their members. Bring an assortment of relevant library materials, bookmarks and bibliographies, and library card registration forms to the meeting at the church. Introduce yourself, and describe any materials or resources that you think will catch their interest. If you have books in Russian, or if you have staff who speak Russian, let them know. If you have any services that will make the library more convenient for them, mention it. For example, does your library deliver books to agencies? New immigrants who are intimidated by the idea of visiting your library might get a library card if they knew they could pick up and return their books at their church. Better yet, can the church staff and the library work out a way to set up a small satellite library in the church? Be sure you use part of your time at the meeting to ask questions and listen. Ask them what services would get them to visit the library. And ask them what services they would like to see offered at their church or other neighborhood location. Would they attend a parenting class, an English as a New Language class, a financial aid workshop? Would the class need to be in Russian? After you have ideas, work with the staff of the hosting agency (the church, community center, etc.) to make the program a reality.

Remember, programs will have to be relevant. Let the target group participate in the planning process. The seniors at the senior center might tell you that they want a book discussion group, but they might not like the title you choose. Let them choose. Use the staff of the senior center as a resource. Ask them questions. Your program will alter shapes many times before it becomes a reality.

The possibilities with outreach programming are almost endless. Frequently, libraries offer a certain program topic or program format both in-house and off-site. A topic such as preparing for U.S. citizenship might be popular at both a library branch and a nonlibrary location, such as a family learning center. Please see chapter 4 of *Managing Library Outreach Programs* for some detailed examples of outreach programs that might work for you.[20]

As you begin to plan your outreach programs, be sure to set more time aside than you would for your average library program. There is probably a reason why you are bringing a program to a group, instead of the group coming to you. Your current in-house program might not be useful to your target audience in its current format. You might have to first modify your program in some way. Modifications take time. You may have to collaborate with someone who speaks Spanish in order for you to bring a computer instruction class to a community center. Finally, you are sending staff in cars, on subways, on buses, or in taxis to other locations. You will have to take commute time into consideration when creating your schedules.

In chapter 6 we explored various ways in which we can select a topic. In this chapter we learned how to gear our programs toward particular audiences, and we learned how to modify our library services and materials to make them more inclusive of all members of our community. We have done a lot of preparation. Now we can have some fun and perhaps spend some money. Let's go out and find some performers who can make our ideas a reality!

NOTES

1. Rhea Joyce Rubin, *Intergenerational Programming: A How-to-Do-It Manual for Librarians* (New York: Neal-Schuman, 1993), 3.

2. *The Whole Person Catalog No. 4: The Librarian's Source for Information about Cultural Programming for Adults* (Chicago: American Library Association, Public Programs Office, 1998).

3. *The State of America's Libraries: A Report from the American Library Association* (Chicago: American Library Association, 2011), 3.

4. D'Vera Cohn and Paul Taylor, "Baby Boomers Approach Age 65—Glumly: Survey Findings about America's Largest Generation," Pew Research Center, December 20, 2010.

5. Beth Dempsey, "LJ Series 'PatronSpeak': What Boomers Want; They're Changing Old Age and Library Service with It," *Library Journal*, July 15, 2007, www.libraryjournal.com/article/CA6457208 .html.

6. Pauline Rothstein and Diantha Dow Schull, *Boomers and Beyond: Reconsidering the Role of Libraries* (Chicago: American Library Association, 2010).

7. RoseMary Honnold and Saralyn A. Mesaros, *Serving Seniors: A How-to-Do-It Manual for Librarians* (New York: Neal-Schuman, 2004).

8. Barbara T. Mates, *5-Star Programming and Services for Your 55+ Library Customers* (Chicago: American Library Association, 2003).

9. "Keys to Engaging Older Adults @ your library: Libraries Can Empower Older Adults with Engaging Programs and Services" (Chicago: ALA Office for Literacy and Outreach Services, 2010), www.ala .org/offices/sites/ala.org.offices/files/content/olos/ toolkits/OAT_largeprint.pdf.

10. Gene D. Cohen and National Endowment for the Arts, *The Creativity and Aging Study: The Impact of Professionally Conducted Cultural Programs on Older Adults* (Washington, DC: National Endowment for the Arts, 2006), www.nea.gov/ resources/accessibility/CnA-Rep4-30-06.pdf.

11. Cohn and Taylor, "Baby Boomers Approach Age 65—Glumly."

12. Library Services to an Aging Population Committee, *Guidelines for Library and Information Services to Older Adults* (Chicago: The Committee, Reference Services Section, Reference and User Services Association of the American Library Association, 1987, rev. 1999, approved in 2008), www.ala.org/ rusa/resources/guidelines/libraryservices.

13. Honnold and Mesaros, *Serving Seniors*, 12.

14. "Keys to Engaging Older Adults @ your library."

15. National Institute on Aging, "Quick Tips for a Senior Friendly Computer Classroom," nihseniorhealth.gov/toolkit/toolkitfiles/pdf/ QuickTips.pdf.

16. Liz Danforth, "Allan Kleiman on Gaming for Seniors," *Library Journal.com*, September 15, 2010, www.libraryjournal.com/lj/ reviewsgaming/886555-288/allan_kleiman_on_ gaming_for.html.csp.

17. ALA RUSA American Library Association, Reference and User Services Association, "Library Services to an Aging Population: 21 Ideas for the 21st Century," www.ala.org/ala/mgrps/divs/rusa/ sections/rss/rsssection/rsscomm/libraryservage/ ideas21stcentury.cfm.

18. William L. Needham and Gerald Jahoda, *Improving Library Service to Physically Disabled Persons: A Self-Evaluation Checklist* (Littleton, CO: Libraries Unlimited, 1983).

19. Gerald Jahoda, "Suggested Goals for Public Library Service to Physically Disabled Persons," *RQ* 20 (Winter 1980), quoted in Needham and Jahoda, *Improving Library Service to Physically Disabled Persons*, 109.

20. Marcia Trotta, *Managing Library Outreach Programs: A How-to-Do-It Manual for Librarians* (New York: Neal-Schuman, 1993), 43.

Identifying the Right Performer

As I was writing this chapter I knew that I would also write a chapter called "Choosing the Best Format: Performances, Lectures, Discussions, and Series." I immediately realized I had a what-came-first-the-chicken-or-the-egg scenario on my hands. Do you need to know what format your program will follow before you begin looking for performers, or do you first find out if there is someone in your community who has expertise in the topic before you spend a great deal of time fretting over the format? I decided that quite a bit of give and take occurs between the program coordinator and the performer. You might call the performer with a great idea for a lecture on the history of jazz. The performer, however, might explain to you that she finds it much more effective to perform certain jazz songs on her trumpet and then give a brief talk on the history of the song afterward. In reality you will need to have a fairly clear idea of what format you are looking for, because the performer will very likely ask you what topic you would like presented and how. The solution to the which-chapter-to-read-first conundrum might be to set aside an hour and read this and the following chapter as companion pieces.

At last: you are ready to bring a performer into the library! This is fun stuff. You have ideas and you have permission to get someone to come into your library and *do* something. Let's see: you've heard a lot of people asking questions about tablet computers at the information desk . . . so, how about a program on buying your first tablet computer? Your uncle knows a lot about computers, but so does the guy at the corner computer store, and you had this great teacher a couple of years ago when you took this continuing education class . . .

Who gets the job? A useful trick might be to think of programming as another aspect of collection development. What would you do if you were looking for a computer book? You would be interested in content, you'd probably want a book from a reputable publisher, and you don't want to spend a fortune. If your programming policy doesn't get into the details of hiring a performer, take a look at your collection development policy. Here's what a typical collection development policy (from Queens Library, New York) says about selecting materials:

> General criteria for selecting material include importance of subject matter, timeliness of the material, permanent value of material as a standard work, prominence of the author, critical reception, suitability of subject and style for intended audience, customer interest.

Most of these qualities—customer interest, timeliness, and the suitability of subject for intended audience—would be applicable to performers. "Prominence of the author" is very similar to the reputation and skills of the performer, and "critical reception" is analogous to what your neighboring libraries have to say about a performer's skills.

Now that you are more comfortable with the qualities you are looking for in a performer, it's time to begin the search.

STAFF MEMBERS AS PERFORMERS

When you are seeking a performer, it will occur to you to look for staff members who can present or perform programs. Be careful here. Let's say that you have identified a need for a job-hunting program. You don't have anyone on staff who is an expert on this topic, but you supervise a librarian who has excellent presentation skills, so you approach her and ask her to develop a ninety-minute job-hunting program. She carefully studies the topic and creates a Power-Point presentation and a bibliography. It takes her eleven hours over the course of three weeks to put this together. She presents the program and the audience

evaluation forms are unanimously positive. Is the program a success?

If patron education classes are within the mission of your library, then the answer is most likely yes. The job-hunting program can be wheeled out again and again when the need arises and can be shared with other libraries. But how many of these staff-produced programs can your library create? They are certainly costly in terms of staffing. If you intend to offer more than one program a month, then you will probably want to turn to local community members, agencies, and associations for potential speakers. The missions of many local and national organizations include community outreach. Frequently these groups (AARP, the Consumer Credit Counseling Service, etc.) will send someone to your library at no cost; rarely will you pay more than $75. The materials and presentation skills that these groups offer are usually excellent.

Let me elaborate a bit here. Library staff are excellent presenters of information. Libraries all across the country and world have librarians presenting programs on genealogy, web-based shopping, basic computer skills, and a myriad of other important topics that are in high demand. But many of the libraries that use their staff as presenters have trained these people to do so. Such training can be elaborate. First, some or all of your staff are trained in the learning patterns of your target audiences—adults, children, young adults, or other populations. Then this cadre of staff learns how to develop the format and content of a program. This involves learning when to use a computer projector versus flip charts and how to break up a program or class with hands-on activities. The staff apply these skills by creating classes and programs. Ideally, a test audience previews these programs—how to shop on eBay and Craigslist, how to conduct genealogy research on the Web, and so on—before they go live. When a program is ready for the public, the staff that developed the program will also train their peers on how to present this program to library patrons. The class can then be taught at a variety of times and locations by several staff members. In the end, you have two wonderful resources. You have a collection of terrific programs that can be scheduled at any time with minimal preparation, and you have a collection of staff who now have the skills to develop quality programs and classes on any topic imaginable. But it takes time to get there. Books such as *Teaching the New Library: A How-to-Do-It Manual for Planning and Designing Instructional Programs*,[1] and *Teaching the Internet to Library Staff and Users*[2] will help you get there.

The other scenario that you will encounter is identifying a staff member who has an expertise in an area that sounds perfect for programming. Your head of circulation is an accomplished rock climber. One of your pages is a popular local zine author. What do you do? Some of your patrons might be more likely to attend the program if a staff person whom they know presents it. The program will undoubtedly be well produced and well received. Are there any cons? Well, again, it comes down to staffing. How much time was spent preparing for the program? Was or will that person be compensated for his or her preparation? Could you have brought someone in from the community at a lesser expense? And last, and this might sound harsh, would your patrons be better served if you brought someone in from a local or national organization? We, as librarians, usually seek to purchase materials from nationally recognized publishers. Should we do the same with our performers? Ideally, your staff member will be affiliated with an organization. Perhaps the rock-climbing staff person is also a member of the Mountaineers. Adding a speaker's affiliation to the publicity can give more authority to the program and thereby increase your attendance.

LOCAL BUSINESSES

The programming policy and procedures you've developed will help determine which performers you seek. Public libraries that receive all or most of

their money from residents' tax dollars might want to be careful about hiring performers who own their own business or work for a business. In fact, there may be laws that address whether your city or county can use tax dollars to promote individual businesses. This means that if you hire someone from Zack's House of Birds to give a talk on birds, you might have to ask Zack to refrain from mentioning his business during his talk. And you will want to make sure you don't give the House of Birds a mention on your flyers or in your newsletter.

Even if no laws are in place, a competing bird store owner may become annoyed if she feels that you are giving Zack the spotlight by asking him to speak. Why didn't you also ask Kim of Kim's Cockatiels to speak? This sort of conflict does happen. Competing businesses will not be pleased with your library if they feel you are producing an infomercial on a competitor's business. If you do seek someone from a local business, you'll want to have a policy in place that states to what extent the performer can mention his or her business. Some libraries ask performers to limit the mention of their business to an introductory sentence. "Hello. I'm Zack and I have a PhD in animal husbandry and in 1982 I opened Zack's House of Birds on 13th Street and 1st Avenue." You might also allow the performer to place a stack of business cards on the table before or after the lecture.

There are benefits to hiring a local business owner. These people work with birds or cars or computers every day, and they are going to be very knowledgeable and extremely enthusiastic. But there are things to watch for. Your local mechanic, for example, might not perform at many speaking engagements each year. Be sure to ask about previous public speaking experience. And remind the person to refrain from plugging the business to the audience. I had a program go completely off the tracks once when a stockbroker began telling patrons ways in which he could make them heaps of money if only they'd use him as their broker. To avoid this worst-case scenario, set the boundaries before the performance, and, if possible, attend the performance yourself to see how the material is covered.

When you contract with a performer who owns or works for a local business, ask him if he belongs to a society or association. Zack may belong to the American Birding Association. If so, you can ask him to use that as his primary source of authority when giving his lecture. Instead of saying, "As an owner of Zack's for the last 29 years . . . ," ask him to talk about his relationship with the association. You can also include this information on the flyer and on your events web page. This approach is probably consistent with your policies in other areas, such as your bulletin board. While you would likely post a flyer from the nonprofit American Birding Association without hesitation, you would most likely not post a flyer announcing a 50 percent off sale at Zack's.

In reality, business owners, stockbrokers, and other professionals will present many of your programs. They know that libraries are good publicity mechanisms. These people are extremely knowledgeable, and most of them are fine speakers. If you establish parameters well before the program, you'll be fine. But remember to set the parameters: ask speakers to limit the mention of their business to an opening introduction, and remind them that they can set a pile of their business cards on the table. Check over their handouts and ask them to tone down or remove letterhead and other materials that promote their business or attempt to recruit clients. Occasionally you will want to find someone from a local business to present a topic. These people are experts; if they weren't they wouldn't be in business. If someone is going to speak to your patrons about computer repair, it's a good idea to hire a professional.

Yes, It's Okay to Say No

If a local business (or a local author or a community group) approaches you and asks to present a program in your library, you might discuss the content of the program and decide to use it. If you decide that the program is *not* appropriate for library sponsorship, but

people in the community are interested in the topic, then you could remind the business owner that she can rent (if there is a fee) a room in the library and hold the event on her own. The program would then become an event sponsored by the business, not your library. The business would be responsible for creating the publicity and handling whatever registration might be involved with the program. This approach can also be used when organizations, such as the American Heart Association, ask if the library would like to sponsor an informational program on heart disease. Because these organizations usually have a comprehensive publicity system in place, it might be appropriate for you to donate the meeting space and let them handle the publicity and other logistics themselves.

There will also be instances when the program is just not the right fit for your library. Regardless of the exact reasons why, there will be times when you will say no to someone who offers his talents. To help you effectively and consistently deliver this message, draft a boilerplate letter that can be mailed or e-mailed to individuals or groups informing them that their programming offer is being declined or kept on file. For example, Multnomah County Library (MCL) asks potential performers to submit an online form if they are interested in working with the library. When submitted, the form generates the following auto-response: "Thank you for submitting a program proposal to Multnomah County Library. You will be contacted if the program meets our guidelines, and fits into our schedule and budget." MCL's program development specialist told me this about the art of saying no: "For the performers that we definitely know we won't hire, I keep their proposal on file with notes as to why we did not choose it—too expensive, too far astray from our mission, etc.—so if they call, and many times they do, I can explain it to them." A set of talking points to use on the telephone when delivering a "no thank you" can also come in very handy.

On occasion a business owner or author might become rather persistent and try to convince you that you are obligated to sponsor her program because the library is a publicly supported agency. Don't fall for this. Your programming policy will help you in such situations. Patiently explain your policy and your decision-making process, and state that the library reserves the right to make the final decision on which programs it produces. If the individual persists, shift gears and offer her access to your public comment process and politely bring the conversation to an end.

OTHER PERFORMERS

Now that we've thoroughly, perhaps painstakingly, explored the pros and cons of staff members and local business owners, it's time to get back to locating our performer. The topic of the program will influence where you look for the performer. A professor who has a great deal of experience in studying and possibly treating depression could present a quality program on depression. Therefore, you're likely to look for someone with an academic background. A local college's speakers' bureau might be a good start. If you are looking for someone to play some jazz during a grand opening of a new library, you probably want someone who plays well; you won't be too concerned with educational background. The newspaper's arts and entertainment section might give you a lead in locating a local jazz band.

FINDING PERFORMERS

If you do decide to seek performers outside of your library staff, you'll be relieved and amazed to discover the places you can turn to for assistance. Here are some strategies you might want to use when seeking performers:

Call the universities and colleges in your area. Funding for many schools is contingent upon these schools offering services—such as volunteer work—to their communities. Ask them if they have a speakers' bureau or a catalog of faculty members willing to speak to community groups. A surprising number of colleges have detailed catalogs listing subjects and faculty members who speak on these subjects. The schools will usually mail these catalogs to you. Ninety-nine percent of the time these professors will speak for free.

Use print and online resources, such as the *Encyclopedia of Associations*.[3] Many national associations have a number of ready-made lectures and workshops that they can bring to your library, most likely at no direct cost.

When you are looking for artistic performers, such as musicians or actors, newspapers are a great resource. Check the "Community" or "Arts" section of the paper. If you see something that coincides with what you are seeking, give the performer a call. Also, check the classifieds for people advertising their services. You might find sections such as "Musicians' Services" and "Musicians Wanted/Available." See if the person would like to perform in your library.

Call or contact other libraries and ask them if they keep a list or database of performers. Ask them to share this information with you. If you have access to the Internet and e-mail, join regional and state electronic mailing lists that discuss library-related issues. ALA's Public Programs Office website (www.ala.org/offices/ppo) is a good place to start when seeking peer input on programming. While visiting this website, you might consider joining the Public Programs Forum electronic mailing list, which offers you the opportunity to ask questions of and exchange ideas with library staff from around the country who are actively engaged in planning and producing library programs.

If you will be working on the phone and via snail mail, then the *American Library Directory* is a good standard source for library addresses and phone numbers.[4] Your state library is also a likely resource for programming ideas, publicity ideas, and potential performers. And while you are investigating at a state level, check the Library of Congress's Center for the Book at www.read.gov/cfb. Your state might have a Center for the Book affiliate that is dedicated to promoting or sponsoring literary events and projects.

You really will be surprised at the number of organizations in your community that will offer performers at little or no cost. And once you begin offering programs fairly frequently, people and organizations will catch word of this, and they will begin calling *you*. Figure 8.1 is an example of some of the performers who have appeared at little or no cost at the Jefferson County (Colorado) Public Library.

NATIONAL TRAVELING EXHIBITS AND INITIATIVES

There is yet another option open to you when seeking a performer: contact your state library or state humanities council to see if it is funding or producing any traveling exhibits or initiatives. For example, the Choices Program is an international issues forum that is currently being held in communities across the United States. This discussion series of historical and current international issues was developed at Brown University. When I worked in Colorado, the National Endowment for the Humanities (NEH) and the Colorado Endowment for the Humanities produced the initiative. A participating library was assigned a scholar at no cost. The library then hosted four discussion series covering such topics as immigration, China, and the environment. The library purchased the materials for the participants ($100 for 25 booklets) and completed and submitted a minimal amount of paperwork at the conclusion of the series. This forum might be ideal if you are seeking a current-events program for your library. Information on this initiative is available at www.choices.edu. The Great Decisions Global Affairs Education Discussion Program is another series that engages participants in conversations about global issues. Check out the Foreign Policy Association's website at www.fpa.org for

FIGURE 8.1 | **PROGRAM PERFORMERS**

Agency that supplied performer	Title of program	Program description	Cost
Colorado Student Loan Program	College Financial Aid Planning	Provided financial aid tips for parents and teens	Free
Colorado State University	Barn Again! Preserving Colorado's Agricultural Heritage	Talked about historic barns in Colorado and the efforts to preserve them	Free
Colorado Division of Wildlife	Wildlife Watch	Provided information on the Colorado Division of Wildlife's program that trains people in wildlife appreciation; offered tips on watching animals in the wild	Free
Rocky Mountain Quilt Museum	Quilts!	Talked about the history of quilts, collecting quilts, and how to care for quilts	$50 per location

Source: Jefferson County (Colorado) Public Library

more information on this series. Both the Choices and the Great Decisions discussion series offer you the opportunity to provide programs that bring members of your community together to discuss complex issues that matter to them.

At a national level, ALA produces many programs funded by agencies such as the NEH. Check ALA's website at www.ala.org/offices/ppo. Here you will find information on opportunities such as a collection development and library programming initiative focusing on Islamic history and culture called "Bridging Cultures Bookshelf: Muslim Journeys." And the Live at the Library! project presents libraries with grant opportunities to bring nationally known authors into their libraries.

The ALA website also provides information on how your library can host traveling exhibits such as "Discover Tech: Engineers Make a World of Difference," a portable panel exhibition. ALA is a good place to look for traveling exhibits, because the association usually offers grants to cover the costs of shipping and security and may also provide funding to help cover the costs of hiring speakers to present accompanying programs on the exhibit's topic. Traveling exhibits offer great programming opportunities. In fact, the ALA exhibit grants usually require that you offer at least one or two programs on the exhibit's theme. So if you are lucky enough to host one of these exhibits, you will probably soon be looking for a speaker to bring it alive for your community. MCL, for example, was selected to host ALA's "Pride and Passion: The African American Baseball Experience" exhibit. A surviving member of the Negro Leagues was living in the community, and when the library first applied for this grant the hope was to get this man to speak about his baseball career in conjunction with the exhibit. Unfortunately, he passed away before the exhibit made its way to MCL.

Many other institutions, including the Smithsonian and the Library of Congress, also offer traveling exhibits. Your library will probably be asked to pay a fee for these exhibits, which may or may not cover

the shipping and security costs. Fees can range from a few hundred dollars to a few thousand dollars for a six- to eight-week exhibit. These exhibits do require a commitment of staff time that ranges from filling out applications and other paperwork to setting up the panels to planning and producing any accompanying programs. But they do offer your library the chance to host beautifully produced exhibits and offer interesting exhibit-related programs that your patrons will surely appreciate, hopefully in large numbers. For more information on traveling exhibitions, be sure to visit ALA's Programming and Exhibitions web page at www.ala.org/programming.

CONTACTING THE PERFORMER

Once you've chosen a topic, selected a format for the program, and identified a potential performer, you're ready to give the performer a telephone call. Chapter 2 discussed guidelines and procedures that are helpful to have in place before you begin offering programs. It's assumed that you've checked calendars and budgets and whatever else first. Before you call, however, it's a good idea to have a checklist in front of you. This checklist will guide you in asking the performer the right questions, such as, "How much will you charge to perform?" and "What days and times are you available?" The checklist in figure 8.2 can be used when negotiating with a performer on the telephone.

The days and times that a program is held can be very important. The makeup of your community will help you determine when to schedule programs. Is your library located within a bedroom community? If yes, then you might want to plan programs for later in the evening, since people will need the time to commute home. Although you cannot stereotype any one group, you do begin to hear some repetition in patrons' comments over time. For example, some seniors will ask that you hold programs in the afternoon. This might be because they cannot see well at night, or they eat dinner early and go to bed shortly

FIGURE 8.2 | **PROGRAM PERFORMER CHECKLIST**

Name of Program: _____

Name of Presenter: _____

Telephone: _____

Before you call, fill out this section as the program coordinator:

Know What You Want from the Performer

Topic of Program: _____

Length of the Program: _____

Format of the Program: _____

Meeting Space Available: _____

Month(s), days, and time of day you have in mind for program:

_____

Other: _____

_____

When calling the performer:

1. Explain your expectations. _____

_____

2. Get the days and times the performer is available within your time frame.

_____

_____

3. Ask what the performer feels is fair compensation (have a ballpark amount in mind—e.g., $75–$125 per hour).

_____

_____

4. Ask if the performer is willing to present at other branches.

_____

_____

5. What is the performer's preferred audience? Adults? Children? Young adults? All ages?

_____

_____

6. Let the performer know if he or she will need to use any assistive technology, such as the microphone from a voice amplifier. Will a sign language interpreter be present?

_____

_____

7. Ask the performer to send you a brief biographical sketch (via e-mail, fax, or USPS). (This will help you determine the authority of the performer. It also provides your public information office with the information necessary to generate publicity.)

_____

_____

8. Ask the performer to send you the names, addresses, and phone numbers of locations where he or she has appeared recently. Let the performer know that you may call these locations as references.

_____

_____

9. Ask the performer to send (via e-mail, fax, or USPS) a brief outline of the proposed program. (This will ensure that you both agree on the content of the program. It also provides your public information office with the information necessary to generate publicity.)

_____

_____

thereafter. If you live in a community that offers great sporting events, music or food festivals, and the like, can your library program compete? Therefore, it is a good idea to have a target audience in mind when scheduling a performer. If the program is going to be held at other nearby libraries, you might want to choose different days and times and compare results afterward.

You and the performer should be specific and in agreement when choosing the program's length. This step is important because you will most likely need to book or set aside a meeting room for the event. It's also nice to either print the length of the program on the flyer or agenda, or announce the length of the program when you introduce the performer. People like to know how long they will be sitting. Ask the performer how much time she feels is needed to cover or perform the material. The format of the program (see chapter 9) will greatly influence the length. People can easily go two hours when involved in a group discussion; most people begin to squirm when a lecture goes beyond an hour.

Let's take a moment here to elaborate on performers' fees. Chapter 5 addressed many of the basics of creating a programming budget, and chapter 2 covered the guidelines and procedures that you will want to put in place as you begin to offer adult programming. So you probably already have something in place that specifies what you are able to pay your performers. Your budget alone will give you a good deal of guidance as to how much you can pay someone to appear at your library. You can't pay Stephen King or Malcolm Gladwell to appear at your library if they charge $10,000 per appearance and your annual programming budget is $5,000! In addition to your overall budget, it is a good idea to keep a document up to date that states what your library currently pays performers. This document will probably stress the upper end of the fee range. Every two years or so, review this document to make sure it still offers reasonable compensation for your performers. As I mentioned earlier in this book, your local business owners and your university professors and your speakers from local agencies and nonprofits may all appear at little or no cost. It is likely that your authors and storytellers and musicians—those who make their living or largely support themselves through performing—will request the highest fees.

You'll want to do a cursory market study to find out what these creative folks are earning when they appear at other libraries and festivals and fairs and base your fee structure on this information. Call your neighboring libraries and your local cultural and music festivals and ask what they offer their local and regional performers. Then, in your performers' fees guidelines document, you might state that you offer a modest stipend (between $50 and $100, depending on your budget and local economy) to cover local travel costs for performers from the local business community and from local agencies and organizations (such as colleges, county government, and museums). Some of your programs will be workshops, so you might want to develop a guideline that states that you will pay a performer $50 of prep time for each hour that he devotes to creating the content for the workshop. You might also specify that you will pay *up to* (but not beyond) one or two hours of prep time. Some workshops will include course materials—handbooks, glue, paper, and the like—and in order to keep the program free for your patrons, you might specify that you will pay the performer $2 to $3 per participant for materials.

You might also specify a second-tier performance fee for cultural programs—authors, musicians, and other self-employed creative types—and then set the high end of the fee range for this type of performer. Stating that you are able to pay up to $175 an hour for a local or regional or even an up-and-coming national performer to put on a one-hour cultural program is a reasonable guideline. Depending on your budget and your local economy, you may want to set the upper threshold a bit higher or lower. And don't forget to review these numbers every couple of years or you will find it more and more difficult to schedule the cultural programs that you want to offer to your patrons because your performers will start saying no to what you offer as compensation.

When it comes to negotiating the fee on the phone, come to the phone call prepared. If you are calling a local chiropractor who first called you and asked if he could offer a program at your library, you know that you are working with someone from the local business community, and it is reasonable to assume that the program will both benefit your patrons and help the performer market his practice. With this in mind, you could either ask him what he charges—and he very likely will say nothing—or you could just offer a modest stipend up front to cover local travel costs. Either way, you should get a fee that ranges from nothing to around $50. When speaking to a local or regional musician or dancer or author who has some name recognition, your best bet is to ask her what she charges for a sixty- or ninety-minute performance. If she states a fee that is within your range and you really want her, then you can agree verbally to the fee and get started on the paperwork. Sometimes, though, the stated fee will take your breath away! This is where I believe that it is completely acceptable to do a little negotiating. It is helpful to remind the performer that your library is a nonprofit organization with a limited budget. You should also mention the various ways in which the program will be publicized and the number of people that this publicity will reach. Some performers are delighted to learn that their event will be listed in a printed or electronic newsletter that reaches thousands or tens of thousands of people. Many performers love libraries and many are aware of our budget challenges, so you will be pleasantly surprised at how effective a reminder of these realities can be when you are talking to performers about money.

So, after making the initial contact with the performer, you will proceed with whatever process you have in place. (An example of the workings of a programming committee is discussed in chapter 2.) Most likely you will submit paperwork (either electronic or hard copy; see chapter 2 for examples) to some person or department. The performer should then receive some sort of written confirmation. You can develop a standard contract to meet this purpose. It's a good idea to use this contract even if the performer is not charging for his services, since it contains details on how and when a performance may be canceled, whether or not a performance may be recorded, and so on. This contract may be mailed or e-mailed from your library's business office. If you work for a smaller library system, or if your programming is done at a branch level, then the person who writes this letter may be you. A sample cover letter (from Jefferson County [Colorado] Public Library) for a performer's contract and the contract itself are included in figures 8.3 and 8.4. The person coordinating the program should sign the cover letter. The contract contains a list of the branches of the Jefferson County Public Library. The dates and times of the upcoming performances would be listed next to the participating branches.

In addition to mailing the performer a contract, it is a good idea to contact the performer at least two other times before the program. If flyers are to be created for the program, you will want to share a copy with the performer. You might want to offer a quantity of the flyers to the performer or send an electronic copy to her via e-mail. She may want to distribute copies to her friends, coworkers, and association co-members.

The final contact you make with the performer before the program date will be a confirmation call. Give her a call a week or so before the program to verify the dates and times. Ask her if she has the directions to the library. Ask again about any equipment needs. Again ask if she will be distributing handouts. Will the performer reproduce these or will the library need to make copies from the originals?

This brings us right up to show time. Now let's backtrack. At the beginning of this chapter we realized that finding a performer and selecting a format (film series, film lecture, filmmaking workshop, etc.) occur almost simultaneously. The following chapter explores the various formats available to you as you plan your program. But before we find the format that fits your particular program, I want to discuss one more type of performer—The Big-Name Author.

THE BIG-NAME AUTHOR

In addition to going after some of the big discussion series and exhibits mentioned earlier in this chapter, some of us will find that our libraries are ready to host our first big-name author event. So how do you score that big-name author? And for the sake of clarity, let's loosely define "big-name author" as someone who has appeared on a *New York Times* best sellers list or has won a national or international award or is someone we studied in our literature anthology in high school or college. You know: A Big Name! So how do you go about getting these big names to appear at your library?

The first strategy that comes to mind involves location, location, location. Your library might just be situated in prime author territory. Many libraries share a community with a well-known author. Frequently we see these authors in our libraries, and sometimes we are on a first-name basis with them. If you have that level of familiarity with an author, you probably have already asked him whether he has an interest in appearing at your library. If not, go ahead and ask. Sometimes the answer will be, "No, thank you." But it's just as likely to be, "Yes." And if it's yes, either you will work directly with the author or he will refer you to his agent. If you are lucky enough to work directly with the author, then the planning of your author program will proceed in the same way as the other programming that you offer. (If you are referred to an agent, keep reading.) If you do schedule your local big-name author, be sure to estimate the attendance. If Stephen King lives down the street from your library and agrees to appear on a Saturday in your meeting room that holds fifty-five people, will you end up with a successful event or a mad adult scrum of musical chairs that ends in chaos and upset patrons? You might need a bigger venue. If that's the case, please see the section on off-site programs later in this chapter.

Another avenue that can lead to success with big-name authors is to find out which authors are on book

FIGURE 8.3 | **SAMPLE COVER LETTER**

Date

Dear _____:

Thank you for agreeing to present _____ at _____ branches of the Jefferson County Public Library.

Contract

Enclosed are two copies of a contract for your presentations. The contracts have been signed by the Library Director. Please review the agreement, then sign and return one copy to me so I can submit a request for payment to the business office.

Jefferson County writes checks each Thursday. Please return your contract promptly in order that your check can be ready for you.

Special Arrangements

In order to ensure the best situation possible for your presentation, please let me know how you'd like the room arranged, how you'd like to be introduced, and whether you'll need any special audiovisual or presentation equipment.

Directions

Please take a moment to look over the enclosed map of library locations. Let me know if you need more detailed directions.

If you have any questions, please do not hesitate to call me.

Cordially,
Name
Program Coordinator
Phone

Source: Jefferson County (Colorado) Public Library

FIGURE 8.4 | **SAMPLE CONTRACT**

Contract

THIS CONTRACT is made _____ by and between the Library Board of Trustees of the Jefferson County Public Library (hereafter referred to as Sponsor) and _____ (hereafter referred to as Speaker) in connection with an engagement sponsored by Jefferson County Public Library, upon the following terms and conditions:

Belmar Library
555 S. Allison Pkwy.
Lakewood City Commons
Lakewood, CO 80226
Phone (303) 235-JCPL (5275)

Arvada Library
7525 W. 57th Ave.
Arvada, CO 80002
Phone (303) 235-JCPL (5275)

Golden Library
1019 Tenth St.
Golden, CO 80401
Phone (303) 235-JCPL (5275)

Standley Lake Library
8485 Kipling St.
Arvada, CO 80005
Phone (303) 235-JCPL (5275)

Evergreen Library
5000 Hwy. 73 (at Buffalo Park Rd.)
Evergreen, CO 80439
Phone (303) 235-JCPL (5275)

Edgewater Library
5843 W. 25th Ave.
Edgewater, CO 80214
Phone (303) 235-JCPL (5275)

Conifer High School
10441 Hwy. 73
Conifer, CO 80433
Phone (303) 235-JCPL (5275)

Wheat Ridge Library
5475 W. 32nd Ave. (32nd and Chase)
Wheat Ridge, CO 80212
Phone (303) 235-JCPL (5275)

Columbine Library
7706 W. Bowles Ave.
Littleton, CO 80123
Phone (303) 235-JCPL (5275)

TYPE OF ENGAGEMENT:_____

COMPENSATION: _____

cont.

FIGURE 8.4 (cont.)

TERMS OF PAYMENT: Payment in full mailed to the presenter five days after last presentation at the _____ Library. If presenter is providing programs over a multi-month time period, payment will be made at the end of each 30 day period for programs completed during that 30 day period.

ADDITIONAL TERMS: None

1. The Speaker shall complete all setup and preparation activities before the engagement's designated start time.

2. If the speaker wishes to sell books or music at a library-sponsored event, the speaker must sign and date the following statement:

    > I understand that I am solely responsible for collecting and paying any and all taxes due from the sale of my books and/or music at programs sponsored by the Jefferson County Public Library.

    _____

    Signature and Date

3. In the event that the engagement covered by this contract shall be prevented by weather, an act of God, physical disability, or any other cause beyond the control of the parties, Speaker and the Sponsor shall respectively be relieved of their obligations stated in this contract.

4. The Sponsor reserves the right to cancel this engagement for any reason at any time prior to 30 days preceding the engagement; voiding this contract and excusing the Sponsor from any payment or other compensation. If this contract is cancelled by the Speaker less than 30 days prior to the scheduled engagement, the Speaker will reimburse the Sponsor the amount of $_____ to help defray the production, promotion and labor costs that are incurred up to the date of the cancellation.

5. The Speaker shall indemnify and hold the Sponsor harmless from any claims or damages which arise from the Speaker's negligent or intentional acts or omissions.

6. No member of the Sponsor or of County government shall benefit from this contract. Violation of this clause shall cause this contract to be void and of no further force and effect.

7. The Sponsor reserves the right to audio or video tape record any lecture, reading or speaking engagement. The Sponsor may retain the tape in its files, may re-play the tape for its employees, and may make the tape available to Sponsor's customers. Sponsor shall make no more than three copies of the tape. Sponsor shall not sell the tape. The Sponsor shall provide a copy of the tape to the Speaker, upon the Speaker's request.

8. The Sponsor will review and approve all materials developed by the Speaker to cross-promote the program in advance of distribution. Additionally, the Sponsor will approve in advance the use of its logo on all materials developed by the Speaker.

9. In the event expense reimbursement is included as compensation, the Speaker shall provide the Sponsor with receipts or similar documentation adequate to confirm the expenses incurred.

10. The laws of the State of Colorado shall be applied in the execution, interpretation and enforcement of this contract, and venue shall be in the District Court in and for the County of Jefferson, State of Colorado.

11. This Contract is a personal services contract, and is not assignable by either party absent the prior consent of the other party.

12. This Contract represents the entire agreement of the parties hereto, and may not be amended except in writing signed by the parties.

SPONSOR:
Library Board of Trustees
of the Jefferson County
Public Library
By _____
Date _____
Marcellus Turner, Executive Director
Jefferson County Public Library
Lakewood, CO 80215

SPEAKER:

_____
Signature

_____
Phone

_____
Mailing Address

_____
Date

Source: Jefferson County (Colorado) Public Library

promotion tours. When an author is on tour to promote a new book, the publisher usually sponsors the tour. The reviews in *Publishers Weekly* are a good source for identifying which new books will include an author tour. Another great source for finding authors is BookExpo America. BookExpo bills itself as "the premier North American publishing event," and *it is huge*. If your library can send someone to this annual event, ask her to look for authors who will be on tour promoting their new releases. Do a good deal of planning *before* you head off to BookExpo. Before a

publisher puts an author in your library, the publisher will want to know that author is in good hands. Have details about your venue and its capacity, as well as details about the level of publicity and marketing that you'll be able to generate for the event. For the publisher, it's all about generating buzz around the book and putting the author in touch with as many fans as possible. I was amazed when more than one publisher told me that there would be no speaker's fees as long as we could deliver on the venue (in our case, an eight-hundred-seat facility) and produce extensive promotion! We might not all have access to an eight-hundred-seat facility, but through partnerships with colleges, hotels, and other community spaces, finding large, off-site space is very doable. In addition, check publishers' websites to see which authors will be going on tour. Contact these publishers and ask them if they would consider sending their author to your library.

The third route I want to mention is the most likely path you'll take to obtaining your big-name author—the agent route. Let's say that my library has decided to launch an annual distinguished author lecture, and to kick off year one we have decided to pursue David Sedaris. So I Google "David Sedaris." After the *Wikipedia* article, I see that the second hit is the Steven Barclay Agency. And, sure enough, David Sedaris is one of the authors that the agency represents. I poke around on the website a little bit and come across this: "If you wish to make arrangements for an appearance, or to receive further information, simply e-mail, phone, or write us." Well, heck, that's pretty easy! Sort of. Things are just about to get interesting . . .

Now that you've found your big-name author, let's cover some of the things to consider when producing a big-name author event. Negotiating and finalizing a contract for Joyce Carol Oates is quite a bit more complicated than contracting with the local beekeeper. And, Ms. Oates will need a limousine and a comfy hotel. She may have dietary specifications that you'll want to honor. And folks are going to be *really* eager to see and hear her, so as in *Jaws* where they needed a bigger boat, you're gonna need a bigger venue.

THE BIGGER VENUE AND OFF-SITE PROGRAMS

There are various reasons why you might choose to produce a program outside your library. Certainly your outreach programs will be held off-site. (Please see the "Outreach" section of chapter 7.) A few of your programs will involve popular performers who will draw large crowds, so in these instances you'll need a larger venue in order to accommodate everyone. The big-name author program in this chapter is an example of an event that will most likely need an off-site venue. Depending on the anticipated size of the audience, your choices in venues could be many or quite few. While I worked for Jefferson County Public Library, we launched a yearly author series called InSight & InPerson. We brought in such authors as Amy Tan and Joyce Carol Oates, and the response was amazing. These author appearances attracted between six hundred and eight hundred people. Because our library was a county system, we felt it was important to partner with a venue within the county, and this decision limited our choices to a handful of options—the fairgrounds, a hotel or two, and an events center. In the end, your choice will probably come down to price, availability, and amenities. You'll want something that you can afford, that's available when you need it, and that offers the lighting, sound, and whatever other conveniences and comforts you need in order to produce a successful event. The prices that you are quoted will probably vary wildly, but with luck, you'll find a venue that will offer you a little lenience in price based on your standing as a vital community institution. The price might come down a little more if you find opportunities to highlight the venue's name as an event sponsor.

Perhaps there's a church or a high school near your library. Form relationships with the administrators and discuss partnership opportunities. You'll know which library programs are likely to draw a good crowd. Would the church be interested in partnering to host a play or bluegrass performance? Would the high school host a battle-of-the-bands program knowing that several of their students are involved in the competition?

So if you do hold some of your programs off-site, how can you ensure that the public knows the library is sponsoring the event? Mary Hurlbert Stein of East Baton Rouge Parish (Louisiana) Library notes:

Off-site programs have real benefits (new audience pool, shared resources, best skill set from each partner, etc.), but there is one major risk: that the Library will not receive the "credit" that is due for the joint effort. We counteract that risk by flooding these types of events with easily-spotted library staff or library volunteers, and by making sure that the Library's brand is on everything, and that the Library is clearly identified as a principal host of the event. (personal communication)

The Bigger Contract

If you are going after a *really* big author, there is a good chance that your author is represented by one of a handful of large agencies, such as the Steven Barclay Agency mentioned earlier. The best piece of advice that I can give to you when working with an agency is to allow yourself the time to place and receive many, many phone calls and e-mails until both sides have all the details ironed out. The agency takes its job very seriously, and the agent you work with will want to be assured that she is placing her author in good hands. In fact, the agency may ask you to submit what is called a "firm offer" to demonstrate that you are serious and prepared on your end. (Figure 8.5 is an example of a firm offer between Jefferson County Public Library and HarperCollins Speakers Bureau.) The agent will want to know which hotel her author will be staying in, what food and beverages will be available, the duration of the book-signing portion of the program, and more. And you will want to be sure that you have thought through all the activities that you want the author to participate in. If you want the author to conduct a telephone interview with the local newspaper or public radio station a week before the program, be sure that this request

is articulated to the agent well in advance because it might need to be included in the contract. The agent will also have very specific requests. For example, the author might need a specific type of microphone and prefer a specific type of bottled water. You'll need to negotiate when the author will fly in and how much downtime he will need before the program. If you want him to mingle at the foundation-sponsored mixer before the main reading event, be sure to specify that as well. It really is a dance of details.

Once these details have been worked out and both sides agree to them, the agency will send you a contract to sign and return. The good news is that after you've booked your first big-name author, the next time seems much, much easier. Each author will bring his or her own creative personality and preferences into the mix, and that's both the challenge and the fun! (For example, Jefferson County Public Library brought Amy Tan in to speak a few years ago, and the agent wanted to be sure that the hotel would accommodate her two dogs, which she brings with her—in a large handbag!—to all her speaking engagements.) Figure 8.6 is a day-of-the-big-event planning worksheet that will give you a good idea of the complexity of a big-name author event.

Your big-name author will almost certainly present his talk from behind a podium to an audience that is seated in rows in front of him. This format works very well with a mostly stationary performer who will primarily talk to his audience. But what about the artist who will conduct a watercolor painting workshop while simultaneously moving about the room with a remote control that advances a PowerPoint demonstration displaying examples of the subjects that she will ask the audience to paint? The next chapter will guide you through deciding which format is the best match for your performer and topic.

FIGURE 8.5 | **FIRM OFFER FOR AUTHOR**

Firm Offer

Date: July 9, 2010

To: *John Doe*
                 VP, Director, HarperCollins Speakers Bureau

From: Marcellus Turner, Executive Director
                 (*Name and title*)

RE: Speaking Offer For   Dennis Lehane
                 (*Name of speaker*)

Sponsor: Jefferson County Public Library
                 10200 West 20th Avenue, Lakewood, CO 80215
                 (*Provide the name of host organization, street address, city, state, zip code.*)

Sponsor Website: jeffcolibrary.org

Event: InSight & InPerson Distinguished Author Series
                 (*Specify Lecture Series, Annual Meeting, etc*)

Event Date(s):   Monday, 09/13/10 OR Tuesday, 09/14/10 OR Monday
                 09/20/10
                 (*If more than one date, give order of preference.*)

Event Time(s):   5:30–6:30 PM Small (200 people) Library fund-raising reception;
                 7:00–8:00 PM Author Presentation; 8:00–8:15 PM Q&A; 8:15–
                 9:15 Book Signing.
                 (*If more than one time, give order of preference.*)
                 NOTE: The times listed above will reflect the schedule listed on
                 your contract. Any changes to these times may require written
                 permission from the speaker's office.

Event Location: MileHi Church Event Center Auditorium (Pictures: www.milehi
                 church.org/about/sanctuary.asp)
                 9079 W. Alameda Avenue, Lakewood, Colorado 80226-2826
                 (*Provide as many details as you know at this time: location,
                 auditorium, street address, city, state, zip code, telephone*)

Honorarium:	$125.00 honorarium; first class travel; ground transportation; premium hotel accommodations
(in US dollars)	*NOTE: In addition to honorarium, Sponsor agrees to pay first class travel expenses (flight, hotel, ground travel at origin and destination cities, meals) unless noted above.*
Book Sales:	We will partner with a local bookseller (Borders *or* Barnes & Noble). Both booksellers have partnered with us for this event since 2004.
	(Please specify how you will handle book sales for this event—local bookseller or direct purchase.)
Topic:	We encourage our guest authors to select and present their topics.
Hotel Accommodations:	JW Marriott Denver at Cherry Creek (www.marriott.com/hotels/travel/denjw-jw-marriott-denver-at-cherry-creek)
Audience Profile (size and demographics):	
	The main portion of the program (Author Presentation, Q&A) will be attended by approximately 1,200–1,400 people. The main program is a free event for our patrons and communities (registration and tickets are required). The small (200 people) fund-raising reception is attended by the Library's supporters. All proceeds go to the Library Foundation to help support this beloved author program. Generally, our programs are attended by our patrons and fans of the author. The age range of our patrons who attend this program varies widely (18–65) and is predominantly women; however, attendee demographics closely follow the age range and gender of the author's fans. Our area is also the nation's baby boomer capital, with one-third of the city between the ages of 35 and 54.
	(include number of attendees, age range, gender ratio)
About Sponsor (background information):	
	Jefferson County Public Library is a large and diverse system of 10 libraries, nestled in the foothills of the Rocky Mountains, minutes west of Denver. We serve a population of more than 525,000 residents. The InSight & InPerson Distinguished Author Series was created to bring nationally recognized authors to Jefferson County, offering local book lovers the opportunity to hear prominent, award-winning authors. The main program is free to the public.
Past Speakers:	Amy Tan, Sue Monk Kidd, Alexander McCall Smith, Anne Lamott, Joyce Carol Oates

cont.

FIGURE 8.5 (cont.)

Speaker Attire (mark one):   ☐ Casual ☐ Business ☐ Business casual ☐ Black tie
☐ Academic Regalia
We encourage Mr. Lehane to dress as he feels most comfortable

Pre-event contact: Betty Crocker, Administrative Coordinator, Office of the
Executive Director
Office: 303-275-XXXX; Cell: 720-299-XXXX;
E-mail: bettyc@jeffcolibrary.org
(phone/cell phone/e-mail/title)

On-site contact: Betty Crocker, Administrative Coordinator,
Office of the Executive Director
Office: 303-275-XXXX; Cell: 720-299-XXXX;
E-mail: bettyc@jeffcolibrary.org
(phone/e-mail)

By signing below you acknowledge that this is a firm offer to invite the speaker to your event to speak and perform any additional activities. The firm offer is needed as assurance that you are serious about inviting the speaker. This is NOT a contract. If the speaker accepts this offer, a binding contract will subsequently be formed, subjecting you to its terms and conditions. This firm offer form must be filled out and signed by someone with the requisite authority and returned within seventy-two (72) hours of their receipt by you. We cannot hold dates or confirm a speaker's availability until we have the firm offer.

Agreed _____ *Date* _____

Please fax or e-mail this form, along with any additional materials you would like us to provide to the speaker (including a letter of invitation) to 212-207-XXXX or john.doe@harpercollins.com. If you have any questions please do not hesitate to contact us.

John Doe
VP, Director, HarperCollins Speakers Bureau
Phone: (212) 207-XXXX
Fax: (212) 207-XXXX
E-Mail: john.doe@harpercollins.com

Source: Jefferson County (Colorado) Public Library

FIGURE 8.6 | **BIG EVENT PLANNING WORKSHEET**

Day of Event Planning

Anne Lamott—September 24, 2008

Time	Item	Task	Responsibility/Status
10:00 AM	Belmar Library signs	Deliver and set up (1) sandwich signage outside BL library, (2) easel sign inside library	Marty
11:15 AM	Loading of event materials	Transport all event materials to Belmar Center	Marty (podium, chairs [2], table [1]—from AR), Amber, Bethany, Paul
12:00	Advance team arrives at Belmar Center—ballroom and stage set up by noon	Check event set-up, make seating adjustments, reserved seating, special needs seating, hang banners, set up easels, signage, etc.	Amber, Marty, Bethany, Paul
12:15	Control room	Control room setup (water, mints, snacks, supplies, etc.)	Amber, Bethany
2:00	Full team arrives	Lunch—BAKER STREET PUB & GRILL	Full team (MT, Bethany, Paul, Marty, Amber, Cindy, Berdina, John)
3:00	Audio check	Set up/check audio system	Audiovisual company, John, Amber
3:30	Advance team—BETHANY—change clothes—get ready	(1) Bethany	Bethany
3:45	Advance team—AMBER—change clothes—get ready	(2) Amber	Amber
3:45	Caterer arrives	Delivery and setup, terrace—Rosaccis 303-662-XXXX	Cindy, Berdina
4:00	Borders arrives	(1) Three 6-ft tables set up in an L configuration for book sales area in vestibule	Borders, Cindy
		(2) One 8-ft table with 2 chairs set up in Alaska Room for book signing	Borders, Cindy
4:00	Complete setup	Walk through and completion of event setup	Full team (MT, Bethany, Paul, Marty, Amber, Cindy, Berdina)
		(1) Ballroom and reserved/special seating	Amber, Paul, Cindy, Bethany
		(2) Ballroom—stage and podium set up	Paul, Amber, Marty

cont.

FIGURE 8.6 (cont.)

Day of Event Planning

Anne Lamott—September 24, 2008

Time	Item	Task	Responsibility/Status
		(3) VIP room—water, etc.	Berdina
		(4) JCPL help table	Cindy
		(5) Book sales area	Cindy
		(6) Book signing area	Bethany
		(7) Water station	Cindy
		(8) Reception area and bar area—set up on terrace	Amber, Paul, Berdina
		(9) Signage	Paul, Bethany
		(10) Stage	Cindy, Paul, Marty
		(11) Interior ballroom curtains drawn	Cindy, Berdina
		(12) Terrace—heating/comfort check—exterior terrace curtains—audio check	Cindy, Bethany, Amber, MT
4:15	Advance team—change clothes—get ready	(3) John (4) Cindy (5) Berdina (6) Paul (7) Marty	John, Cindy, Berdina, Paul, Marty
4:30	Sam Scinta arrives	Greet Sam—make introductions—go over event	Bethany, Amber, John
4:45–4:50	Limousine arrives at hotel	Pick up Ms. Lamott	Limo 303-470-XXXX
4:45	Volunteers begin to arrive	Volunteer orientation	Cindy
5:00	Paul (aka photographer)	Prep work for photos	Paul
5:00	JCPL help table	Make sure help table is set up—and ticket registration information is available	Vicki, Deb
5:00	MT—podium microphone/ instruction	MT—podium microphone instruction and check	MT, John, Amber
5:15	Reception/ticket checkers	Volunteers in place at terrace entrance to greet and check tickets	Cindy—Nancy and Vicki Ponce
5:15	Microphone check for Q&A	Main ballroom—John check microphones for Adrianne, Priscilla, and Suzanne	John, Berdina (Adrianne, Priscilla, Suzanne)
5:15	Ms. Lamott arrives at Belmar	Bethany introductions—Bethany escort Ms. Lamott to VIP suite	Bethany, Sam, MT

Day of Event Planning

Anne Lamott—September 24, 2008

Time	Item	Task	Responsibility/Status
5:30	Reception begins		Note
5:45	Volunteer ticket takers and brochure givers	Volunteers in place at ballroom doors (4 ticket takers on outside and 3 to 4 brochure givers on inside)	Cindy
5:50	Advise Ms. Lamott—10 minutes to interview and microphone setup	Bethany (with assistance from John if necessary)	Bethany (John)
5:55	Mic setup for interview	John ready at terrace stage to monitor audio setup	John
5:55	Bethany escort Ms. Lamott to terrace stage for interview		Bethany
6:00	Introduction of Ms. Lamott	Sam	Sam
6:00	Interview begins		
6:00	Doors open to public		Note
6:25	Place volunteers to assist in seating reception guests		Nancy and volunteers, Cindy
6:30	Interview ends		
6:30	Bethany escort Ms. Lamott to VIP suite for 30 minute break		Bethany
6:40	Final audio check	Final audio check—make sure everyone has a microphone check and instruction and all systems are working	John, Amber
6:45	Interpreter arrives	Show interpreters to their area/seat (Alyssa 303-321-XXXX)	Cindy
6:50		Advise MT 10 minutes to introduction	MT, Amber, Cindy

cont.

FIGURE 8.6 (cont.)

Day of Event Planning

Anne Lamott—September 24, 2008

Time	Item	Task	Responsibility/Status
6:50		Bethany advise Ms. Lamott 5 minutes until time to head to stage	Bethany
6:55	Bethany escort Ms. Lamott to terrace for entrance to event		Bethany
7:00	Event begins	MT on stage for welcome, introduction, etc.	MT
7:40	LMs in place for Q&A session	LMs in each aisle stand up, make sure microphones are working	Priscilla, Suzanne, Adrianne
7:45	Q&A begins	Ms. Lamott will move into this portion on her own	Bethany confirm
7:50	Advise Borders—10 minutes to book signing	Borders prepares for book signing	Cindy
7:55	Bethany watch time for transition to book signing announcement		Bethany
7:55	Advise MT 5 minutes to thank you and book signing announcement		MT, Amber, Cindy
8:00	MT thank you and book signing procedure	MT thank you and brief explanation of procedure for book signing	MT
8:00	Bethany check for break and then escort Ms. Lamott to book signing area	Bethany—check w/Ms. Lamott on preference for location of break—if any	Bethany
8:00	Volunteers in place to thank people		Cindy
8:05	Book signing begins		Note

Day of Event Planning

Anne Lamott—September 24, 2008

Time	Item	Task	Responsibility/Status
8:30	Check on limousine	Check and make sure limousine is en route	Amber
8:30	Determine volunteer needs for rest of evening	Release volunteers as appropriate	Cindy/Amber
8:45 (?)	Event ends	Bethany escort Ms. Lamott to limousine	Bethany
9:00 (?)	Event center walkthrough and cleanup	Take down event signage, walk through, pick up envelopes, etc.	Cindy—volunteers—Advance team
9:30 (?)	Team end of event check	Meet to check all is well	Full team (MT, Bethany, Paul, Marty, Amber, Cindy, John, Berdina)

Source: Jefferson County (Colorado) Public Library

NOTES

1. Cheryl LaGuardia et al., *Teaching the New Library: A How-to-Do-It Manual for Planning and Designing Instructional Programs* (New York: Neal-Schuman, 1996).

2. William D. Hollands, *Teaching the Internet to Library Staff and Users: 10 Ready-to-Go Workshops That Work* (New York: Neal-Schuman, 1999).

3. *Encyclopedia of Associations: Regional, State, and Local Organizations* (Detroit, MI: Gale Research, published annually).

4. *American Library Directory* (Medford, NJ: Information Today, published annually).

9

Choosing the Best Format

If you are reading this book from front to back—and bless you if you are—then this chapter might seem out of place. Shouldn't you know what format you want your program to take *before* you go out and find a performer? Well, perhaps. Certainly if you know that you want to conduct a book discussion group, you have this format in mind when you begin your search for a discussion leader. When looking for a jazz band, you probably have a live performance in mind. At other times you might know that you want to present information on a topic, such a buying a tablet computer. Yet you are open to whichever format is most effective in conveying the information to your patrons. After you've found your computer expert to present the program, you consult with her on the best way to present the topic. She might suggest a sixty-minute lecture, or she might suggest a two-hour hands-on workshop where patrons actually get to play with three or four different tablets. After some discussion, the two of you decide that, with a workshop, she has more opportunity to interact with the patrons. She could bring a few examples of tablets to the program and allow the patrons to spend some hands-on time determining which models they like best.

WHAT ARE YOUR CHOICES?

Which format is best for your program? Some of your programs will blend two or more formats. A classical guitarist might preface the performance of each piece with a brief story (lecture) about the history of the song. Other format choices will be straightforward, such as your book discussion group. Let's attempt to put names to our choices in formats. There seem to be (at least) seven programming formats that recur frequently: speakers (lectures) and panel discussions, instructional presentations, workshops, demonstrations, live performances, discussion groups, and film series. I will define these formats, list some of their strengths and weaknesses, and give some tips that will help you when producing a program in a particular format.

Speakers and Panel Discussions

Definition: Speakers tend to be experts on a topic. They usually arrive, speak on a topic, answer some questions from the audience, and leave. Panel discussions usually consist of several speakers seated behind a table. They each speak in turn, answer some questions from the audience, and then head home. Panel discussions are sometimes facilitated by a moderator who poses certain questions to the panel.

Pros: The speaker format is an excellent venue for an author or someone giving a personal account. For example, a Holocaust survivor's personal story would probably be presented in this format. Panel discussions can also be a very powerful medium. Fairly controversial topics can be addressed, such as immigration and the environment. Experts with differing points of view can express their beliefs and question the beliefs of the other panel members. Patrons can leave these discussions with a new perspective on a topic. Because speakers and panels frequently work without a script, you can ask them to tailor their discussions to your audience's particular interests.

Cons: The speaker/lecture format offers little audience participation. If your lecturer doesn't have strong speaking skills, your audience is going to lose interest quickly. Panel discussions take a great deal of time to organize. You must select all the speakers on the panel, and then you must make sure that each person understands what his role is on the panel. You might have to find a moderator as well to keep the program on track.

Tips: Begin planning a panel discussion several months in advance. At least one member of the panel will end up canceling. Have alternates in mind. Provide everyone involved with a list of the panel participants (including the performers' names, telephone numbers, and e-mail addresses), so that you and the participants can work out the details of the program's content. Send the participants an outline of the discussion that breaks the sections down into time periods. This agenda will help keep them on schedule during the program. Try to have a staff person sit in the front row during the program and act as a timekeeper. She can hold up a "1 more minute" sign when appropriate, so that the speakers know when to move on to the next section. Last, remember that people's attention span is shorter when they are not actively engaged. Your lecture or panel discussion should probably not go for more than an hour—ninety minutes if questions are taken at the end.

Instructional Presentations

Definition: Instructional presentations are similar to the speaker/lecture format. In fact, presentations essentially are dynamic lectures. The goal of an instructional presentation, particularly in libraries, is usually to teach the audience how to do something. Presentations frequently incorporate handouts, PowerPoint slides, audio or video samples, practice exercises, and limited interaction with the audience. An example of a program in this format is a college financial aid presentation. The presenter might speak about specific scholarships and grants. She could then project a financial aid form onto a screen via a computer projector and demonstrate how to fill out the form. She might end the program with a practice exercise for the audience members. For example, she could distribute some books on financial aid to the audience and ask them to identify scholarships that seem tailored to them or their children.

Pros: Presentations are a great way to convey a great deal of information in a short period of time. People love this type of program when you hit on the right topic. A job-hunting-on-the-Internet presentation might attract a large audience, especially if the participants are able to access the Internet during the presentation. If library staff conduct the presentation, the library will have copies of the agenda, an outline of the presentation's content, and handouts. This means that the presentation can be reproduced fairly quickly and easily by staff the next time around.

Cons: Because these programs take a great deal of preparation—creating PowerPoint slides, agendas, outlines, and exercises—they can be very staff-intensive when produced by library personnel. Try to bring in outside presenters if possible. Unavoidably, someone in the audience will either know much more or much less about the topic than the rest of the audience and will then comment afterward that the program was either too advanced or too simplistic. Use these comments as the basis for developing another program at a different skill level. Perhaps a patron comment regarding the simplicity of "Finding a Job on the Internet" will encourage you to pursue a program called "Marketing Your Resume on the Internet." Last, presentations can overwhelm people with information. People will then comment, "Too much stuff covered in too little time." Create an agenda that has three or four objectives. Less *is* more . . . or at least less is enough.

Tips: You will want the audience to receive an agenda. A printed outline allows the patron to look at what will be covered and bail out at the beginning if it isn't what he had in mind. If time allows, ask each audience member to tell the presenter why he is attending the program. This overview gives the presenter the opportunity to slightly alter the presentation in order to meet the expectations of as many patrons as possible. Remember that many adults learn through practice and examples. Don't just say, "There's millions of jobs on the Internet." Show them how to use a specific Internet site to

find a particular job, and then, if possible, let them find a job that is relevant to them.

Workshops

Definition: If instructional presentations are dynamic lectures, then workshops are dynamic instructional presentations. Workshops will contain the same elements as presentations: the handouts, the PowerPoint slides, the lecture component, and the exercises. The additional element is the "work." There will be many more hands-on opportunities. In a fiction-writing workshop, participants will get an opportunity to write something. In an introduction to social media workshop, the participants will have opportunities to create their own Twitter and Facebook accounts. Workshops are usually at least two or three hours in length. In the case of a fiction-writing workshop, the program might be best offered as a three-part series. This format will ensure that everyone has a chance to write a piece and have it critiqued by the instructor and other participants.

As I wrote the revised edition of this book from 2010 into 2013, I can't tell you how many library staff told me that "how-to" and "hands-on" programs have become the bread-and-butter of their libraries' programming calendars. Adults love to learn, and we *need* to learn in order to remain healthy and successful in our lives. And frequently the best way to learn how to download apps to your iPad or to learn how to file your taxes online is through a hands-on, interactive learning experience (which we librarians tend to call a program or workshop).

Pros: Workshops allow participants to learn by creating something. Even computer workshops on Excel or Google Docs tend to have participants create their own spreadsheet or slide presentation. It's amazing to see people go into a workshop with reservations about their skills and come out with pride in what they've accomplished.

Cons: The same potential "cons" listed for instructional presentations also apply to workshops. It is essential that the presenter is knowledgeable about the learning patterns of adults.

Tips: If you don't treat adults like adults, they will become upset, perhaps angry. In *Training Teachers,* Margie Carter and Deb Curtis offer ideas and strategies on training adults to become effective teachers. They state that "in any workshop we offer, participants have the opportunity to see things written down, hear ideas in a variety of ways from a variety of people, and move around and try things out (using methods such as props, case studies, and role plays)."[1]

Some adults learn best when taking notes from a PowerPoint presentation. Others understand a concept better after role-playing. Try to present the material in a variety of ways. Patience and respect are essential when teaching adults. Adults don't like to make mistakes, and they may be reluctant to ask questions. When an adult does make a mistake or ask a question, integrate these into the learning experience. Say things like, "That's a great question," or, for a mistake, "This happens all the time with PowerPoint. This is a good example. Let me mention this glitch to the class." If the workshop lasts longer than ninety minutes, work a break into the agenda. Give plenty of opportunity for the participants to practice what they have learned. Be receptive of questions. Questions allow adults to get what they need from the workshop. Break the workshop into distinct sections and summarize what was learned after each section. "Okay, what did we learn?" Let the participants summarize what they just learned. Try to make some one-on-one contact with each participant, and try to make the learning experience relevant to the individual. Make it a personal experience. Have the learner design a PowerPoint slide that reflects a hobby. If he loves the beach, design a slide show around a day at the beach.

Demonstrations

Definition: A demonstration is a show-and-tell program. The presenter talks about a topic while she creates something right before your eyes. An example is a program in which an origami expert stands in front of the audience and explains what she's doing as she creates various animals and shapes.

Pros: First off, demonstrations are fun. This is the format where your imagination (and perhaps your meeting room's seating capacity) is the only limit. You can bring in a black belt expert to give a karate demonstration. You can bring in an Italian chef to give a demonstration on making pasta. Demonstrations, when you hit on the right topic, are extremely popular. They will bring people into your library—perhaps for the first time. Demonstrations can tap into all those "how-to" sections of your collection: how to cook, how to train your dog, how to salsa dance . . .

Cons: The performer's fees for a demonstration can be costly. Some demonstrations, such as the cooking demonstration, include materials (food, plates, silverware, etc.), and the performer will add these costs into the overall fee. You might need to distribute tickets or keep a registration list in order to regulate the attendance. Insurance policies and programming policies might need to be reviewed or rewritten before you host a cooking program at which people eat the results or a dog-training program to which people bring their own dogs that might or might not bite.

Tips: Demonstrations can cause the occasional reality check with your programming policy and mission statement. The purpose of a demonstration is usually to relay information in an enjoyable manner. Demonstrations are recreational-slash-informational. You could argue (and I believe correctly) that a winemaking demonstration is educational, but you'd probably be more accurate if you said that you were offering an informational program for the recreational wine enthusiast. If your programming policy says that you pursue recreational and informational programs, then you're all set.

You will want your presenter to be an expert on his topic. The topic itself might call for a presenter who possesses a specific, uncommon skill, such as airbrushing T-shirts. Ideally, your expert can both *speak about* airbrushing and *create* the T-shirts. These performers can be costly unless you can find a business owner who will perform at a reasonable price in exchange for the publicity. Or maybe you are lucky enough to have an art school down the street with faculty and students who offer demonstrations free-of-charge.

Live Performances

Definition: Live performances are demonstrations without the talk. Examples include a play, a concert, or a ballet.

Pros: Live performances are entertaining. They can draw a crowd. They may introduce a topic to someone for the first time. And, most important, they present the material in the way that the author intended—through a human performance witnessed by an audience. A performance can be an exhilarating experience for someone who is hearing Celtic music for the first time or seeing Hamlet struggle over whether "to be, or not to be." Audience members are likely to exit the performance and walk right over to the information desk and ask for a copy of *Hamlet*.

Cons: As with demonstrations, you might have to make your play or concert a ticketed event to ensure that two hundred people don't show up and compete for fifty seats. The musicians or actors you identify in your community might earn their living by performing at events such as library programs. Performer's fees exceeding $100 an hour are fairly common. Last, a concert of drums can be noisy; a tap dancing performance requires a hard surface.

In other words, certain performances require certain facilities. Make sure that the performance you have in mind is compatible with the intended site of the performance.

Tips: Be sure that you work closely with the performers. Ask a lot of questions about their needs. What equipment will they need (such as speakers and microphones)? And try very hard to get references. Bad performances can be really, *really* bad. Bad opera or bad Shakespeare can result in someone's first and last visit with *La Bohème* or the Bard.

Discussion Groups

Definition: A discussion group consists of a number of people who get together to explore something. A facilitator usually leads the group. A book discussion group is an example of this format.

Pros: Discussion groups are a great way for people to learn from other members of the community. Because the participants are other library patrons and (usually) not subject experts, the participants feel comfortable expressing their thoughts and opinions. People often comment afterward that the discussion caused them to think of the book or topic in a new way. Discussion groups can become mainstays in your library. The core participants of a book discussion group will faithfully arrive—with book in hand—month after month, year after year.

Cons: Discussion groups take a great deal of planning. When working with scholar-led discussion series, such as the Choices Program (see chapter 8), you will need to select the discussion topics, attend an orientation session, coordinate the program dates with the scholar, read the accompanying materials, and then perform the standard in-house paperwork and preparations. Book discussions take a fair amount of preparation as well. The books must be selected, the facilitator must read the books, and questions or discussion points must be created to stimulate the discussion. Occasionally, only two or three people will show up because everyone hated, *really* hated the book.

Tips: Plan far in advance. If you plan to lead the discussion yourself, try to get some facilitator training. The function of a lecturer and a facilitator are almost the exact opposite. A lecturer talks; a facilitator gets others to talk. The Great Books Foundation (www.greatbooks.org) offers training in what it calls the Shared Inquiry method. This is a wonderful method that levels the playing field so that everyone can participate equally. The leader or facilitator poses basic questions to the group, and the group uses these questions to initiate discussion. Leaders do not offer their opinions, nor do they bring in outside materials, such as reviews. Participants are asked to support their opinions with examples from the text. This method makes everyone in the group feel equally qualified to offer insights and opinions.

Because so many great resources already exist on planning and leading book discussion groups, I've avoided replicating that information here. Ted Balcom's *Book Discussions for Adults: A Leader's Guide* is a great place to start when planning a discussion group at your library.[2] Lauren John's *Running Book Discussion Groups* will also get you started.[3] *The Whole Person Catalog No. 4* lists agencies that can help you get started with a book discussion program.[4] And the *Reading America Toolkit* offers great advice on how to plan and produce successful intergenerational and intercultural discussions.[5]

Civic Engagement

Many of our patrons are looking for opportunities to participate in community dialogue and address issues of public concern. Deborah A. Robertson mentions the term *community dialogue* several times in her book *Cultural Programming for Libraries: Linking Libraries, Communities, and Culture*.[6] A facilitated discussion can be one of the best ways to bring people together to have these community dialogues. And

libraries are in a unique position to do this. People see us as an objective, safe place to pursue ideas and information. And we can bring that same environment of objectivity and civility to our programs. We live in a society that is politically polarized, and this polarization is amplified when we turn to sources—friends, television programs, blogs—that merely verify and reaffirm our beliefs rather than challenge us to examine them. We can play a role in positioning our libraries as places where complex, civil dialogue occurs around topics that are of crucial importance to our communities. Rather than hosting a lecture on police brutality, we can host a discussion on "the police in our community" and frame the discussion in a way that allows people with all points of view on the topic to feel safe in expressing their thoughts.

Civic engagement–type programming can fall along a continuum, ranging from a program that comes very close to being a lecture to a true civic engagement discussion developed by National Issues Forums (www.nifi.org). When the director of Multnomah County Library (MCL) selected "facilitating civic engagement" as one of the library's priorities in 2009, one of the first things we did was to see if we could reshape some of the programs that we would have normally presented as lectures into discussions. Rather than have someone from the local college come in and give a lecture on the local service economy, we could ask him to structure his program in a way that provided opportunities for the audience to ask questions and share experiences with him and fellow audience members. A program like this probably gets a 2 or 3 on a scale of 10 in terms of civic engagement. While I was at Jefferson County Public Library, the director and I tracked what was happening in Denmark with the Human Library (humanlibrary.org) and some of the programs that were coming out of that project, such as "Borrow a Person You Don't Like." We decided to try something similar at Jefferson County. The following case study describes how we ran with the borrow-a-person idea, making it into something that worked for our community called "Trading Shoes."

A Case Study

Sometimes the right book can make you think deeply about your own opinions and beliefs and even help you change your perspective of the world. Can a library program achieve similar results? I decided to give it a try.

I had read several articles about libraries in Denmark and elsewhere that were hosting "Borrow a Person" programs. Librarians located individuals in their communities who could speak to an alternative world view—for example, an adoptee, a gay person, a war veteran, or someone who had spent time in prison. They worked with these individuals and brought them into a "Borrow a Person" program. A patron could browse through a Rolodex, find a person representing a group of interest, borrow him or her, and learn something new. It sounded pretty cool—and also pretty complicated.

My director was already sold on the idea, but I still had a lot of thinking to do. Although I knew the program had been done successfully, it seemed unlikely that we could build up a compelling Rolodex, market the program effectively, and then create a way to ensure a safe and successful experience for everyone. So I decided to go a slightly different route: structure the program as a facilitated conversation.

Locating the right people proved to be a challenge. I identified a number of organizations I thought might help. I started by drafting a document describing the format and purpose of the program: to create a facilitated conversation between guest speakers and an audience from which new ways of thinking might emerge. Chairs would be set up in a circle, with speakers seated at various intervals. I stated that I would begin the program by introducing the speakers and then asking them to tell a little about themselves and the group they represented. I explained that I would then ask the speakers very broad questions—for example, "What exactly is an animal rights activist?" Audience members could ask questions at any point during the program, and the speakers were welcome to ask

questions of each other or the audience. When the group seemed to be interacting easily, I would turn the conversation over to them, sit back, and listen. Last, I wrote a few ground rules reminding the audience to be respectful and listen and reminding the speakers to refrain from lecturing or using the conversation as a soapbox. I made it clear that I would end the program if the rules were ignored. To accompany this description, I created a cover letter introducing myself, briefly outlining the program, and explaining that I was writing because I felt that this organization might be a good source for a speaker. I ended with my contact information. Now I just needed someone to mail these letters to!

At this point I started developing lists on my own. What groups of people have been in the news lately? What ethnicities, belief systems, or occupations are feared or misunderstood by more than just a handful of people? I knew that I wanted to work with community organizations instead of individuals, so I also started making lists of organizations that might prove good resources for speakers. I then sent the letter to twenty or thirty of them. Some groups called back, but I could never quite explain what I was trying to pull off; a few thought the program might put their speakers at risk of being verbally attacked.

While I continued the hunt for speakers, I took time to brief our library system and get our programming committee on board. I also spoke with the head of our marketing and communications department. I then sent an e-mail to staff. Some were uneasy; they feared the library would be seen as perpetuating stereotypes instead of challenging them. I understood the reaction, but I was confident that with the right speakers and the proper framing of the conversation, we could make the program a success.

Eventually I found three organizations willing to send speakers my way. The first program would include an animal rights activist, a gay person, and a Latina. I spent time with each of them on the phone, going over the details of the program and reviewing the ground rules. I thought it would be helpful for them to get to know each other beforehand, so we collaborated on designing the flyer and promoting the program. They were all active members of the community and helped get the word out on the program. One of them even suggested a better name for the program: "Trading Shoes."

The day of the program finally arrived . . . and one of the speakers canceled. I needed a gay person, and fast! A coworker agreed to participate with almost no advance notice. And she was fantastic. The turnout for the program was modest. We probably had ten people in the audience, not counting the four of us. I welcomed everyone. I gave a little background on the program and stated that we were there to listen to each other, to ask each other questions, and to have a conversation, which I hoped would challenge a few long-held beliefs and make it apparent that we all had more in common than we might think. Then we were off and running. Some of the speakers' stories were just incredible. Our Latina representative wondered if we would ever get to a point where people would be able to move across the world unrestricted. The animal rights activist described how an arrest during a demonstration helped him realize that protestors didn't need anger or violence to contribute to something they believe in. And when my coworker was asked if someone who is gay could also be religious, she told of being denied visiting rights at a Catholic hospital when staff members discovered she was the patient's partner. In no time the audience was asking questions. I was amazed at how interested the patrons were, and as they relaxed, I noticed they were laughing and leaning in. After the program I thanked each speaker for participating. I was awed by the courage it must have taken to be so honest and so vulnerable during the evening. And I was certain that some folks in the audience were on their way home feeling good about the fact that these three people were members of their community.

So that's how "Borrow a Person" became "Trading Shoes." In May 2011 MCL began its own series titled "Mile in My Shoes: The Human Library." Figure 9.1 is the program flyer for that series.

National Discussion Forums

The "Trading Shoes" program is probably a 6 or a 7 on the civic engagement scale, since this is a program that really does allow people to talk, listen, share their stories, and begin to transcend some of their long-held convictions in order to feel some commonality with those who previously they may have only seen as different. And then there are the full-blown civic engagement discussion series such as the Choices Program (www.choices.edu) and Great Decisions (www.fpa.org) and the discussions developed by the National Issues Forums (www.nifi.org) and Everyday Democracy (www.everyday-democracy.org). These programs get a 10 on the civic engagement scale. They frame an issue in a way that does not lead the participants down any predetermined path. The group might meet for three hours at a time for six sessions over six weeks. As the dialogue and deliberation progress, some areas of agreement will emerge. In addition to building trust and understanding among the participants, some discussions also lead to action. A series might end with the group members submitting "ballots" that state their position on issues. For example, in the Great Decisions series, the ballots are tabulated and compiled into the *National Opinion Ballot Report* (NOBR), which is then distributed to the U.S. public, policymakers, and other Great Decisions participants.

Recently, the Kettering Foundation named ALA as a Center for Public Life. This designation means that ALA's Center for Public Life will train librarians from different types of libraries to convene and moderate deliberative forums and frame issues of local and national concern, using National Issues Forums materials and processes. This program should provide library staff with a great opportunity to receive training and support materials for leading discussion forums on issues such as privacy, health care, immigration, Social Security, and ethnic and racial tensions. By hosting such complex forums at your library, you

FIGURE 9.1 | **MILE IN MY SHOES FLYER**

MILE IN MY SHOES:
THE HUMAN LIBRARY

You can borrow all sorts of things from the library—how about borrowing a fresh perspective? Emily Harris of OPB's *Think Out Loud* will moderate a series of conversations where we'll attempt to answer the question, "what's it like to be someone else?" Bring your questions and your curiosity.

Muna Abshir Mohamud
What's It Like to Be Muslim?
Saturday, May 7, 1–2:30 p.m.

Originally from Somalia, Muna settled in the west 11 years ago as a refugee of her war-torn homeland. Since then, she has worked on refugee rights and resettlement issues, post-9/11 education and advocacy work, and provided policy and cultural expertise to schools, local and state officials, law enforcement and community organizations. A passionate educator, Muna believes that education through honest and respectful dialogue is an effective way to counter prejudicial and intolerant attitudes in our communities.

Terris Harned
What's It Like to Be Homeless?
Saturday, May 21, 1–2:30 p.m.

Terris is 32 years old, bipolar, and a student of life. He has been experiencing houselessness off and on for 9 years.

Jessica Richardson
What's It Like to Be a Victim of Sex Trafficking?
Sunday, June 5, 1–2:30 p.m.

About 300,000 youths are trafficked for sex each year nationwide, according to the U.S. Justice Department. When Jessica was 17 she became a victim of this illegal industry and was trafficked throughout the west by her pimp. She has since escaped that life and now runs a successful business.

All programs held at:
Central Library, U.S. Bank Room
801 S.W. 10th Ave. | 503.988.5123

Emily Harris
MODERATOR

Emily Harris hosts *Think Out Loud*, OPB's daily public affairs talk show. Prior to helping launch *Think Out Loud*, she was based in Berlin for National Public Radio, covering central and Eastern Europe and contributing to coverage of the Iraq war. Before moving to Germany, she reported from Washington for NPR and for the public television program *Now* with Bill Moyers.

Made possible by the National Endowment for the Humanities Fund of the Library Foundation. Space at programs is limited. Seating is available on a first-come, first-served basis.   04.11

MULTNOMAH COUNTY
LIBRARY

Source: Multnomah County (Oregon) Library

will contribute to bringing people together to discuss difficult issues, come to some common understandings, and agree on some unified actions to pursue in order to build a better community. For a wonderful example of how a library has partnered with various agencies to create an ongoing dialogue around a topic that is essential to the well-being of a community, take a look at Howard County (Maryland) Library and the Choose Civility initiative at www.choosecivility.org. An article in *Programming Librarian* titled "Civic Awareness Month" reminds us that September is Civic Awareness Month and gives some examples of what other libraries are doing to foster civic engagement.[7] Also be sure to take a look at the National Coalition for Dialogue and Deliberation's *2010 Resource Guide on Public Engagement* for some great information on how to get started with civic engagement discussions.[8] The National Issues Forums has a news page (www.nifi.org/news) that's worth a visit as well for examples of public forums that are occurring across the country.

Now that we've *thoroughly* covered discussion groups, let's move on to . . .

Film/Video Series

Description: A film series, at the very least, involves an audience and a film. The audience usually views one film (or several "shorts") during a certain day and time over the course of several weeks, such as every Tuesday in June from 2 to 5 p.m. Film series can be thematic (Great Silent Comedies or '40s Film Noir). They can occur with or without discussion. You can use a film in conjunction with other materials. For example, if the film is based on a novel, then the participants could be asked to read it beforehand. They could then discuss both the film and book after the viewing.

Pros: Just about everyone loves films. If your library has a film (as in celluloid) collection, you may have classic films that are not yet available on DVD. People may come up to you afterward and say that they hadn't seen that film since they were children.

Film discussion series can be very popular. The audience does not have to prepare as they do with a book discussion.

Cons: If you are using films, be prepared for the film to break, get stuck, melt, wobble, and unravel. If you are renting a movie from your local video store, chances are that you will need to obtain public performance rights before you show it to your audience. You will need to find the firm that handles that movie's public performance rights and pay a small fee to show the video. An example of such a firm is the Motion Picture Licensing Corporation. And remember, with movie theaters, television, Netflix, and video stores, you have some competition out there. Consider adding a component to your series that might draw in an eager audience and add value to the experience. For example, you might invite the movie critic from the local newspaper to introduce the film.

Tips: Try to offer a unique experience. Offer titles that are hard or impossible to find on television and at your video store. Or create a theme. Create a month-long film series on Saturdays called Saturday Afternoon Fever. Show *Grease, Saturday Night Fever, Can't Stop the Music* . . . (all right, perhaps some of your patrons would consider this a horror series). Or host a scholar-led, film discussion series. Please be sure that you are familiar with your equipment. What is the best room for the program? If the room is too large or if the floors and walls are bare, the sound might echo. Be creative with the equipment you do have. If you don't have a film projector, try hooking your LCD projector to a DVD player and project the video onto a movie screen, or play the DVD on a laptop and project the image onto a screen with a computer projector. *The Whole Person Catalog No. 4* (see note 4) lists agencies that can help you get started with a film series.

Miscellaneous Formats

The preceding formats will encompass most of the programs that you will offer in your library. But, there are even more ways in which you can serve up activities and events that engage your patrons. You might want to organize a three-hour chess or poker tournament or create a monthly ninety-minute open house where local inventors share their gadgets and ideas. All you might have to provide is the publicity, meeting space, and perhaps some refreshments.

The "meet-up" is another possible format. Use Facebook and other social networking applications to create meet-ups and gatherings. For example, it's Friday afternoon and you notice that the geese are beginning to migrate through town. You hop onto the library's Facebook and Twitter accounts and post that you will be in the local park on Tuesday from 2 until 4 p.m. On Tuesday you show up with a pair of binoculars, an iPad with a data plan/Internet connection, and a few books to help patrons learn more about the geese that are landing in the nearby pond.

"Passive programming" is yet another format that can bring patrons and staff together to converse and collaborate on a topic. For example, set up a flip chart near the information desk with the first line of a mystery story written in marker: "It was a dark and stormy night." Patrons then contribute the next line and continue to build on the story. Not only is this fun for staff and patrons alike, it will also get people talking to one another and building new relationships. (Although its focus is on youth programming, take a look at *DIY Programming and Book Displays* by Amanda Moss Struckmeyer and Svetha Hetzler. Their book includes some great examples of what they call DIY—do-it-yourself—programming.)[9]

As you can see, your programs will take shape in a variety of formats. And that's part of the fun for both you and your patrons!

MAKING YOUR DECISION

After weighing the pros and cons of each format, you will make your decision. Most of the time, the decision will be a straightforward one. A magic show can't really be anything other than a demonstration. But let's say you want to offer a program on maintaining a healthy diet. Do you ask someone from the American Heart Association to give an instructional presentation on healthy eating, or a local chef to give a cooking demonstration on the preparation of healthy dishes? There isn't a right answer. Perhaps you could try one of the two this year, the other next year. Just keep in mind that different programming formats tend to result in different program lengths. Lectures usually run about an hour; discussion groups, ninety minutes to two hours; workshops for several hours or days. Keep the length in mind when negotiating fees with the performer, when booking the meeting room, and when creating the accompanying publicity materials.

THE ROOM AND EQUIPMENT

The format you choose will affect the way you set up your meeting room. A lecture, for example, can accommodate seventy-five or more people. You will probably want to set up the room in an auditorium style, with chairs arranged in rows. Of course, the room you have available to you will also affect the format you choose. We don't all have rooms that can accommodate seventy-five people! A book discussion, however, is a much more intimate setting. This format calls for a round table with chairs or just chairs alone arranged in a circle.

The size of your audience will also influence the type of equipment the performer uses to present the information. *Program Planning: Tips for Librarians* gives some guidelines to keep in mind when using projection equipment to display information to your audience.

- Flip charts are recommended for audiences of less than 25 people.
- Overhead transparencies are recommended (using at least 20-point type) for audiences ranging from 75 to 200 people.
- Slides are best with audiences ranging from small to large (25 to 200 people).

- An audience up to about 25 people can clearly see a single video monitor.
- LCD panels are used to project information from a computer screen or to project presentation software such as PowerPoint. These are best used with audiences ranging from 25 to 50 people.
- LCD projectors are used for the same purposes as LCD panels. They have a much higher resolution, however. They are recommended for audiences ranging from 25 to 200.[10]

The formats we've discussed here are fluid. Think of them as colors on a palette. Experiment with and mix them. While someone is presenting information on common sports injuries in your meeting room, have a massage therapist in the lobby offering neck and back massages. If you have an embroidery exhibit in your display case, invite members of an embroidery club to come in and set up a table in front of the case. The public can view the exhibit, watch experts work on embroidery projects, and ask any questions they might have. Your patrons will appreciate your creativity.

NOTES

1. Margie Carter and Deb Curtis, *Training Teachers: A Harvest of Theory and Practice* (St. Paul, MN: Redleaf Press, 1994), 5.
2. Ted Balcom, *Book Discussions for Adults: A Leader's Guide* (Chicago: American Library Association, 1992).
3. Lauren Zina John, *Running Book Discussion Groups: A How-to-Do-It Manual* (New York: Neal-Schuman, 2006).
4. *The Whole Person Catalog No. 4: The Librarian's Source for Information about Cultural Programming for Adults* (Chicago: American Library Association, Public Programs Office, 1998).
5. Libraries for the Future, Americans for Libraries Council, and MetLife Foundation, *The Reading America Toolkit: How to Plan and Implement an Intergenerational and Intercultural Reading and Discussion Program at Your Library* (New York: Libraries for the Future, Americans for Libraries Council, 2005), www.aging.unc.edu/programs/nccolle/lff/ReadingAmericaToolkit.pdf.
6. Deborah A. Robertson, *Cultural Programming for Libraries: Linking Libraries, Communities, and Culture* (Chicago: American Library Association, 2005).
7. "Civic Awareness Month," *Programming Librarian*, www.programminglibrarian.org/library/events-and-celebrations/civic-awareness-month.
8. National Coalition for Dialogue and Deliberation, *Resource Guide on Public Engagement* (2010), ncdd.org/files/NCDD2010_Resource_Guide.pdf.
9. Amanda Moss Struckmeyer and Svetha Hetzler, *DIY Programming and Book Displays: How to Stretch Your Programming without Stretching Your Budget and Staff* (Santa Barbara, CA: Libraries Unlimited, 2010).
10. Gail McGovern et al., *Program Planning: Tips for Librarians* (Chicago: Continuing Library Education Network Exchange Round Table, American Library Association, 1997), 13.

10

Programming
and Technology

When I wrote the first edition of this book back in 2001, technology had a definite role to play in library programming. Back then someone giving a lecture at your library probably had a PowerPoint presentation running as she spoke. You had your PA system. You publicized your programs on your library's website. Much has changed since then. Facebook, Twitter, and You-Tube came along. Technology, such as geo-demographic mapping, has emerged that helps us learn more about our communities in much less time than ever before. Online programming is now possible. Social networking allows us to not only publicize our programs but also interact with our patrons before, after, and even during our events. We can record our programs and then offer them to our patrons over the Web via podcasting and video. Spontaneous programs are possible by quickly planning and then promoting timely, last-minute events via our Facebook and Twitter accounts, inviting people to come together to connect and learn. Viral marketing now occurs when our patrons find a recording of a program on YouTube and send it to their friends who send it to their friends who . . . We have event software products that help us promote and manage our programs. It's exciting! And a little overwhelming. So where do we start with all this technology, and which tools are right for your library and community?

ONLINE PROGRAMMING

The Internet has changed quite a bit over the past ten years. It has gone from a fairly static environment to an interactive environment where the user expects to help create and add content to the sites that he visits most often. Online book discussions were one of the first library programs to transition to an online environment as libraries began taking advantage of chat in the late '90s. Book discussions continue to thrive online, and the emergence of applications such as Skype now allow us to host live events that bring people in various locations together to hear and see one another in real time.

Online Book Discussions

Technology gives you several different ways in which you can provide opportunities for your patrons to interact and share ideas online. Some libraries create web pages dedicated to book discussion groups and readers' advisory. (Take a look at Hennepin County [Minnesota] Library's site at www.hclib.org/pub/bookspace.) In addition, some libraries create a blog where both library staff and patrons contribute content. For example, the Multnomah County Library (MCL) maintains a site called "An Embarrassment of Riches" at multcolib.org/blog/embarrassment-riches. And Palm Beach County (Florida) Library System has a Spanish Reading Club (Club de Lectura) with an accompanying blog (pbcclubdelectura.blogspot.com) where members exchange ideas and comments on the books. Your library might also want to consider starting an online readers' advisory service. An example is Charlotte Mecklenburg (North Carolina) Library's "What to Read" service on their Reader's Club page at www.cmlibrary.org/readers_club.

But how do we capture the exchange of ideas—the *discussion*—and bring that to the Web? How can we bring voices and faces onto the Web? Audio recordings of book discussion groups can be problematic, because it will be somewhat difficult for the listener to discern who is involved in the conversation. But audio recordings of authors talking can translate very well to the Web. You might want to record an appearance by an author at one of your book discussion groups. If you then post this recording to your readers' advisory blog or to iTunes, your patrons will go online to listen. (Please see the section on podcasting later in this chapter.) If you expect a

well-known author at one of your book discussions, or if you expect a particularly lively discussion, you might consider video recording (with audio as well!) the discussion and then providing a link to that discussion from your website. Another possibility is to video record and post short book reviews or book talks. Fort Vancouver (Washington) Regional Library District named its collection of short video reviews the "One Minute Critic" (www.fvrl.org/findabook/oneminutecritic.cfm). Staff record the reviews on a simple Flip camera (www.theflip.com). (In April 2011 Cisco announced that it would stop making the Flip camera. This is probably because most smartphones now have built-in high-definition video cameras.) These approaches to readers' advisory and book discussion bring literature to your readers via new delivery methods such as blogs and e-mail and YouTube.

Live Online!

Today's technology allows patrons to see and hear library programs in real time at whatever location they choose via a computer and Internet connection. Not only can patrons see and hear your programs, but with the right technology, they can also speak to the performer and interact via chat. Thomas Peters's book *Library Programs Online* is a great resource for detailed information on the various technologies that you can use to provide online programming.[1] Peters also coordinates OPAL (Online Programming for All Libraries). Visit OPAL at www.opal-online.org to see the variety of programs—discussion programs, interviews, special events, library training, memoir writing workshops, and virtual tours—that can be presented with web conferencing software. OPAL uses software from Talking Communities. (OPAL ceased operating in 2012, but the archive of previously recorded programs is still available on the website.) Other commonly used software for online events includes WebEx, Glance, and Adobe Acrobat Connect. But when I asked libraries which application they were using for their live, online events, just about every library that responded told me that they were using Skype (www.skype.com).

Skype is a software application that allows users to make telephone calls, conduct video conferencing, and perform instant messaging over the Internet. Although Skype does offer conference calling (which makes attendance from patrons' homes technically possible), you must register with Skype in order to place and receive calls from a computer. The most common use of Skype with library programming still involves patrons gathering at a library meeting room. The library then calls the performer via Skype on a library computer and, when connected, the video of the performer is projected onto a screen with a computer projector and her voice is amplified with external computer speakers. Patrons can then communicate with the performer via the library computer's microphone and camera and type questions via Skype's chat feature. Here are three libraries' experiences with Skype:

> The Hagen Ranch Road Branch Library got rave reviews from patrons when we presented an author program via Skype. The author was on the *New York Times* best-sellers list at the time, and the staff knew that our patrons couldn't get enough of her books. Unfortunately, the author lives in France. Fortunately, however, she mentioned that she does book discussion groups via Skype. For a week before the program, we asked patrons to submit their questions for the author. We also asked patrons to come a little bit early, so that I could explain the technology and how it worked. Even though our connection to the author dropped a couple times, patrons were ecstatic that they could have a personalized event with an author who lived on another continent. The setup for the program was simple, the hardware required is fairly cheap (or was already owned),

and because of the patron response, we plan on doing similar programs with popular authors that won't be traveling through Palm Beach County any time soon. —Adam Davis, Manager, Hagen Ranch Road Branch, Palm Beach County (Florida) Library System

> Our book club did a live Skype discussion with the author of one of the books we read. It was pretty easy—all we needed was a decent laptop, a working high-speed Internet connection, speakers to boost the sound on the computer, and we were in business. We kept it very informal, but he basically talked a little about his book and then the club members asked him questions and commented on some of their favorite parts. —Sharon Blank, Public Services Librarian, Screven-Jenkins (Georgia) Regional Library System

> The Highland Park Public Library (located in the northern suburbs of Chicago) recently held our first Skype event. The program was part of the "Rise and Shine" humanities lecture series that we present in conjunction with the Highland Park Senior Center. The programs are held two Wednesday mornings a month at the Library from September through May and feature humanities-related topics.
>
> The Skype event was a conversation with author Philippa Gregory about her new book *The Red Queen*. Ms. Gregory is based in England and this was her only U.S. event. The program was arranged by a local bookstore that needed a venue to hold such an event. The event was held in our auditorium, so Ms. Gregory was featured on a large screen. She talked to the audience and then took questions from audience members. Her books were sold during the event with bookplates that had been signed by her. Attendance was about 20–25.

Judging from patron comments, the event was a success (although we were hoping for a larger turnout). Those that attended thought it was a great use of technology and enjoyed the event. We would definitely use the format again for a high-profile speaker we were interested in hosting that could not appear at the Library. I think it opens new doors in terms of programming as a way to host high-profile or esteemed speakers that aren't able to travel to the Library or perhaps whose personal appearances we can't fund. —Beth Keller, Marketing Specialist, Highland Park (Illinois) Public Library

ARCHIVING YOUR PROGRAMS

Technology not only enables us to present programs in innovative ways, it can help us preserve them as well. A library board member once asked me if there was a way for him to get the information that was conveyed in a program that he was unable to attend. This question might on the surface appear to be strange, since we tend to think of our programs as live events that live on only in memory after they occur. And, yes, some of us post the accompanying PowerPoint slides and handouts to our websites for some of our programs. But the human element that draws us to live events in the first place and causes us to lean in as someone speaks or plays a note on an instrument, that part isn't captured on a slide or handout. So I was happy to be able to tell this board member that we had audio recorded the program and that he could now access it at any time via our website. He thought that was pretty cool—and it is! By recording your programs and making them available on the Web, you bring your programs to an audience that can choose to listen to or view an event at a time and place that is convenient for them. You just might end up with someone downloading your retirement planning program to her iPod and listening while she goes for her morning run.

So let's start with podcasting. The word *podcast* is really a blending of the words *broadcast* and *iPod*. With podcasting, you are recording something, uploading it to a website, and making it easily available for listening online or downloading onto a personal device such as a laptop or iPod. (Please see the resource directory at the end of this book for titles that provide in-depth help on the technology and know-how needed to get started with podcasting and other technical processes covered in this chapter.) MCL has been recording a percentage of its programs and offering them as podcasts for a few years now. The podcasts are available at multcolib .libsyn.org.

To get started with podcasting, you will need some equipment that you can use to record the program as a digital file that can be stored on a computer. Edirol (now owned by Rowland) makes the digital recorder used by MCL. Sony, Sanyo, Olympus, and others make similar devices. Prices on these devices start around fifty dollars and go up into the hundreds. You'll want to buy something with a sensitive, high-quality microphone. The better devices look something like a men's electric razor; the microphones sit atop the device and look like silver, perforated tubes. Once you've purchased the device (or devices), you might consider developing a short class outline that allows you to train others on the device. MCL offers two classes. One covers how to record with the device and how to save the recording as a digital file on a computer, and the second class teaches staff how to edit recordings. The more staff you have trained the better the chances that you'll have someone around to record that big-name author event when it occurs.

Now that you have your recorder and know how to use it, you are ready to pick the best events to capture on audio. Think of what types of events play well on radio. Poetry readings, storytelling, and talks and lectures come to mind. Demonstrations—cooking, crafts, computer classes, and the like—will probably lose too much of their how-to value when reduced to audio alone. To make sure that certain programs get recorded, it is helpful to work podcasting into your overall programming process and insert a step that asks you to decide whether you will record a program. For example, if your library uses some type of programming request form, you could include a box on this form to be checkmarked if the coordinator of the program would like the program to be recorded. You'll also want to be sure that the contract with your performer states that the program may be recorded. (The sample contract in chapter 8 includes such a statement.) Last, you'll want to create a web page for your podcasts (such as multcolib.libsyn.org) or find a company that will host your podcasts (such as Liberated Syndication, libsyn.com) and create some content for the page that guides your patrons on how to listen to and download the audio files. And as your confidence in podcasting builds, you can begin to explore how to do such things as submit your podcasts to iTunes so that your patrons can find your library's programs right alongside the music they download to their computers and music players.

On the day of the program, be sure to work with your performer and let him know how far he can wander from the podium if he chooses not to use a lavalier. Announce to the audience that the program will be recorded and made available as a podcast. Some members of your audience *will* listen again from home or work. After you have recorded and uploaded a few of your programs, ask your web folks or IT folks or your web hosting service if they can tell you which programs have been listened to most often. At MCL, author talks, programs targeted toward baby boomers (such as a "Perspectives on Positive Aging" program and a "Caring for Your Aging Parent" program), and sixty-minute brown bag lunchtime topics such as conflict resolution and understanding business relationships all do very well as podcasts, averaging ten to thirty downloads per month. With podcasting, not only do you retain much of the information that was shared during your program, you also open up your programs to a whole new audience beyond your physical library.

TECHNOLOGY AND MARKETING

We humans continue to develop technology and tools that help us communicate. Radio and television and the Internet not only entertain us and send information our way but these mediums can provide the opportunity for people to get their stories and ideas out to the world. The Internet emerged as primarily a one-way medium that presented us with pages with links to other pages. Then Web 2.0 came along, and the Web evolved into a truly collaborative medium where terms such as *creator* and *user* lost meaning in this highly interactive environment. Today the user creates the content of many sites. This is certainly the case with YouTube. One user posts a video, and then other users watch and some comment on that video, which then leads to a conversation that continues for pages and pages and weeks and weeks. Nowadays a well-crafted tweet or a playful video might get more attention than that beautifully written library newsletter piece. Libraries everywhere are finding that social media—Facebook, Twitter, and YouTube—offer an opportunity to not only promote library events but engage with our patrons before, after, even *during* these events.

Social Networking

Social networking technology, Web 2.0, Twitter and Facebook . . . these terms and tools seemed to appear very quickly and just as quickly change how people use the Web. Twitter (twitter.com), which reduces communication to 140 characters, is a great tool to use to promote your programs. (You can get a crash course on Twitter by reading the *Wikipedia* article at en.wikipedia.org/wiki/Twitter.) One thing that you will get if you begin to use Twitter is instant access to your patrons. Many Twitter users, called tweeters or twitterers, keep Twitter continuously running in the background on their computers. Twitter also offers an option to have some Twitter messages or "tweets" sent to their cell phones, so Twitter can be a great application to use to remind patrons of a program that will occur in the next twenty-four hours. Because tweets are limited to just a few characters, they are very straightforward. You can mention the event and provide a link to the event on your website. A sample tweet can look like this: "Meet author Michele Serros Tue & Wed http://insertURLhere," or "Charlotte Lewis exhibition opening reception: Sun. 2 p.m. North Portland Library http://insertURL here." When I worked at MCL I'd receive tweets via my cell phone for events at MCL's Central Library (where I worked), and I'd spontaneously take a break and walk down to the meeting room to catch a portion of the program. I'm convinced that Twitter is a great tool to nudge me and others toward those events that are just about to occur in your libraries.

And then there is Facebook (www.facebook.com). If you are familiar with blogs, then Facebook will look somewhat familiar to you as well. You can learn more about Facebook by reading the *Wikipedia* article at en.wikipedia.org/wiki/Facebook. Facebook will allow you to amass a group of followers (or "friends") that can read and view (via any photos or videos that you include) and comment on your postings. Take a look at MCL's Facebook page (www .facebook.com/multcolib) to see how one library uses this web application. One of the primary purposes of Facebook is to create online communities of friends, and you'll notice that most Facebook postings are more informal than what you see on a library flyer or press release. Here's a sample posting on MCL's Facebook page:

> Dude, That's Gross: The Wonderful World of Mucous & More! That's the compelling/repelling title of what is sure to be an "engrossing" program. *snort* Join Bart King, author of the popular books "The Big Book of Boy Stuff" and "The Big Book of Girl Stuff" and most recently of "The Big Book of Gross Stuff" as he discusses his work and all things gross. This program is open to all ages, but is most appropriate for kids 9–13. Hollywood Library,

> Oct. 18th from 6:30 to 7:30 p.m. http://insert URLhere

On Facebook you might accompany a posting such as this with an image of the book's cover, or you might insert a YouTube (www.youtube.com) video of the author reading from his book. But, what makes Facebook *really* cool is that it allows the library and your patrons and friends to all interact and contribute content to your online library community. For example, *Ghost Map* was the featured book for MCL's "Everybody Reads" program in 2010. In addition to our community reading the book together and discussing it together at various book discussion groups throughout the library system, we were also lucky enough to bring in the author, Steven Johnson, to speak. We posted information about the event to Facebook, and Mr. Johnson commented to our Facebook page both before and after the event. And then our patrons commented on his comments, and he responded. It was a wonderful way for the author and our patrons to come into contact with each other and have a conversation around issues presented in *Ghost Map*.

Sometimes patrons will post a comment that can be very helpful to others, such as "Hillsdale is out of tickets as of yesterday . . . Northwest is the closest on the west side that has them . . ." Patrons will also post with questions: "Dear MCL: I've been trying to find the adult summer e-reader drawing results, but can't seem to get anywhere. Were the winners announced? Thanks!" And you can post with answers: "Hi! The winners are on the Read 4 Life web page here: www .multcolib.org/events/read4life.html. Thanks for asking!" Sometimes your patrons will post information that adds value to your programs. Patrons will post information about related programs and events that are occurring around your community or in neighboring library systems. They will post information on books or films or TV programs that tie into your programs. And sometimes they will just post to tell you that you are on the right track: "I LOVE the Multnomah County Library system—it's the best!"

I also want to mention Flickr (www.flickr.com) as a social networking application that can help you, through images, convey the vibrancy of your library programs. Posting photos of patrons enjoying your programs just might persuade others to attend a program in the future. (If you are going to take photos of your patrons and post them on the Web, it's a good idea to get permission beforehand. I've included a sample photo release form for you to use in figure 10.1.) If you have a performer who is appearing at multiple locations over a week or more, you can take some photos at one of the first performances and then post those photos to Flickr to entice others to attend that same program later in the week. Take a look at Christchurch (New Zealand) City Libraries' Flickr page at www.flickr.com/photos/christchurchcity libraries and MCL's page at www.flickr.com/photos/multnomahcountylibrary and McCracken County (Kentucky) Public Library's page at www.flickr.com/photos/mclibdotnet. Flickr is interactive in the sense that people can comment on photos and easily share photos from your page with friends and family (which amounts to great publicity for your library and library programs).

All these tools—Twitter, Facebook, Flickr, and the like—give you the opportunity to strengthen relationships with your patrons by continuing the conversation with them beyond your physical buildings. Someone might attend a program at your library, love it, tell you so, and then go home, check your Facebook page, view a brief video snippet from that program, add a comment about how much fun he had at the event, and then forward the link of the video to friends. You might then see his comment and post a comment of your own: "If you loved tonight's program, please come back next Tuesday when a similar and even more awesome program will be held, same place/same time!" These tools are just plain fun to use, and they offer you opportunities to experiment and use your creativity. MCL had huge library cards made (see figure 10.2), and library staff started bringing them to programs and outreach events. Before a program

begins, MCL staff ask people in the audience if they would like to take a photo with the humongous card. Staff and patrons really enjoy these interactions, and patrons love visiting the Flickr and Facebook pages to see these photos. Some of the photos posted to Flickr have been viewed hundreds of times!

Be sure to check out *A Social Networking Primer for Librarians* by Cliff Landis for even more information on how you can begin using social networking to enhance your library services and further engage with your patrons.[2]

Going Viral!

With online social networking, a video posted to a website can be viewed by thousands or even millions of people in just a few days if it goes viral, because people will e-mail and tweet about what they've just seen to friends, and those friends will tell others, and so on and so on . . . And because all this networking is happening so effortlessly through people sharing the video from their phones and laptops and iPads, a video can get forwarded thousands of times very, very quickly. Check out the *Wikipedia* article on viral marketing at en.wikipedia.org/wiki/Viral_marketing.

People love your library, and they trust your staff. They turn to you to provide materials and assistance on topics that remain safe within that confidential bond between them and their library. And they certainly feel connected and invested in their library through the taxes that they contribute and through the personalized assistance and services that they receive in return. Facebook and Twitter can build upon this social capital and allow you to connect with your patrons throughout the day by bringing the library to the handheld devices that travel with them both day and night. And as you build up your following on Twitter and Facebook, you position yourself to begin using these applications to try new ways of marketing your library and its programs and services. Although you may have limited time and resources,

FIGURE 10.1 | **PHOTO RELEASE FORM**

Jefferson County Public Library
Photo/Video Release

I hereby agree and consent to the use of my photograph (and/or child's photograph) in news coverage or publicity concerning the Jefferson County Public Library.

I am aware that I may refuse to be photographed in the library.

Today's Date _____

Name of Minor _____

     Minor's Signature _____

Name of parent or responsible adult _____

     Adult's Signature_____

If not parent, please describe relationship_____

Library where photo was taken _____

News media _____

We ask you to sign this release because Colorado Statute 24-90-119, Privacy of User Records, protects your privacy in use of the library unless we have your written consent to disclose your use.

Please send signed release to Public Information Office.

Source: Jefferson County (Colorado) Public Library

FIGURE 10.2 | **SAMPLE PHOTOS**

Source: Multnomah County (Oregon) Library

you can still experiment with creating videos that offer teasers of upcoming programs. You can work with your performers ahead of time and video record a few moments that offer a glimpse into what an upcoming program offers. Canton (Michigan) Public Library created a nice teaser for its "Living Books" program (www.youtube.com/watch?v=6WK4Va8vIoc). And you can create videos that present your library as a fun, vibrant place just bursting with creative people and events. For some great examples of library videos that have gone viral, take a look at the *Huffington Post* article "Librarians Go Gaga: 9 of the Funniest Library Videos Ever."[3]

QR Codes

When I attended the ALA Midwinter Meeting in San Diego in 2011, many of the vendors were wearing T-shirts with QR codes printed on the front. Librarians were walking up to the vendors, snapping a picture of the T-shirts with their smart phones, and then seeing what information the QR codes contained via the QR code readers on their phones. The codes usually contained information about the vendor's company or products. QR (or Quick Response) codes are similar to traditional barcodes, but they can contain a lot more information—up to thousands of characters.

(Check out the *Wikipedia* article at en.wikipedia.org/wiki/QR_code.) They also add convenience for those who are familiar with using them in combination with a QR code reader on their smartphones. People with iPhones and Android phones with cameras can download free QR reader apps that take a photo of the code and then display the information that is included in the code. QR codes are being used more and more for marketing purposes: the librarian snaps a photo of the QR code on that vendor's T-shirt, and the QR code contains a URL that pulls up a YouTube video introducing the vendor's new product line. All this happens seamlessly on the librarian's smartphone. So how can *you* start using this technology?

QR codes can be used in libraries in various ways. If your library lists all its programs on an events web page, consider placing a QR code with the events page's URL in the upper right corner of that page. A patron can walk up to one of your public computers, call up your events page, snap a photo of the QR code with her smartphone, leave the library, and then scroll through your upcoming events on her phone as she's riding the bus home. Many libraries are starting to place QR codes on their newsletters and flyers. These codes link patrons to the library's events page, a booklist, a map to the library's location, and so on. Figure 10.3 is an example of a library flyer with an accompanying QR code. Do you have a smartphone with a QR code reader? If so, take a photo of the code and see where it takes you! For some good basic information on QR codes, take a look at Contra Costa County (California) Library's QR code page at guides.ccclib.org/qr.

GOING MOBILE

In May 2010 the *New York Times* ran an article titled "Cellphones Now Used More for Data Than for Calls." The article noted that more than 90 percent of all U.S. households now have mobile phones, and people are using these phones to listen to music, watch videos, send texts, and surf the Web. (Worldwide, 81 percent of people own a cell phone, while only 50 percent have access to a computer.)[4] Are people in the United States using those same phones to place calls? Not so much these days. More and more people are using their mobile phones to stay connected with news, friends, and local events. The point is that the mobile device is becoming the primary computing device for an emerging majority of our patrons. And our patrons are using these devices to send and receive texts, to log in to their Facebook and Twitter accounts, to listen to audio and watch videos, and to record video of their own that they then post to Facebook. So if we embrace Facebook and Twitter and YouTube and become skilled at recording, producing, and distributing our podcasts and videocasts, we will reach many of our patrons through devices that they carry with them wherever they go. Our programs will join our online catalog and our databases as part of our online library. For further reading on mobile devices and libraries, check out *Mobile Technology and Libraries* by Jason Griffey.[5]

EVENTS SOFTWARE

Events software tools are wonderful resources that can do much to enhance how your patrons interact with your program offerings. As of 2013, examples of such products included Events by Evanced Solutions and EventKeeper by Plymouth Rocket. Most of these products will integrate nicely with your current website. They will attractively display your upcoming programs in various formats, such as a calendar view or a list of upcoming programs. This list can usually then be sorted by topic or age group or library location. Figure 10.4 shows an example of how Jefferson County (Colorado) Public Library uses events software to list and promote its programs.

In addition to displaying your programs online in a calendar or list, these tools have some very useful bells and whistles. For example, if a patron finds a

FIGURE 10.3 | **SAMPLE PROGRAM FLYER WITH QR CODE**

Meet Elyssa East, author of

DOGTOWN

DEATH AND ENCHANTMENT
IN A NEW ENGLAND GHOST TOWN

Winner of the 2010 L. L. Winship/P.E.N. New England Award in Nonfiction

Dogtown -- an isolated colonial ruin and surrounding forest in Gloucester, Massachusetts -- has long exerted a powerful influence over artists, writers, eccentrics, and nature lovers. But its history is also woven through with tales of witches, supernatural sightings, pirates, former slaves, and drifters. In 1984, a brutal murder took place there: a horrific event that continues to haunt Gloucester even today.

Author Elyssa East interlaces the story of this grisly murder with the strange, dark history of this wilderness ghost town and explores the possibility that certain landscapes wield their own unique power. Join us as she takes us to an unforgettable place brimming with tragedy, eccentricity, and fascinating history.

THURSDAY
MAY 20 @ 7:00 P.M.
IN THE LARGE MEETING ROOM

scan this with your smartphone!

CARY MEMORIAL LIBRARY • 1874 MASSACHUSETTS AVE • LEXINGTON, MA • 02420 • 781-862-6288 • WWW.CARYLIBRARY.ORG

Source: Cary (Massachusetts) Memorial Library

FIGURE 10.4 | **EVENTS SOFTWARE**

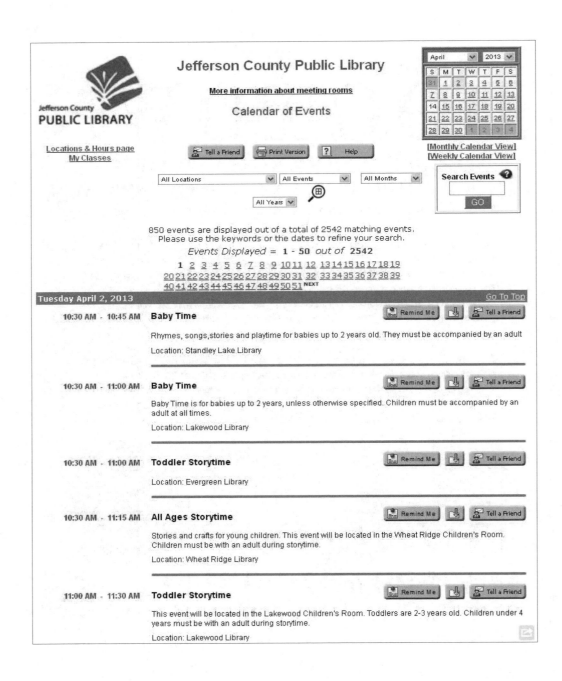

Source: Jefferson County (Colorado) Public Library

program listing that interests him, he may be able to click on a button to request that a reminder be sent his way as the program date approaches. Or he may be offered the option of sending a friend a heads-up about a particular program. Some of these products allow patrons to register for programs online, and some even create waiting lists when programs reach a specified capacity. Library staff will enjoy the benefits of features such as attendance lists and various statistics reporting functions.

Finally, these events tools frequently offer for purchase modules that allow you to manage your summer reading clubs online as well as offer and manage a cultural pass program online. Most of the summer reading modules allow patrons to sign up online, log their reading, and print a certificate that they can redeem for a prize at a library service desk. Examples of such modules include Summer Reader by Evanced Solutions and The Summer Reading Program Manager by LibraryInsight. As for cultural pass or museum pass programs, these passes can be a great way to allow your patrons to attend a cultural event or other off-site experience. Rather than bringing someone from the art museum or the opera to your library to present a program, you can put passes to those cultural institutions into the hands of your patrons. The time that it takes to work out the logistics and agreements with the various institutions can be intensive on the front end, but once these partnerships are established, you have created the ultimate "program" for your patrons by giving them a seat at an actual venue. Take a look at Jefferson County Public Library's "Culture Pass" program (jeffcolibrary.org/culturepass) to see how the library allows patrons to view and request passes online via EventKeeper.

DEMOGRAPHICS AND MARKET ANALYSIS

The Web allows us to easily access statistical data about our cities and regions through sources such as American FactFinder (factfinder2.census.gov) and ERsys (www.ersys.com). These can be great resources to learn more about the age range, racial makeup, and income level of your community. This information is valuable when you are planning a program for a particular audience. Subscription services such as DemographicsNow (www.demographicsnow.com) give you demographic information as well as consumer profile information that tells you such things as how much your patrons earn and where and how they spend their money. A similar subscription product, Civic Technologies (www.civictechnologies.com) provides customer analytics through GIS (geographical information system) technology. This product integrates various demographic data sources with consumer information data that describe your patrons' behaviors (such as spending behaviors). SimplyMap by Geographic Research, Inc. (geographicresearch.com/simplymap) is yet another subscription application that generates thematic maps and reports using extensive demographic, business, and marketing data. These products use GIS technology to overlay demographic and behavioral data about your patrons onto maps, so that you can see, block to block, how certain behavior patterns cluster within your neighborhoods. (For an overview of GIS, take a look at the *Wikipedia* article at en.wikipedia.org/wiki/Geographic_information_system.) For example, you can generate a map that shows how many people in your neighborhood are spending their money on travel or restaurants or a new computer. You can even pinpoint where these new computer owners live. If you learn that many of your patrons who live within five blocks of the library eat out several times a week, then a program with several local chefs participating in a cooking demonstration followed by a Q&A session might prove to be very popular. Your library can also load its own statistical data—circulation data, building data such as square footage—and this allows you to create charts and graphs and maps that illustrate, for example, how the sizes of your meeting rooms are keeping pace with the population growth of your service area.

Jefferson County (Colorado) Public Library used the Civic Technologies product to analyze its communities. Each library manager then used the information generated through this product to write a report about the community her library serves. The next step was for each library to develop a service project based on this report. One library decided to launch a joint project with the local food bank. This library will begin providing books at a local summer lunch program as well as providing a literacy class for the parents attending this lunch program. This wonderful service resulted from the library's using a tool to learn more about who lived in its neighborhoods, how many of these residents were parents, what their income and literacy levels were, and where they congregated to take advantage of a warm lunch. Of course not all our libraries can afford the subscription costs of some of these tools. Fortunately, some of our local colleges and universities are compiling some of this information for us. Check with your local colleges to see what demographic and behavioral data they have collected on your community. For example, Portland State University maintains the Population Research Center (www.pdx.edu/prc). Please be sure to refer to chapter 4 for even more information on getting to know your community.

ONLINE SURVEYS

There are tools out there to help you gather feedback from your online users. For example, a tool such as SurveyMonkey (www.surveymonkey.com) can help you quickly generate online surveys and evaluation forms. As mentioned previously in chapter 7, Redwood City (California) Downtown Library used SurveyMonkey to involve patrons in the selection of titles for a film series. And Christchurch City Libraries in New Zealand provides a link on its events page to an evaluation form created with SurveyMonkey (see figure 10.5). You can use these tools to gather the same information that you would via a paper survey.

You can ask patrons about what topics they would like to see presented as programs. You can ask what days and times are preferable for programs. But these tools can also be used to ask timely questions that create a collaborative relationship between your library and your patrons. For example, you could propose two or three potential titles for an upcoming program and let your patrons choose which title to use on your flyers and other publicity. You could do a quick survey to ask your 12- to 18-year-olds whether they prefer to be called "teens" or "young adults" and then use the results to influence how you refer to this audience in your library's communications—newsletter, flyers, and the like. You can place online surveys and evaluations on your library events web page, and you can also push these surveys to the e-mail lists that you have compiled from patrons who have voluntarily offered their addresses to you via print and online program evaluation forms. These online survey and evaluation tools provide you with yet another way to interact with your past or potential programming audience.

PUTTING IT ALL TOGETHER

So let's take a look at a library that is using much of the technology mentioned in this chapter. Christchurch City Libraries in New Zealand embraces technology in a big way! Take a look at its website at christchurch citylibraries.com. You'll find an interactive blog, a Flickr site, an online events calendar using Trumba, a Twitter feed, a Facebook page, and various RSS feeds including a library events feed. The library podcasts its programs and has purchased webcams and video equipment that allow it to transmit some programs via Skype to schools and sister-city libraries. It also offers classes on technology, including an introductory class called "Coffee and Computers" and a Technology Tasters series in which patrons are introduced to current technology topics such as online book clubs. In 2009 Christchurch City Libraries celebrated its

FIGURE 10.5 | **ONLINE SURVEY**

Login - Groups

Learning Centre Computers and Coffee Evaluation Form

Click on the link above to give us feedback on the programme you have just completed.

Which Learning Centre Centre/Library did you attend for this course?: *

[select...   ▾]

Which programme did you attend?:

[select...   ▾]

How much did you enjoy the programme?:

[select...   ▾]

What new skills did you learn?:

[   ]

Were the instructions easy to follow?:

○ Yes

◉ Sometimes

○ Not at all

What days/times would suit you best?:

[   ]

What other courses/topics would you be interested in attending?:

[   ]

Other comments::

[   ]

(Submit)

Source: Christchurch (New Zealand) City Libraries

150th anniversary with a video contest. Aspiring filmmakers created videos, submitted entry forms, and then uploaded their videos to YouTube where they were viewed by a library panel that selected winners and awarded prizes to adults, teens, and youth. You can view some of the library's past events at www .flickr.com/photos/christchurchcitylibraries.

NOTES

1. Thomas A. Peters, *Library Programs Online: Possibilities and Practicalities of Web Conferencing* (Santa Barbara, CA: Libraries Unlimited, 2009).

2. Cliff Landis, *A Social Networking Primer for Librarians* (New York: Neal-Schuman, 2010).

3. Caroline Eisenmann, "Librarians Go Gaga: 9 of the Funniest Library Videos Ever," *Huffington Post*, July 16, 2010, www.huffingtonpost.com/2010/07/16/ librarians-go-gaga-9-of-t_n_648177.html?.

4. Jenna Wortham, "Cellphones Now Used More for Data Than for Calls," *New York Times*, May 13, 2010, www.nytimes.com/2010/05/14/technology/ personaltech/14talk.html.

5. Jason Griffey, *Mobile Technology and Libraries* (New York: Neal-Schuman, 2010).

Generating Publicity

Planning a program is a lot like planning a party: you plan and plan and plan, but it's no fun unless people show up. Don't forget to invite your friends/ patrons to your party/program. Create a guest list/mailing list. Send out the invitations/flyers. And then guarantee success by doubly or triply inviting people. Send print and electronic mailings, followed up by phone calls and press releases. Make it appear obvious that your event is *the* event to attend.

Remember just ten to fifteen years ago when publicizing a program mostly meant creating some print flyers for the event, listing it in your event newsletter, and sending out a press release to the local newspaper? And then the Internet came along and then Web 2.0, and now many of our patrons stay informed about what we do via our websites and Facebook and Twitter accounts. Our patrons might still read about an upcoming library program in a newspaper, but there's a good chance that they read that newspaper online. Most of our patrons now browse our program listings through our libraries' websites. The previous chapter is called "Programming and Technology," but I had to initially ponder whether it made sense to create a separate chapter on technology because so much of what we do now in libraries is intertwined with technology. Ultimately I decided to dedicate a chapter to technology. So, before you read about the more traditional forms of publicity in the following sections, please be sure to read "Technology and Marketing" in chapter 10.

FLYERS

Let's start with the basics. Just as you create an invitation to a party, you'll create an invitation to your program. This is your flyer. Whether it will be made by hand and photocopied, created at a computer in your branch, or mass-produced in your marketing office, a flyer is usually an essential marketing tool for a new program. People are accustomed to things being announced on flyers. "Missing Cat" flyers are tacked to telephone poles, "Band Mate Wanted" flyers are posted in record stores, and "Help Wanted" flyers are taped to restaurant windows. Patrons will notice the program flyers you post on your bulletin boards and place at your information desks.

When creating your flyers, keep in mind these key elements:

- Display the title of the program prominently.
- List the presenter.
- Include a brief description of the program.
- If the presenter is an author, consider including a quotation from one of his works.
- List the day, date, and time of the program. Include a beginning and end time.
- List the library or libraries where the program occurs. Include the address and phone number of the library as well.
- Include your snazzy library logo.
- Include the universal symbol for wheelchair accessibility, if your library is accessible to people using wheelchairs. If you offer interpreters for the hearing impaired or other services, give the patrons a telephone number they can call for further information.
- Placing the word *free* on the flyer can be helpful. Some of your patrons will always be surprised that your programs are free.
- Mention whether tickets are required.
- A cool graphic relating to the event never hurts either. The eye is always attracted to interesting images, such as clip art, a photograph of the performer, and so on.

There are a few formatting decisions to make as well. Do you make a separate flyer for each branch that hosts the program, or do you make one flyer and list all the branches hosting the program, along with all the dates and times? Your choice might depend on the number of branches hosting the program and the distance between the branches. Someone who lives in Staten Island, New York, for example, might not be terribly interested in wading through a list of the Bronx branches that are hosting the same program. Some libraries list all the programs for the month on one flyer. This approach can result in a cluttered flyer if you do a lot of programming. A trifold or brochure would be better. The brochure in figure 11.1 was created by printing on both sides of an 8½-by-11-inch piece of paper and then folding that paper in half. The brochure includes all the young adult summer reading programs for June, July, and August.

Be sure to check with your state library, your state library association, and ALA (www.ala.org) for sample flyers. Check these organizations' websites to see if they have publicity kits (with flyers) available for events such as National Library Week and Banned Books Week. They may have programming ideas as well.

NEWSLETTERS

Print newsletters are a vanishing breed. Many libraries now promote their events via e-mail blasts, Facebook, and online events calendars. That said, your newsletter—if you still have one—is also a great place to promote your programs. Just as there are those patrons who rely on flyers, so there are others who use your newsletter as their guide to library events. This is particularly true if your library e-mails or snail mails your newsletter to patrons who have asked to be placed on a mailing list. Frequently, libraries will divide the programming section of the newsletter into adult, young adult, and children's listings. The programming information you include will be similar to what you included on the flyer. You can even use the same clip art. Consider listing the names, addresses, and telephone numbers of your library

FIGURE 11.1 | **SAMPLE PROGRAM FLYER**

Source: Jefferson County (Colorado) Public Library

branches on the final page of the newsletter. This will save space. Your programming listings will include each program's title, the description, and the names of the branches hosting the program, and perhaps some clip art specific to the program. Your patrons can look on the final page of the newsletter for branch locations and telephone numbers. You can further condense the programming portion of your newsletter by including certain publicity elements only once. The library logo, the universal symbol for wheelchair accessibility (if it applies to all the program locations), the telephone number for interpreters, and the "all programs are free" reminder can take up quite a bit of space if you include them with each program listing. Instead, include them either at the beginning or end of the programming listings. If your library foundation and Friends group also publish newsletters, send your programming information to them as well so that they can publicize your events in their publications. Figure 11.2 contains an example of an adult programming section of a newsletter. If your library has a robust programming calendar, consider creating a monthly newsletter devoted entirely to library events and programs. Take a look at Palm Beach County (Florida) Library System's *Happenings* publication at www .pbclibrary.org/publications.htm.

MAILING LISTS

Now is a good time to talk about mailing lists. Do you want to build an entirely electronic mailing list of e-mail addresses, or will you send some mail via USPS for those who do not have or prefer not to use e-mail? Either way, your library probably already has a public relations or marketing office that maintains various mailing lists. A mailing list built for programming purposes usually includes all the local schools, colleges and universities, chambers of commerce and visitors bureaus, local newspapers and magazines, some local businesses and organizations, community leaders, and individuals who have requested to be placed on the list. If your library hasn't created a mailing list, you can build one yourself (preferably using a spreadsheet or e-mail client), or you can ask for help. Your chamber of commerce or economic council has the resources to generate mailing lists and labels. The software that the organization uses may allow it to limit the data by zip code or business type. Ask the organization if it can sell the data to you as a data file. You can then use the data on your own computers. At the very least, the chamber or council will be able to sell you the mailing labels.

As you build and maintain your database, look for ways to divide it into subsections. For example, do certain programs appeal to certain businesses or organizations in your service area? Can you identify associations, clubs, and businesses in your database that are frequently visited by seniors? If so, perhaps you can create a smaller database called "seniors." If you offer a dog-training workshop, does your database allow you to limit your search to pet stores and kennels? This feature would allow you to write an invitation for the program and include it with those mailings—either via e-mail or USPS—that you send to the pet stores and kennels. (Figure 11.3 is an example of an invitation to a library program.) You might also want to investigate a product such as Constant Contact (www.constantcontact.com) to help you manage your e-mail contacts and market your events via e-mail, Facebook, and Twitter.

Last, you will have to decide who gets what. For example, do you send your newsletter and flyers to everyone? Do you send flyers to everyone but the newsletter to only those who have requested it? Do you send multiple copies of your flyers to groups, such as colleges and recreation centers, that have agreed to post and distribute them? Time and experimentation will help you answer these questions. Also consider working with your web and IT folks to create a form on your events page that allows patrons to select topics that interest them via a drop-down menu. A bit of web development on the front end will result in your website doing a great deal of personalized marketing for you!

FIGURE 11.2 | **SAMPLE NEWSLETTER**

June 2011

Especially for **ADULTS**
I want to enrich my reading experience. Can the Library help?

Arvada

Thursday Night Book Group

7 p.m. June 9

Empire of the Summer Moon: Quanah Parker and the Rise and Fall of the Comanches, the Most Powerful Indian Tribe in American History by S.C. Gwynne

Family Movie Series

1 p.m. Saturday, June 11

Star Wars: Episode IV – A New Hope (PG)

Belmar

Thursday Night Book Group

7 p.m. Thursday, June 2

Orange Mint and Honey by Carleen Brice

Become a Garage Sale Wizard

1 p.m. Sunday, June 5

Garage sales, yard sales and estate sales can often net some serious profit for those putting them on and some great deals for those doing the shopping. In this workshop you'll learn about buying and selling, advertising, displaying items, setting prices and more.

Belmar Film Series Presents: Inside Job

5:30 p.m. Saturday, June 18

This is a free program. Seating is limited to 50 patrons.

Art wall

Lakewood Arts Council

Columbine

Tuesday Afternoon Book Group

2 p.m. June 7

Girl with the Dragon Tattoo by Steig Larsson

Colorado Screenwriter's Forum

7 p.m. Tuesday, June 14

Learn about the art of screenwriting with moderator Mark Krekeler and special guest speakers as they discuss various techniques in screenwriting. The group will have the opportunity to critique one screenplay. Reservations are not required. Space is limited, so arrive early.

Great Decisions

Nonproliferation

6:30 p.m. Wednesday, June 1

Is there any chance that sanctions will help to curb North Korea and Iran from continuing to develop nuclear weapons?

Crisis in the Caucasus

6:30 p.m. Wednesday, June 15

How does living in the shadow of Russia, Iran and Turkey influence the countries of the Caucasus today? How does the energy resources of the Caucasus play into their relations with the outside world?

Global Governance

6:30 p.m. Wednesday, June 29

How has an increasingly interconnected and shrinking world affect the viability of existing agreements and institutions worldwide? What economic, social, political and security concerns are on the agendas of intergovernmental bodies?

Source: Jefferson County (Colorado) Public Library

FIGURE 11.3 | **PROGRAM INVITATION**

Orland Park Public Library
14921 Ravinia Avenue
Orland Park, IL 60462

Friday. July 15
7:00-8:30 p.m.

You're cordially invited

A Fine Romance

Jewish Songwriters, American Songs, 1910–1965

Opening Reception

Featuring performances by the premiere interpreter of
the American Songbook, Peter Oprisko and his ensemble.
A special thank you to Ortigara's Musicville for support
with the grand piano. The reception will be sponsored by
The Great American Bagel and Panera Bread.

A Fine Romance: Jewish Songwriters, American Songs, 1910-1965 was developed by Nextbook, Inc., a nonprofit organization dedicated to supporting Jewish literature, culture, and ideas, and the American Library Association Public Programs Office. The national tour of the exhibit has been made possible by grants from the Charles H. Revson Foundation, the Righteous Persons Foundation, the David Berg Foundation, and an anonymous donor, with additional support from *Tablet Magazine: A New Read on Jewish Life.*
Image credit: The composers and leading ladies of South Pacific. Courtesy of Photofest.

Source: Orland Park (Illinois) Public Library

PRESS RELEASES

Press releases are used to relay your programming information to newspapers and radio and television stations. The sample press release in figure 11.4 was copied from ALA's website (www.ala.org). This sample prompts you for all the key ingredients of a press release: your library's letterhead, a catchy program title, a library contact person, and a "release" date. Many press releases have "For Immediate Release" written in bold letters right under the library letterhead. Others will have a time specified, such as "For Release After July 1." The release should be sent out at least two weeks before your program. Ideally, you will send your release to a particular contact person, or at least a particular department or office, at the newspaper or television station. Most newspapers and radio and television stations will run press releases free of charge. But expect the unexpected. An editor might cut words from your release. The radio station might run your releases this month but not next month. And the TV station might run the releases a little too far in advance this month and a little too close to the event next month. If you want more control over your publicity, please read the "Paid Advertising" section of this chapter.

PUBLIC SERVICE ANNOUNCEMENTS

Public Service Announcements (PSAs) are read on the air at television and radio stations. The key

FIGURE 11.4 | **SAMPLE PRESS RELEASE**

For release National Library Week
April 10–16, 2011
Contact: (name, title, phone number)

Celebrate National Library Week and Create your own story @ your library® at the [name of your library], April 10–16

(CITY, STATE)—Libraries are places for new beginnings. Whether you are getting your first library card, learning new computer skills or planning a trip, the library is the place where your story begins. This National Library Week, join our nation's libraries and librarians and Create your own story @ your library.

The [*name of library*] is celebrating National Library Week by [*describe programs, activities here*].

"Every day, libraries across the country are helping people create their own unique stories," says [*name and title of spokesperson*]. "Whether it is by opening a book and exploring distant lands, or by learning how to use new technologies to find a job, people at our library are creating new stories for themselves."

First sponsored in 1958, National Library Week is a national observance sponsored by the American Library Association (ALA) and libraries across the country each April.

For more information, visit the [*name of library*] at [*address*], call [*phone number*] or see the library's website at [*provide URL*]. Libraries' hours are [*list times*].

Source: American Library Association, www.ala.org

elements are very similar to those of the press release. PSAs differ from press releases in that they include the time needed to read them on the air, and they are written in language that appeals to the ear. The type itself should be easy to read. Consider typing the announcement in all capital letters. PSAs are also a free source of advertising, and the same adventures and inconsistencies apply to them as were mentioned with press releases. Sometimes your local cable station will invite *you* to read the PSA on the air. The four samples in figure 11.5 come from ALA's website (www.ala.org).

PAID ADVERTISING

Much of the publicity we've talked about so far—PSAs, press releases, mailings—can also occur as paid advertising. Why pay for it if you can get it for free? You are more likely to get what you want, when you want it, if you pay for it. Paid publicity allows you to determine when your PSAs and news releases will run. If you pay a newspaper to run your press release, you know that it will run the entire release, uncut. You can pay for an exact piece of advertising space in the newspaper of your choice. Let's say that you decide that you want a 3-by-5-inch space. You can create the text, the font types, and the graphics (including your library logo) that you want to run in that space. You can then send this information to the newspaper as a camera-ready press release, and the paper will run it as is. With paid advertising, you really do get what you pay for.

An advertising budget allows you to try such things as renting billboard space to promote your summer programs or renting the advertising space on the sides of buses to announce an upcoming film series. You can also conduct massive mailings. For example, you can work with a mailing house to send a letter announcing your spring programming lineup to every home within your library's zip code.

DIRECT PUBLICITY

Sometimes you can advertise your program in all three local papers and run off five thousand flyers and still have five people show up for the program. Why? Somehow you still didn't tap into your target audience. Perhaps the motorcycling enthusiasts didn't attend the "Motorcycling in the Rockies" program because this group just doesn't read the "Community" section of the newspaper. You need to make a more personal contact to target this group.

Direct publicity is usually done over the telephone. It should begin early in the planning process. The program committee or the program coordinator should identify those programs that might be a tough sell. The "How to Buy an e-Reader" program will have folks banging on your meeting room door. The "Know the Warning Signs of Alzheimer's Disease" program might need a publicity boost if it's going to attract the people who will benefit most from its message. Find a way to identify those programs that will need an additional publicity push. Comparing the program topic to the books you have on the subject is a good place to start. The circulation doesn't reveal the importance of the topic, but it does signify its popularity. People are attracted to the materials and programs that cover popular topics. Other topics might need a little extra promotion in order for them to get the attention that they deserve.

Once you've identified a program that will need additional publicity, assign someone the task of identifying groups or people in the area that might be interested in attending the program. Are you presenting a program on how to bike cross-country on a motorcycle? Are you concerned that the turnout might be low? If yes, then check your local, state, and national directories, such as the *Encyclopedia of Associations*, to see which motorcycling associations exist in your area.[1] You probably also have a local directory of clubs and societies. Does a nearby college offer a course on motorcycle repair? Check the phone book and do a

FIGURE 11.5 | **SAMPLE RADIO PSAS**

National Library Week 2011
Radio Public Service Announcements

:10

Celebrate National Library Week! Visit the [*name of your library*] this week to create your own story @ your library.

A message from the American Library Association's Campaign for America's Libraries and [*name of your library*].

:20

Public, school, academic, and special libraries help millions of Americans begin the next chapter in their lives every day. National Library Week is April 10–16. Celebrate today by visiting your library—in person or online—and create your own story @ your library.

A message from the American Library Association's Campaign for America's Libraries and [*name of your library*].

:30

Looking to start the next chapter in your life's story? Check out the resources available to you at your library. With tools to help you search for a new job, resources to help your kids with their homework and, of course, books to expand the horizons of your dreams—it's all free at your library. Celebrate National Library Week, April 10–16, and create your own story @ your library.

A message from the American Library Association's Campaign for America's Libraries and [*name of your library*].

:30

Looking for a place full of adventure and excitement that's educational too? Why not visit your library? It's the perfect place to discover new worlds and begin the next chapter in your life's story. This is National Library Week, so visit your library today—in person or online. Create your own story @ your library.

A message from the American Library Association's Campaign for America's Libraries and [name of your library].

Source: American Library Association, www.ala.org

quick Google search for motorcycle dealerships. Jot down the telephone numbers of the associations, clubs, businesses, and colleges that might be able to help you with your publicity efforts. This information needs to be gathered at least three weeks before the program.

Figure 11.6 shows a form that you can use when placing your calls. The form will give you some talking points to refer to as you describe your program over the telephone. It can also be filled out and then e-mailed, mailed, or faxed to the groups you have identified. If you are speaking to people on the telephone, be sure to ask them if they can promote your program to their students, customers, or members. The attendance at a particular program will go up dramatically if you can get a professor or club president to announce your program to his students or members. Also ask if the individual can distribute your flyers. If the answer is yes, e-mail an electronic copy or mail or fax the print flyers to that person's attention, or do both. Or, ideally, offer to hand-deliver any print flyers to your contact person.

ODDS AND ENDS

Sometimes the little things, like placing a stack of flyers at the checkout desk, count the most. So, without further ado, here's a list of miscellaneous things you can do to increase the likelihood that your patrons will notice and attend your program:

- Consider whether your program can be viewed as a human-interest story. Is a popular or intriguing community figure presenting the program? If so, write the human-interest story and submit it as a press release three weeks or so before the program.
- Place flyers at all service desks.
- Two or three days before the program, ask the circulation staff to include a flyer with the materials they check out to your patrons.
- Order some plastic stands that can vertically display a copy of your flyer.

- Place flyers in the library windows the day of the program. Write "Today!" across the tops of the flyers.
- Tweet about the program the day before or the day of the program (see chapter 10).
- Post a "teaser" podcast or video about the program on your website (again, see chapter 10).
- Announce upcoming programs during your introduction of the current program.
- Create a colorful banner for your program and hang it on the outside of your building.
- Write a review or summation of the program immediately after it occurs. Publish your comments on your events web page and in the library newsletter and consider sending the item as a press release to the local newspapers. This won't help the attendance at your program, but it might increase the attendance at the next branch that is offering the same program.
- If you audio recorded the program and took photos, get the podcasts uploaded to the Web and get your photos on Flickr ASAP—again, see chapter 10—because this might also increase attendance at the other locations that are offering the program.

NOTES FROM THE FIELD

Frequently, as I wrote this book, I turned to peers for advice, or just for a reality check, to make sure that I was on the right track. To hear from as many people as possible, I formed a virtual discussion group of librarians from around the United States and beyond who had an interest in or involvement with adult programming. When I was planning this chapter on publicity, I e-mailed group members and asked them what types of publicity they used in their libraries. Susan Akers—then a librarian with Anderson (Indiana) Public Library, now the executive director at Indiana Library Federation—responded with some

FIGURE 11.6 | **TALKING POINTS FOR DIRECT PUBLICITY**

Hello, my name is [*name*] and I'm a librarian at [*my library*]. Our library offers a variety of programs for children and adults. I'd like to tell you about an upcoming program.

Program title: _____

Presenter: _____

Of interest to: _____

Description of presentation (content, visuals, audience interaction—what the audience will see and hear):
_____

Why the library is offering this program: _____
_____
_____
_____

Locations hosting the program:
Library _____ Telephone _____
Address _____
Time: From _____ to _____ Day/Date _____

Library _____ Telephone _____
Address _____
Time: From _____ to _____ Day/Date _____

Library _____ Telephone _____
Address _____
Time: From _____ to _____ Day/Date _____

Library _____ Telephone _____
Address _____
Time: From _____ to _____ Day/Date _____

Library _____ Telephone _____
Address _____
Time: From _____ to _____ Day/Date _____

Library _____ Telephone _____
Address _____
Time: From _____ to _____ Day/Date _____

Tickets required: _____ YES _____ NO
For tickets, call the library at which you'd like to attend the program.
Library contact: _____ Phone: _____

extremely insightful comments. She also included a yearlong publicity calendar. The calendar struck me as a terrific idea. Both her comments and the calendar are included in figure 11.7 and figure 11.8.

In this chapter we've looked at some techniques we can use to get our programs noticed by our patrons. Over the course of eleven chapters we've explored policies, budgets, demographics, topics, target audiences, formats, performers, technology, and publicity.

It's getting very close to show time. We have a little time yet before the curtain rises. Let's move forward with our final preparations.

NOTE

1. *Encyclopedia of Associations: Regional, State, and Local Organizations* (Detroit, MI: Gale Research, published annually).

FIGURE 11.7 | **PUBLICITY TIPS**

Review your library logo. Is it old/outdated? Work with a professional designer to brainstorm a new look. Libraries need to break out of the stereotype of only promoting books in the design element of their logos. I wouldn't recommend having a logo-design contest, though. They aren't generally very good and make for poor community relations for the ones whose designs don't win!

Take a walk through the library with fresh eyes. Is the signage ragged/old-looking? The inside and outside of the facility should be neat and clean with no trash and should be as clutter-free as possible. Flyers, etc., should be placed in information racks or in plastic holders that keep them from blowing around and becoming litter in the building. Display areas should be used to promote various displays and stay interesting and exciting! We're a visually oriented society and as such enjoy looking at neat displays!

Renew relationships with local reporters, editors. This is one of your best resources to reach the community. Submit news releases (well written and according to standard guidelines) on a regular basis. They usually prefer it by faxing; don't generally call the reporters to see if "they received the news release." If you used the correct address and/or fax number, they received it. They may not always use it, but if it was sent in a reasonable time frame and is newsworthy and well written, they will be more apt to use it.

Try to participate in information fairs, home shows, senior events, etc., that give you a chance to promote the library "on the road" through being out in the public eye.

Source: Anderson (Indiana) Public Library

FIGURE 11.8 | **PUBLICITY CALENDAR**

JANUARY—Call or write to local service clubs, Rotary/Exchange/Optimist, etc., and get the director on the speaking circuit in the community. Create a display with books and videos promoting "New Beginnings" that focuses on New Year's resolutions (improve marriage communication/weight issues/finances/ stress management/physical fitness/slowing down/getting in control of one's life/ parent-teen communication). Invite a speaker on a popular topic.

FEBRUARY—Black History Month. Promote and celebrate culture/history. Create programming that will attract people that don't otherwise visit the library. Brainstorm for creative programming for April.

MARCH—Improve or build on relationship with your Friends group. Brainstorm activities and promotion of library for April's National Library Week. March (Women's History Month) is an excellent time to promote library resources on that topic. Travelogues on trips to New Zealand, Hawaii, Alaska, and Australia are always good this time of year. Find someone in your community, a retired teacher perhaps, with good speaking skills who has traveled and can discuss highlights of the trip as well as what to know about/plan for before the trip. We always have thirty to forty people at these types of programs.

APRIL—Invite your contact with the local newspaper to visit and write a story highlighting the community's use of the library. Thank your Friends during National Volunteer Week and hold a reception for them with punch and cookies, etc. This allows staff from various departments to bring cards and notes of thanks to the Friends for their work throughout the previous year.

MAY—Hold a gardening program (or can be done in late March or early April)—these types of "how to" programs always attract people.

JUNE—Book a traveling display that will be of interest to your community. The state's historical society usually has high-quality displays for loan.

JULY—Assess your library's signage, print material, flyers, etc. Are they left up past their date? Get rid of handwritten signs and use only computer-generated signs for a professional look. Your library's guide should be given out to every new library customer and be an overview of what the library offers, complete with phone numbers and short blurbs describing each department. Your print material should always look nice/professionally done with an up-to-date, exciting logo highly visible.

AUGUST—Make a list of community and/or church groups in your district to which you can submit short blurbs to promote the library services and/or events periodically. Send them things periodically! Try to work with local schools to be on hand for kindergarten sign-up at the schools. Parents can get kids their library card at the school's site that day also!

SEPTEMBER—Look for opportunities to piggyback with universities for speakers and authors. This can cut down costs and make speaker fees more affordable.

OCTOBER—Begin planning the following year's budget. Set aside budget money for promotional, inexpensive items, such as magnets, pens, and pencils. These go a long way—especially magnets with the library logo and phone number with hours.

Source: Anderson (Indiana) Public Library

Producing the Program

At last, finally, the time has come to host your program. Let's assume that as you begin this chapter, your program is about three weeks from today. There isn't much left to do. Someone (probably you) has taken responsibility for coordinating the program. A topic has been chosen. You've found a performer and agreed on the topic, fee, and format. You've chosen a location, date, and time. You've submitted the required paperwork, requesting publicity and the necessary equipment. During your planning for the publicity, you also decided whether you would require tickets or preregistration. Everything looks good and in order. Are we forgetting anything?

The Multnomah County Library produced the checklist included in figure 12.1. You probably completed the items in the "Two to Three weeks prior to program" section months ago. If you see any tasks here that still need to be done, you will have just enough time to complete them—even with only three weeks remaining—before the program occurs.

PRE-EVENT

The checklist in figure 12.1 pretty well covers all you need to do immediately before and during your program. Let me elaborate on a few of the other items included in the checklist. For some last-minute publicity ideas, please refer to chapter 11. Program evaluations will be covered in chapter 13. The speaker confirmation is the heart of this checklist. Try to call your speaker three weeks before the program occurs. This is your final chance to make sure that you and the speaker are on the same page. Verify all the dates, times, and

FIGURE 12.1 | **HOSTING A PROGRAM—CHECKLIST**

Program/Event Best Practices Checklist

TWO to THREE weeks prior to program

☐ Check Systemwide Programming MINTS site to see if a pdf flyer is available for the program

☐ Post pdf flyers promoting the program

☐ For branch locations, contact Lisa Canavan (x12345) if your program will involve using the outside lawn (to coordinate mowing and/or watering), will draw very large crowds (to coordinate additional cleaning if needed), or any other questions that you may have about the building.

☐ Contact Cindy Strasfeld (x98765) to request sound system, AV needs, etc.

ONE to TWO weeks prior to program

☐ Contact presenter/programmer to confirm directions, equipment and other arrangements. Let them know who will greet them if you won't be there that day.

☐ Review potential room setup; need to be sure all are available or ordered:

- Tables
- Chairs
- Name tags
- Sound system
- TV/VCR/DVD

- Projector
- Screen
- IT/computer services re: laptop, support drive access or other functions
- Other

☐ Photocopy any needed materials

ONE to TWO days prior to program

☐ Check AV/computer needs if the program requires these. Be sure all necessary cords are available, required software is loaded on laptops, batteries are charged, etc.

☐ Pull books/materials relating to the program topic for display during the program

Day of program

☐ Arrange book display on a table by the door

☐ Display @ your library flyers and other materials

☐ Provide program evaluations and pencils

☐ Provide bottled water for speakers/musicians

☐ Greet presenter/programmer

☐ Follow ticket system guidelines if using tickets

☐ Announce upcoming programs

☐ Introduce presenter/programmer

Source: Multnomah County (Oregon) Library

---

locations. Let him know that you will e-mail, fax, or mail the directions to him. Explain to him when and where he can collect his check. Many libraries like to pay the speaker after the performance. This practice gives the speaker an extra incentive to appear. This phone call is also your opportunity to verify all the speaker's needs. Make sure that you are clear on what equipment and technology he needs. Which pieces of equipment will the library supply? What equipment will the speaker bring with him? Will he bring his laptop and you will provide the computer projector and screen? Let the speaker know if he will be asked to use any assistive devices, such as the microphone to an FM personal hearing system. After you verify the equipment with the speaker, double-check to make sure that you have requested everything that is needed. What materials will the speaker distribute to the audience? Make sure that you are both in agreement as to who will make the photocopies. Will the speaker drop the originals by your library for you to copy?

Although you probably discussed the target audience with the speaker several months ago, you should briefly discuss the audience again on the telephone. The two of you should try to estimate the number of people who will attend the program. This estimate will help you decide how to set up for the program. Will you use auditorium-type seating, expecting a large audience, or will you set up the chairs in a circle, expecting a smaller, more interactive audience? Does the speaker want a table to himself? The room configuration can greatly affect the tone of the program. Circular seating, for example, sets the tone for a discussion, not a lecture.

By now the flyers for the program should be printed and available to the public. Let the speaker know that you can e-mail or mail him a copy. If you'll be mailing the flyer, ask him if he'd like several flyers to distribute to friends, clubs, and local businesses. Ask him if he would like you to introduce him. If he would, then ask him to give you two or three pieces of information about himself that he would like to have included in the introduction. Offer to e-mail or fax the introduction to him before the program occurs. You might want to wrap up the telephone call by informing him of anything that you think might affect him during the performance. Will you have an interpreter on hand? If yes, then let him know, only because he should know that he will be sharing the stage with someone else. (Also make sure that you call and verify the day and time of the program with the interpreter.) Will you serve refreshments? This can cause some commotion at the beginning of the program. If you decide to serve snacks, you should tell the speaker that there will be some conversations and networking among the audience before the program begins. Before you hang up, it doesn't hurt to let the performer know how much you and your patrons are looking forward to the program. Not all performers have experienced the enthusiasm of an audience of library patrons!

After your telephone call and before your program, you have a few loose ends to wrap up. You will be following through with your obligations to the speaker. You'll be sending library addresses and directions to him, along with copies of the event flyers. You'll be verifying equipment, including the necessary tables and chairs. Decide who will present the check to the speaker. In fact, verify that the check has already been drafted! Do you need to make any photocopies before the program? How's the speaker's introduction coming along? Have you sent him a copy?

If your program relies on the help of others, verify with these people as well. Give the sign language interpreter a call. Give your caterer a call to verify the delivery time of the lunches. Does the library staff have the information they need to explain the details of the program to someone on the telephone or in person? If your program has any special components, such as pre-registration or accompanying reading materials, then make sure that the staff understand how to register people and distribute the materials. If you are charging an attendance fee, let staff know the details about how the money will be collected. Decide whether you will accept checks and, if so, who the checks should be made out to. Can patrons pay online? If so, be sure that staff can talk patrons through this process. You can help your coworkers by typing up some instructions that will help them make the program a success.

Double-check your own schedule to make sure that you will be working the day or evening of the program. If not, then hopefully you can find a coworker who can introduce the speaker, set up a book display in the room, and distribute and collect the evaluations. Ideally, you will be able to give the introduction, the books, and the evaluation forms to your coworker in advance. And, finally, ask yourself whether you can do everything yourself the day of the program. Do you need someone to collect tickets while you make last-minute preparations with the speaker? Perhaps you should consider scheduling a library page or volunteer to work part of the program with you.

THE CONTINGENCY PLAN

What do you do if the performer cancels or, worse, just doesn't show up? Rather, what do you do after your initial hysteria subsides? In the literature I've read while writing this book, I've come across some authors who advise that the library have some backup plan in place. The implication in these articles and books seems to be that the program coordinator should actually have an alternate *program* ready, in the wings. This seems a bit farfetched. I just can't imagine finding an alternate performer who is willing to appear at each program in the event that the original performer cancels. It also seems unrealistic to expect a staff person to step in and improvise an entire program.

Having a contingency *plan* in place, however, is always a good idea. The same plan can then be used for all cancellations. If your library maintains a programming manual, then you could place this plan there for staff to locate in the event of a cancellation. Or you could introduce staff to the plan during a programming workshop. Whatever plan you devise, it will probably be relatively brief and straightforward. It could be as simple as:

1. Let the audience know that the program has been canceled.
2. If there is a reason, such as the performer's being ill, let the audience know.
3. Apologize.
4. Let the audience know if the program will be held at other locations soon.

5. If you have the staff to follow through, ask for the names and telephone numbers of the audience members. Tell them that you will call them and let them know if you can reschedule the performer at your location.

6. Tell the audience about upcoming library programs and events.

7. Offer to give them a tour of the library or take them to the materials in the library that relate to the program topic.

8. Apologize again.

SHOW TIME!

All your work is about to bear fruit. The few hours before the program will be spent with housekeeping tasks—setting up equipment, arranging tables and chairs, and so forth. You will probably set up a display of related library materials in the program's meeting room. You will set the program evaluations, flyers for upcoming programs, and other handouts on the chairs. (If you have not yet developed patron and staff evaluation forms, then you might want to jump ahead to chapter 13.) Walk around the branch and remind all the staff of the program and its room location. This information will help them field last-minute questions from patrons. As the start time approaches, you'll pour a glass of water for the speaker. A staff person will show people to the meeting room as they arrive. This staff person will also collect any tickets or admission fees.

When the speaker arrives show her the room setup. Remind her that you've written an introduction for her, and verify that she *does* want to be introduced. Many performers prefer to introduce themselves. If she wants to introduce herself, ask her if she could also point out the table of library materials to the audience. Also ask the performer to ask the audience to fill out their evaluation forms. If you do introduce the performer, point out the evaluation forms and materials beforehand and announce any upcoming library programs. Then introduce the performer and let her do her stuff.

Before we move on, let's pause a moment and enjoy the program. If you can attend the entire program, do it. Even if it involves rearranging your schedule or calling in a substitute, try to attend. Staffing situations probably will prevent you from attending all the programs that you coordinate, but at the very least, pop in and out of the room and catch what you can. The primary reason for doing so is to view firsthand the quality of the performer's presentation skills and the program's content. This experience will allow you to write a staff evaluation of the program. The secondary reason is far more personal: a library program is an incredible experience. Not only do you get to immerse yourself in the performance, you also get to witness the audience as they learn and laugh and listen to one another. Programs energize your audiences. They'll energize you, too. Sometimes we can get lost in the planning and the procedures. When you actively attend a program, you can't help but think, "Yeah, this is why we do this." Reward yourself. It'll keep you in touch with your desired outcome: quality programs for your patrons.

After the program, thank the performer and, if you have it, hand over the check! Write down the number of people who attended the program. Many libraries and branches submit program attendance figures in a monthly report. And last, if time permits, glance at the patron evaluation forms and write your evaluation of the program while it is still fresh in your mind.

WRAP-UP

There's not much left to do now. The big event is over. It's like waking up the day after hosting a New Year's Eve party. The room needs to be cleaned and set back to its original layout. At least with a New Year's party people send you thank-you cards. When hosting a library program, you are the one writing the thank-you cards. But it isn't so bad. Your performer did a terrific job, and a thank-you note is a sincere way to show your and your patrons' appreciation. You might even want to quote or paraphrase some patrons' comments to show how much the audience enjoyed the program. Confirm whether you are supposed to send these evaluation forms to your program committee or your programming or marketing office. If yes, put them in the interoffice mail. We'll have a closer look at evaluating programs in the next chapter, but first . . .

Pause . . . and take the time to congratulate yourself and those involved for a job well done.

Evaluating the Program

So, how did you do? Let's hear from you and your patrons. Gather up those audience program evaluations and look them over. They will help you determine whether the program was beneficial to your community. The staff program report—your evaluation form—will help determine whether the program was cost effective.

THE AUDIENCE EVALUATION

Let's begin with your patrons' perspectives. What did they tell you on the evaluations? What did you ask them? Most audience program evaluations seem to be a cross between a demographic questionnaire and a program evaluation. This approach makes sense. We want to know what our patrons thought about the program, yet we also want to know if the program reached its intended target audience. The trick is achieving a balance. If you ask too many demographic questions, such as a patron's age and sex, then you have less opportunity to ask questions about the program itself. And expanding the evaluation form won't help you. If it exceeds one page, people are much less likely to fill it out.

Most audience program evaluations contain a few key elements. They ask the patron to rate the content of the program. The patron can be asked to rate the content as "poor," "fair," "average," "good," and "excellent." Or, the patron might be asked to rate the content on a scale of 1 to 5. The audience program evaluation can also ask the patron to rate the performer on his skills or presentation style. The patron may also be asked to rate the accompanying materials, such as bibliographies and other resources. In order for you to learn which forms of publicity are effective, the evaluation should ask the patron how she learned about the program—through the library newsletter, the library website, a flyer, the newspaper, and so on. The evaluation should give the patron an opportunity to suggest future programming topics. You will also be surprised at the number of adult patrons that comment on the environment—the lighting, the seating, and the acoustics of the room. You might want to include a question that allows the patron to comment on the comfort level of the room.

We have begun to construct an audience program evaluation form that asks the patron some questions about the performer, the program's content, the publicity, and the meeting room. We haven't, however, asked the patron anything about herself. Do you want to know the overall age of the audience? Is it important to know if more men or women attended the program? Do you want to know which branches your audience visits most frequently? Perhaps you want to ask each patron if this is the first time he has visited the library. This question, for example, could help you determine if the program attracted first-time users to the library. Such questions help you determine if you've reached a particular target audience. Just remember that no one wants to sit and fill out a long questionnaire after a program. Try to keep it short. Ask the questions that are most important to you. In a moment, we'll explore how we can answer some of these demographic questions through the staff program report (instead of placing them on the evaluation that your patrons will complete).

Your best approach might be to distribute a paper evaluation immediately after the program that captures information about the program's content, the speaker, the effectiveness of the publicity, and any information you want to know about the attendee (such as age, sex, zip code, etc.). You will want to gather this information immediately after the program while the content and the speaker are still fresh in the mind of the attendee. But in order to measure whether your program brought people in the audience together, or whether it put attendees in touch with agencies or groups that heightened their sense of community, you will have to give attendees time following the program to make these connections. Let six

weeks or more pass. Then, to measure the program's impact on attendees' lives, you could send out a short survey a few weeks or months after the program that asks attendees to rate statements on a continuum from "strongly disagree" to "strongly agree." For example, your survey might say, "As a result of attending the 'Meet Your Neighbor' event at the library: (1) I feel more connected to my community. (2) I met new friends." The rating continuum for each statement could include "Strongly disagree / Disagree / Neither agree nor disagree / Agree / Strongly agree."

Be sure to explore whether technology can help you conduct this follow-up evaluation. If your library uses event software—see chapter 10—then you should definitely explore the options the software offers for registering patrons and collecting e-mail addresses from those who wish to provide that information. The event software may be able to push a survey out to attendees after a specified number of weeks or months have passed. Or you might want to go a bit more low-tech and just ask folks to write their e-mail addresses on a sheet of paper that is passed around the room during the program. You could then send a survey to that group of people at a later date. The point is to let some time pass and then ask people how the program has affected their lives.

By gathering this information from our patrons, we will better understand their preferences, and we will become even better at delivering programs that add value to their lives. And that, in turn, builds upon the library's role in the community as a place of culture and value. Let's take a look at Richland County (South Carolina) Public Library's evaluation form for parents in figure 13.1. Even though this survey is designed for children's programs, I have included it because it contains a great example of a question intended to gather information about whether the program has positively influenced the attendee's quality of life ("Since attending storytime, have you noticed your child having a greater interest in books or a larger attention span?"). Figure 13.2 provides another example of an audience evaluation form used at Palm Beach County (Florida) Library System.

FIGURE 13.1 | **AUDIENCE PROGRAM EVALUATION, EXAMPLE A**

Storytime at RCPL

RCPL GROWING READERS

Richland County Public Library
Parent's Evaluation

We would appreciate your comments about our storytime/children's program so we may continue making it a worthwhile, enjoyable program for you and your child.

We attended on (date) _____

Since attending storytime, have you noticed your child having   YES   NO
a greater interest in books or a larger attention span?

Did you find this program helpful in selecting library materials   YES   NO
for your child?

What information shared by staff in storytime did you find useful? _____
_____

What did you find most enjoyable? _____
_____

What would you suggest to make this program better? _____
_____

How did you find out about this program?   Library Staff   Calendar of Events
Newspaper/Media   RCPL Web Site   Online/Social Media   Friend
Other: _____

Had you used the library prior to this program? _____
_____

Additional comments/suggestions? _____
_____
_____

Yes! E-mail me about free library programs and services:

Please include your e-mail address: _____

Thank You!
www.myRCPL.com

(phone) 803.929.3434   1431 Assembly St.   (fax) 803.929.3448
                              Columbia, SC 29201   08/2011

Source: Richland County (South Carolina) Public Library

FIGURE 13.2 | **AUDIENCE PROGRAM EVALUATION, EXAMPLE B**

Adult Program Evaluation Sheet

Name of Program: _____

Library Branch: _____ Date: _____

Strongly Agree	Agree	Disagree	Strongly Disagree
4	3	2	1

1. I found the presentation interesting		4	3	2	1
2. The information presented was useful		4	3	2	1
3. There was adequate time for questions		4	3	2	1
4. I would like more programs on similar topics		4	3	2	1

I prefer programs held in the: ☐ evening ☐ afternoon ☐ morning ☐ weekdays ☐ weekends

How did you find out about this program? ☐ poster in library ☐ flyer ☐ *Happenings* (library newsletter) ☐ newspaper ☐ friend ☐ *Books & Bytes* ☐ Library website ☐ Other _____

I would attend programs on the following subjects: _____

_____

Comments? _____

_____

If you would like to receive our electronic newsletter "Books & Bytes," and a listing of upcoming programs, please complete the following:

Name: _____ E-mail: _____

The Friends of the Palm Beach County Library support adult and children's programs in the library. All members of the Friends have the library's newsletter and calendar of events, "Happenings," mailed to their home every month, with information about library programs throughout the Library System. Ask a staff member how you can join!

In accordance with the provisions of the ADA, this document may be requested in an alternate format. *07/10*

Source: Palm Beach County (Florida) Library System

THE STAFF PROGRAM REPORT

Ideally, the person who planned the program will be able to view all or part of it. If this isn't possible, try to schedule another staff person to at least pop into the program for a few minutes. Library staff know a quality program when they see one. And they recognize when things go off track. Their input is crucial if you are going to get a solid, overall view of the performer and the material she presents. They will relay this input by completing a staff program report.

Be sure to use your staff program reports to their best advantage. Some demographic-type questions can be placed on the staff program report instead of the audience program evaluation. For example, many audience evaluations ask patrons to mark their age range—"17 and under," "18–24," "25–39," "40–54," and "55 and older." Patrons are also asked to mark whether they are male or female. You can pose these questions to your audience and still end up with data that are difficult to use. For example, if you host a program that is targeted toward single moms, a staff person may have to sort through the audience evaluations and try to guess—based on the age and sex of the attendees—whether the program reached the target audience. You can probably obtain better data by having a staff member observe the audience. Construct your staff program report in a way that asks the right questions. For example, you can include a line on the staff report that asks the staff member to identify the target audience. The staff member can take a look around the room and then write a note or check a box stating whether the intended target audience was reached.

As you begin to create the document that will become your staff report, keep the following in mind. The report should combine several factors. It will summarize the patrons' responses to the program. It will include the staff person's comments about the program. It will document the amount of staff time and library resources spent on planning, promoting, and executing the program. Later, when you review these data, you will weigh factors such as the amount of time and resources that went into producing the program against the number of people who attended the program and their reactions to the performer and the content in order to determine whether you consider the program successful and cost-effective. I've included an example of a hard-copy staff evaluation form in figure 13.3 and an example of an electronic form in figure 13.4.

Programming is, in many ways, a collection development process. Just as staff determine the desirability of library materials, so they have the responsibility of determining the quality of library programs. Look at the staff program reports very carefully. Ask yourself many of the same questions you ask yourself when ordering or deselecting a book or video. Is the information accurate? Does the item/performer cover the materials it/he purports to cover? Most performers create wonderful programs that impress both the audience and the staff. Rarely do you get an inferior program. But when you do, you must then make the tough decision about whether you should ask the performer back or whether you should seek a replacement.

WHAT DOES IT ALL MEAN?

Now that you have collected the evaluations, it's a natural impulse to look them over carefully, perhaps share them with your coworkers, and then enter the data into a spreadsheet or file them snugly away in a three-ring binder called "Program Evaluations." They will stay untouched in that binder until the paper itself biodegrades. Please don't let these evaluations be looked at once and then fall into a void. It *is* a good idea to keep some type of file—three-ring or otherwise—that tracks programs. This file will consolidate information you have gathered from your patrons and staff. This file, whether on paper or in a spreadsheet, can track

FIGURE 13.3 | **STAFF PROGRAM REPORT (PRINT)**

STAFF PROGRAM REPORT

Program coordinator complete this section before sending to branch.

Program Coordinator for JCPL _____

Program title _____

Intended target audience _____

Program description (include length of program):

Publicity received from PIO _____

_____

Hours spent: planning _____   promoting _____

To be completed by branch staff

Name _____ Date _____ Branch _____

Publicity done by branch _____

_____

Branch setup time _____

Library Resources (list material used during program – book displays, videos, bibliographies):

Equipment (list equipment used and if there were any problems):

Number in audience: Adults _____   Teens _____   Children _____

Was intended target audience reached?   Yes   No

Audience evaluations/reaction:

Your comments:

Source: Jefferson County (Colorado) Public Library

FIGURE 13.4 | **STAFF PROGRAM REPORT (ELECTRONIC)**

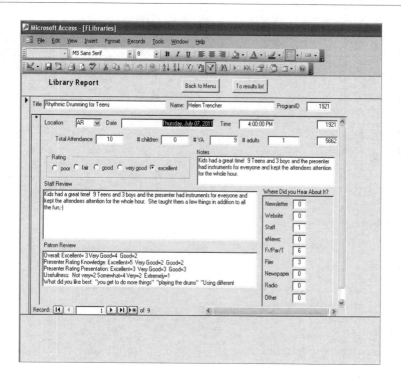

Source: Jefferson County (Colorado) Public Library

performers, what they do, how many patrons attended their performances, the cost, equipment needed, and excerpts from patron comments. A sample file, created in Excel, is included in figure 13.5. (If you store the data from your evaluations electronically, you might want to consider adding this information to the program database mentioned in chapter 2. This option will eliminate the need to maintain two separate electronic files.)

Another file or list that can be developed from the evaluation forms is a simple wish list from your patrons. Keep a list of what they say they would like to see as future programs. You will be surprised at how many clever ideas your patrons come up with.

And this list will help take some of the guesswork out of your future programming.

The staff and audience evaluation forms really are surveys. They can be powerful tools to refer to when you are seeking funding from your library foundation or any funding source. You can create a presentation that includes the number of people who attended your programs, opinions about the programs and performers, suggestions for future programs, and actual patron comments. Include a few comments in your presentation. Comments show your funders that they will be backing a winner when they contribute to future library programs.

FIGURE 13.5 | **PROGRAM EVALUATIONS SPREADSHEET**

Name	Address, phone, e-mail	Tax # or SS #	What they do	Avg. status	Attend.	Cost	Equipment	Comments
Dan Daniels	The Greasy Grill 123 Four St. Denver, CO 80220 (303) 111-1111 dan.daniels@greasy.net	000-11-2222	Holiday eating tips, nutrition, and controlling holiday binges	Request Approved	32	$125.00	None from the library	Positive reviews from both patrons and staff. "What a wonderful program to have during the holidays! Thank you!" Many patrons asked that the program be repeated next year. Enjoyed by a wide range of age groups (mix of men and women).
John Johnson	6 Seven Circle Castle Rock, CO 80104 (303) 222-2222 johnj@ victoriansojournprogram. com	123-45-6789	Victorian Sojourn	Request Approved	20	$125.00	None from the library	Rave reviews from patrons and staff. "Very delightful and informative and entertaining." Presenter used a number of props, costumes, cooking, etc. Patrons suggested that he come back for other programs. Enjoyed by a wide range of age groups (mostly female).
Patty Patterson	1234 Fifth Way Boulder, CO 80302 (303) 123-4567 ppatterson@poetry-programs.org		An evening with Patty Patterson	Request Approved	26	$0.00	Slide projector	Audience enthusiastic per staff evaluation. "A great way to promote poetry reading." Patron and staff requests for more programs on similar topics (i.e., author readings and/or signings).

NEGATIVE COMMENTS

Negative comments should be given just as much consideration as the positive comments. It is hoped your evaluation form will ask the questions that help you to determine the problem. Perhaps you can fix the problem before the same program is held again at another location. If a patron is offended by a program topic, handle the problem in a manner that parallels your reconsideration procedure for library materials. Provide the patron with a copy of your programming policy, offer her a comment card, let her explain her concerns about the program, and so on. Unless you are offering a photography workshop on the wonders of Mapplethorpe, you will probably never have a patron who pursues a complaint with a program. If it does happen, however, refer to your materials reconsideration process as a guideline. Because most programs occur once or just a few times and then disappear, the chances of someone lodging a formal complaint are fairly slim. Most people who pursue such things usually want an item removed from the collection. This result automatically occurs with a program: there is a performance, and then the event is over.

AT THE VERY LEAST . . .

Perhaps you don't have the time to hand out patron evaluations during the program and fill out staff reports afterward. At the very least, take a head count at each program. Write down the name of the program and the attendance. If at some point someone asks you for a status report, you can generate a simple document that lists the programs you have hosted and the attendance figures. You can use program attendance figures to create a variety of persuasive statistics. *Output Measures for Public Libraries* gives some guidance on how you can generate statistical data by using your program attendance figures.[1]

Reading evaluation forms can be a delight. It's like receiving a thank-you card after hosting a party. The responses are nearly always positive. The forms have a way of bringing you full circle. You see which programs were huge successes, and you get suggestions for future programs. And this feedback gets you to thinking about what you will offer next. The planning begins anew.

NOTE

1. Nancy A. Van House et al., *Output Measures for Public Libraries*, 2nd ed. (Chicago: American Library Association, 1987), 71–72.

Looking toward the Future of Adult Programming

Before I started writing the first edition of this book, I posted a message to the electronic mailing list PUBLIB.[1] I asked my peers to tell me what they would like to see included in a book on adult programming. They gave me many wonderful suggestions. One particularly interesting suggestion was to include some information on where adult programming was headed in the future. Prognosticating the future sounded like fun, so I decided to work this aspect into the book. Knowing, however, that I did not possess any exceptional divination powers, I thought of again turning to my peers for help.

The days when we could submit raw data such as door counts or books checked out or reference questions asked (and, it is hoped, answered!) seem to have passed. Libraries must now demonstrate that they add value to their communities. Librarians now measure things in terms of outcomes and output. We don't merely count the number of people that attended a program, but we ask people if they feel more connected to their community as a result of, for example, attending a series of programs designed to link people with volunteer work that aligns with their personal goals and interests. So, in the coming years, we must find new ways to demonstrate the value that library programs can bring into our patrons' lives.

> When I think of the next 5–10 years, my thinking is not so much about "what" and "how" but "why." I personally believe that adult programming should be a core service much like children's programs, reference, and others [have] been for many decades. Many people still think of it as an extra service and as a result they do not put the resources needed into it and it gets cut when times are hard. Libraries don't need to put major resources behind adult programs to make them successful, they just need

to change their thinking about why they are providing them and how they can go about it. We did over 100 programs last year with a budget of less than $5,000. So our commitment was more about philosophy, energy, and priority than finances.

More library personnel and administrators need to recognize the intrinsic value in providing adult programs. The programs we've been doing for the last three years have really changed how our community views and interacts with the library. I believe the biggest change to providing adult programs in libraries in the future is not funding, partnerships, topics, or any of these things, but a fundamental change in attitude and perception. Adult programs are not something we could do, but something we should do. I would like to see people coming out of library school with specialties in adult services the same way we have turned out youth services specialists for years now. I would like to see in more libraries the kind of excitement in providing adult programs as I see in summer reading programs. Think of this: there once was a time when preschool storytime was a new service. Now it is expected and valued by nearly every public library in the country. I believe that if libraries want to remain valuable to their communities and meet the diversity of needs of adults, the day needs to come when adult programs will enjoy the same support, rank, and enthusiasm as other core services. —Jennifer Baker, St. Helena (California) Public Library

Everyone agrees that funding will be challenging for the foreseeable future. To continue to provide quality programming, we will need to pursue relevant grant opportunities and work collaboratively with neighboring libraries and organizations to pool and optimize resources. The recovering economy and transitioning job market will also affect the types of programs that we offer our patrons as we look for ways to assist them through the transitions in their lives.

Library funding will be shared by creating consortia, grants, and sharing resources. For example, the Louisiana State Library has created a model program called "Louisiana Libraries: Connecting People to Their Potential." It will provide job skills and training at 68 public libraries throughout the state, and patrons may register online or by a toll free number. Computer skills are vital to a job search. Many jobs are only found online, and some employers only look online for resumes. To quote from Andrew Reiner's article "Nail That New Job!" in *AARP: The Magazine*, "If you are not online, you will not be noticed, or it will be assumed you are behind the times."[2] — Mimi Nothacker, St. Tammany Parish Library, Covington, Louisiana

Library programming has always relied on partnerships. We've always turned to our local colleges and associations for potential speakers and performers. And during these tough economic times, partnerships have become even more vital as we strive to continue offering valuable programs for our patrons but with diminishing resources. Libraries will continue to look for opportunities to collaborate and share with other organizations to ensure that we have the expertise, venues, publicity, and funds needed to create programs that contribute to the health and success of our communities.

We've tried to do a lot of adult programming here at the Austin Public Library on a shoestring budget. We have benefited greatly by community partnerships especially since we have the University of Texas (UT) in town. We have worked on joint programs with the UT Humanities Institute (guest discussion leaders for our Mayor's Book Club events and cosponsorship of film series), Texas Performing Arts (brown bag Q&A lunches in library locations with the casts from various Broadway Across America productions and other events), UT Harry Ransom Center (library book clubs read Poe's works in conjunction with an HRC Poe exhibit), and various other UT departments like the Polish Film Festival that we had in our branches cosponsored by the Polish study society on campus. We've partnered with the local Community College on their Big Read project. Community groups such as the Literacy Coalition of Central Texas have also partnered on special programs. So adult programs continue on primarily through community partnerships and I suspect that many of those will continue. So the future will probably depend on continuation of community partnerships that have made a great deal of adult programs at the library possible. They also have provided staff with energy and inspiration. It also shows how support of arts and cultural institutions throughout the community multiplies the possibilities for public libraries to connect our mission with the larger mission of building, disseminating, and preserving all of our cultural resources. —Tom Moran, Austin (Texas) Public Library

New target audiences will emerge in the future. As our communities shift, we will welcome new residents, and some of these residents will bring new languages and cultures with them. And we will design programs that appeal to them. Our boomers will become seniors, and we will offer programs on topics that appeal to them, too. We will also have to ensure that we are delivering the content in ways—clear and crisp fonts, amplified sound, enlarged images—that ensure that our boomers can see and hear and enjoy these programs that we develop with them in mind.

At our library, the Plymouth District Library, Plymouth, Michigan, we have made a point

of improving our services to our low-vision patrons. Demographic statistics show that low vision (i.e., vision loss which can no longer be improved by correction of glasses) is significant in the senior population. Of course, seniors have long been an important component of our audience and many longtime users do develop vision problems. We have already presented several programs directed to a general audience, explaining low vision services and technology that are available at the library or in the general community. The programs were well-received and then led to our creation of a monthly "INFO Session," facilitated by a librarian (me) and featuring presentations by experts on a wide variety of topics of interest to seniors with vision loss. It is my hope that more libraries will see this topic as a valid one for adult programming as there is much information to be had that most ophthalmologists do not address with their patients. One of these days, I hope to write a "how-to" article for publication in order to spread the word of the need for this programming! —Ellen Stross, Plymouth (Michigan) District Library

Libraries and librarians have always embraced and integrated emerging technology into our work and services. What we know is that technology keeps evolving, and our patrons turn to us to both adopt this technology and help them learn to use it. It's no surprise then that your peers had a lot to say about the role that technology will play in the future of adult programming.

I think we'll continue to use more technology for programming. For instance, a regional library hires an online speaker or performer, and each branch receives it, live and interactive, for their audience. The audience and performer can both see and hear each other. Maybe state- or national-level consortiums will subscribe to programming, both educational and other types, in this way. —Mary Beth Conlee, Burlington (Washington) Public Library

We will certainly use technology to promote as well as expand the reach of adult programming . . . We can now do podcast teasers for programs, tweet before the program, and post pictures after the program on Facebook, and even capture the program as kind of a digital workshop and stream it from the website or even catalog it and upload it to OverDrive's community collection. Major events receive prominent "ad" space on our website's home page, and the online calendar feeds upcoming events to the home page.

We are blending programs with library technology whenever possible—such as incorporating the use of our Digital Archive with live programs and workshops which celebrate local history, scrapbooking, etc. We also try to link programs with library resources whenever possible, including digital resources. For example—we recently offered a program that dealt with volunteers for the Haiti relief effort, and we cross-promoted our new addition to the Mango Languages database that teaches Haitian Creole. It is the same concept as having the books on a particular topic on display before, during and after the program.

We might push for the online book club to complement our regular book clubs.

As a subject, technology will certainly remain of keen interest to our community, who regularly attend our free computer/technology classes. Even our new bookmobile can offer small technology classes. —Mary Hurlbert Stein, East Baton Rouge Parish Library, Baton Rouge, Louisiana

TOPICS OF THE FUTURE

I love hearing other librarians predict which topics will be popular in the future. A lot of folks mentioned that people would continue to ask for programs and classes that assist them in developing and maintaining their computer and technology skills. The job market will continue to shift, and as some career fields, such as those in industry, shrink or disappear, patrons will appreciate programs and workshops that will help them develop skills needed in emerging careers. Many people also thought that patrons will look to us for opportunities to explore and learn and experience new things throughout their lives. Patrons will particularly welcome interactive programs. So how-to programs where people can learn a new dance or practice with watercolors will remain popular and continue to fulfill our needs as humans to continually learn and grow.

> The demand for job skill classes is almost unmeetable. I anticipate ever more money from the traditional "book & print" budget being funneled into programming. In fact, I tell my practicum students from the University that the best thing I can do for them is give them programming experience. The library is (has) morphed into a job/computer center with entertainment/education as a bonus (IMHO). —Liz Dannenbaum, Middleton (Wisconsin) Public Library

Overall I think what will be of interest will vary from community to community. Technology and life skills classes will always have a place in libraries. However, I think most libraries should be looking for opportunities to meet more cultural needs. Our library does a variety of programs (2–3 a week) for adults. The most popular have been cultural in nature (music, dance, lifestyle, film, food, art, etc.). We have also worked on forming partnerships with the local community college, senior center, chamber of commerce, etc. and have hosted programs at various places throughout the community in addition to doing things on site. —Jennifer Baker

As a subject, technology will certainly remain of keen interest to our community, who regularly attend our free computer/technology classes. Even our new bookmobile can offer small technology classes. We are also seeing more community "living room" type programs . . . casual programs which allow adults (or teens) to come and go. —Mary Hurlbert Stein

As I've mentioned before, libraries are now being asked to demonstrate how they add value to their communities. Fortunately, we also now have the technology at our disposal—see chapter 10—that allows us to learn much more about the demographics and interests and habits of the people in our neighborhoods and communities. We can use this knowledge to develop programs that contribute to the overall health and well-being of our patrons. We should also develop evaluation techniques that ask our patrons whether these programs have created opportunities or made connections or provided information that resulted in improvements in their lives. In the future we will want to be sure that we are conversant in both the demographics and the habits and preferences of our community members, and we will want to be able to demonstrate how our programs result in making our patrons feel more productive and connected in their communities.

Utilization of evidence-based evaluation tools for all programming that demonstrates a focus on demographics, patrons' interests, the performer's presentation skills, and suggestions for new programming will become essential. —Carol Ann Attwood, Patient and Health Education Library, Mayo Clinic, Scottsdale, Arizona

Library staff must evaluate their programs regularly by listening carefully to patrons and having them occasionally complete questionnaires to measure and demonstrate their value. Their responses will help us design new or alter existing programs. —Mimi Nothacker

So that's what your peers see as they look to the future. What do you see as you rub your chin and anticipate where your programming path will lead your library in the years to come? I wish you the very best as you begin planning *your* programming future! To help you with this planning, part 2 of this book tosses a few ideas your way. These programs have been road tested—from your peers to you. Have fun!

NOTES

1. WebJunction, *PUBLIB Electronic Discussion List*, resourcesharing.webjunction.org/publib.
2. Andrew Reiner, "Nail That New Job!" *AARP: The Magazine*, March/April 2011, 58–62.

PART II

A Collection of Five-Star Programs

Your peers have given the following programs their seal of approval. I asked around for examples of excellent library programs for adults. These are the responses. Think of these programs as recipes: modify them to your patrons' tastes, alter the portions to fit your budget or your level of staffing, and then serve them up to your patrons. Bon appétit.

Evenings Upstairs @ your library: Culinary Tourism in Kentucky
McCracken County (Kentucky) Public Library

Description of Program

The program began with Dun Manus kicking off the event with Celtic music in celebration of St. Patrick's Day. This musical duo—led by a Western Kentucky Community Technical College professor—shared a bit of Irish history and entertained the audience with traditional tunes.

Chef Albert Schmid, Le Cordon Bleu Master of Arts and author of *The Kentucky Bourbon Cookbook*, provided a multimedia presentation on the development of Kentucky cuisine, placing several dishes in historical perspective. A lively Q&A session preceded his talk.

Door prizes of *The Kentucky Bourbon Cookbook* and a basket of shamrocks were awarded to lucky attendees. The programs were free and open to the public. Both programs were videotaped to air on educational Comcast Cable Channel 7, MCLIB TV, reaching thousands.

Target Audience

Adults of all ages, culinary arts students, foodies, and Kentucky history buffs

Partner Organizations

The Kentucky Humanities Council, The Friends of the Library, and Western Kentucky Community and Technical College

Cost

$530 (lodging for Chef Albert Schmid, Kentucky Humanities Council [KHC] Speakers Bureau presenter: $70; refreshments: $60; advertising: $400)

Number of Staff Persons Needed

Plan the Program: One

Promote the Program: Two—One Program Coordinator and one PR Assistant to provide press release and promotions

Produce the Program (set up the room, introduce the speaker, distribute and collect evaluations, create displays in meeting room, etc.): Three—Program Coordinator makes introductions, acts as host, distributes evaluations, and is responsible for KHC report; Technology Coordinator provides technology setup in community room, does video production, and is responsible for MCLIB TV coordination; Video Assistant edits the program for cable television.

Hours Spent

Planning: 3; Promoting: 4; Producing: 4

Publicity Methods

Friends of the Library newsletter and e-mail news release, library website, Facebook, flyers, press release, bookmarks, Public Radio paid advertisements, local newspaper calendar listing, County Convention and Visitors Bureau calendar, fax listing, Educational Access TV Channel, Paducah Parenting and Family, mailings

Accompanying Library Resources

(types of books, videos, etc., used to create displays)

First- and second-floor staff prepared March displays of fiction and nonfiction books, CDs, and videos by Irish poets and writers, as well as materials on Irish culture and history, including St. Patrick's Day.

Equipment and Technology Used

The community room is equipped with seating for 100, microphone, laptop and projector, screen, video equipment, and tables.

Refreshments Served?

Yes (Irish soda bread, snacks, drinks)

Average Attendance

35

Audience Evaluations/Reactions to Program

The live music and Irish food set a festive tone. The speaker was informative while captivating the audience with his food travels. The program emphasized the unique culture and heritage of Kentucky. The program engaged diverse participants and encouraged the visitors to attend other library programs and events. It was a good opportunity to partner with organizations leading to future endeavors. We received positive feedback regarding the program.

> "These evenings are one of a kind experiences, in-the-flesh, live—that we could not otherwise enjoy if they were not being furnished by our library."
>
> "Enjoyed the presenter's story of how he came to write the Kentucky cookbook and developed such recipes as the angels share biscuits."
>
> "The Irish soda bread was great!"
>
> "Thank you for Thursday Night at the library."
>
> "What is next in program lineup?"

Who Shot the Librarian? A Centennial Mystery (2010)
Death of a Diva: A Twinsburg History Mystery (2011)
Twinsburg (Ohio) Public Library

Description of Program
An interactive mystery evening of entertainment, performed on two nights after the library closed for the day. Guests enjoyed catering of a full spread of appetizers, nonalcoholic drinks, and desserts, then watched a twenty-minute scene performed by the eight characters. After questioning the characters, guests turned in their guesses, and then watched the resolution of the mystery.

Target Audience
Adults

Partner Organizations
Red's Place—local restaurant (provided catering); Mavis Winkle's, Blue Canyon, Fresh Start Diner—local restaurants (provided door prizes); several authors donated signed copies of their books for the silent auction on Friday night, including Louise Penny, Karin Slaughter, Joanne Fluke, Elizabeth George, and M. C. Beaton.

Cost
$12 per person paid directly to Red's Place, plus approximately $300 for other costs

Number of Staff Persons Needed
Plan the Program: One main person with help from four others
Promote the Program: Two
Produce the Program (set up the room, introduce the speaker, distribute and collect evaluations, create displays in meeting room, etc.): Seven staff members plus seven volunteer actors and a volunteer director

Hours Spent
Planning: 20; Promoting: 6; Producing: 25

Publicity Methods
Advertisement on our website, library electronic mailing lists, Facebook, and blog; in-library flyers and inclusion in our bimonthly events sheet; promotion on electronic sign in front of library

Accompanying Library Resources

(types of books, videos, etc., used to create displays)

If desired, you could easily do a display of mystery novels and true crime, along with accompanying DVDs and audiobooks.

Equipment and Technology Used

Stage and lighting, HD camera to record DVD (already owned by the library)

Refreshments Served?

Yes (see above)

Average Attendance

110 was the cap, with a waiting list of 10

Audience Evaluations/Reactions to Program

Patrons loved our 2010 Centennial mystery so much, we wrote and produced a new mystery for 2011. We do not do a formal evaluation, but the comments we have received have been extremely positive. We plan to write a new mystery for 2012 as well. If you do not have a writer on staff, mystery plays can be bought from sources online. The DVD of our show is available to check out in the library as well.

What's Underneath Candlewood Lake?

New Milford (Connecticut) Public Library

Description of Program

Ray Crawford, experienced diver, will present his discoveries after 25 years of diving Connecticut's largest man-made lake.

Target Audience

Adults

Partner Organizations

None

Cost

$25 for food

Number of Staff Persons Needed

Plan the Program: One

Promote the Program: Two

Produce the Program (set up the room, introduce the speaker, distribute and collect evaluations, create displays in meeting room, etc.): One

Hours Spent

Planning: 1; Promoting: 3; Producing: 4

Publicity Methods

Press releases, bulletin boards surrounding libraries, Library newsletter, website, and in-house display

Accompanying Library Resources

(types of books, videos, etc., used to create displays)

The display cabinet had a selection of the items Ray has discovered. This was a part of our One Book, One Community read, so the books for the program were the only ones on display.

Equipment and Technology Used

Digital projector, laptop, PowerPoint software

Refreshments Served?

Yes

Average Attendance

94

Audience Evaluations/Reactions to Program

We are offering an updated version this April due to the popularity of this program.

Meet, Learn, and Discover Series
Norfolk (Virginia) Public Library

Description of Program

Norfolk Public Library (NPL) has partnered with AARP Virginia to offer a series of programs targeted at the 50 and older audience. Programs are offered on the third Wednesday of the month, and they offer participants an opportunity to come together to hear a presentation and meet other people. The Meet, Learn, and Discover (MLD) Series was created for an Age in America grant that NPL received from the Libraries for the Future organization. The grant will be depleted by the end of 2011, and we plan to continue the program using library funds. In the beginning, AARP was heavily involved with topic selection, and they provided refreshments. AARP is now primarily a sponsor in name only, and they continue to assist in some program topic selections.

Target Audience

All adults, but it is mainly for the 50 and older audience. We do have several adults who bring their parents to the program.

Partner Organizations

AARP Virginia, Age in America Grant

Cost

Depending on topic, speaker, and publicity materials, anywhere from $50 to $200

Number of Staff Persons Needed

Plan the Program: We have a committee of four people who develop the schedule of programs.
Promote the Program: One—Public Relations Coordinator
Produce the Program (set up the room, introduce the speaker, distribute and collect evaluations, create displays in meeting room, etc.): One or two, depending on program

Hours Spent

Planning: 5; Promoting: 5; Producing: 5

Publicity Methods

Flyers; E-Newsletter blast sent to participants who have signed up to receive updates about the MLD program; postcards sent to participants a week in advance; information posted on NPL's website and online events calendar; information posted on the digital screens at the Pretlow Anchor Branch Library, which is the location for the programs. We take out a full-page ad in our local paper's city section magazine, called the "Compass."

This is done in coordination with the City of Norfolk's Communication Department, and the price is reduced drastically. By far, this method of advertising has been the most successful.

Accompanying Library Resources

(types of books, videos, etc., used to create displays)

We provide library information about upcoming programs at each event. We do not set up any elaborate display, unless it is a program that requires it.

Equipment and Technology Used

Presenters can use our computer system and projector as needed.

Refreshments Served?

When we first started the program, AARP provided a fruit, cheese, and cracker tray. We no longer serve refreshments because AARP was not able to continue funding it.

Average Attendance

The attendance varies a lot. We have had anywhere from two to one hundred people attend. It has been interesting to see which program topics have been successful. Our most successful topics have been on history, genealogy, decorating your home, and travel.

Audience Evaluations/Reactions to Program

We have a steady group of about ten people who attend almost all the programs. Participants often comment that they enjoy coming out every month and learning something new.

Kickoff Storytelling Festival

Newport News (Virginia) Public Library

Description of Program

The Newport News Public Library presented the program series What's Your Story? Share it at your Library! from January 10 through June 6, 2009. The program series encompassed a broad understanding of storytelling, as well as different funding sources and Library departments, with the goal to inspire and teach a cross-section of Newport News residents to share their "story" in a variety of media. It included storytelling performances, workshops, and presentations. The series began with the Kickoff Storytelling Festival on January 10, 2009: Presentations by leading professional storytellers Valerie Tutson and Kim Weitkamp and by StoryCorps, a national nonprofit organization that records the stories of everyday Americans and encourages listening to personal stories, to inspire residents. Weitkamp set the stage for later workshops by teaching participants how to choose and cultivate their own stories.

Target Audience

Adult and teen residents of Newport News

Partner Organizations

StoryCorps

Cost

$2,661

Number of Staff Persons Needed

Plan the Program: Two—the library system's Community Relations and Program Coordinator and Special Projects Officer, who worked in consultation with a committee of the Library's Board of Trustees

Promote the Program: Two—the Library System's Community Relations and Program Coordinator and Special Projects Officer

Produce the Program (set up the room, introduce the speaker, distribute and collect evaluations, create displays in meeting room, etc.): Five—the Library System's Community Relations and Program Coordinator, Special Projects Officer, Administrative Assistant, Library Branch Manager, member of the Library's Adult Programming Committee

Hours Spent

Planning: about 40; Promoting: about 20; Producing: about 20

Publicity Methods

The series of programs was promoted through news releases, mass e-mails to city employees, posts on the library system's website, online calendars, and a paid radio advertisement. It was also publicized through printed bookmarks, posters, flyers, and brochures, which were available in the libraries and passed out at other library programs. Brochures and posters also were displayed throughout the community in waiting areas at schools, other city departments, doctors' offices, car repair shops, stores, churches, and community organizations. A large banner was displayed on a busy city overpass. The library system worked with the Newport News Public Schools to distribute materials to students and post announcements on their website and electronic signs.

Accompanying Library Resources

(types of books, videos, etc., used to create displays)
None

Equipment and Technology Used

Chairs, tables, flip charts, writing instruments, paper, overhead projector, laptop, CD player

Refreshments Served?

Yes (bottled water)

Average Attendance

60

Audience Evaluations/Reactions to Program

Participants were asked to fill out evaluation sheets and make comments and suggestions about the programs. Evaluations were overwhelmingly positive, with patrons giving the programs high marks for quality of the presenters, enjoyment, and educational value.

Comments included:

"It is a great review of our lives and instills a strong desire to appreciate what you have."
"I believe that storytelling is a powerful tool and this kind of program is invaluable to the community."
"The Library is providing a very vital service in such a program. It helps us to assess ourselves and also our place in our community."
"This program made me think about the value of every person's story."

Anime Night at the Library

Mid-Manhattan Library, New York (New York) Public Library

Description of Program

A monthly screening of dubbed anime films, this program takes place on the first Wednesday of every month. Initially, screenings started at 8:00 p.m. (the library is open until 11:00 p.m. four nights a week), but they have recently started earlier at 7:00 p.m. This was by viewer request and in hopes that it would attract a greater audience at an earlier time. A pretty straightforward movie program, FUNimation Entertainment provides the DVDs via their Operation Anime website (www.operationanime.com). We tried initially to include repeat viewers in deciding which anime would be selected ahead of time, but they are generally happy with whatever series we pick. DVDs are generally raffled off or given to repeat attendees as an incentive to come back to future screenings.

Target Audience

Adults, primarily in their early to mid-20s

Partner Organizations

FUNimation Entertainment (www.funimation.com)

Cost

Free

Number of Staff Persons Needed

Plan the Program: One, with the support of the library's programming committee
Promote the Program: One
Produce the Program (set up the room, introduce the speaker, distribute and collect evaluations, create displays in meeting room, etc.): One. This person also sets up the multimedia equipment for the screening, briefly introduces the film, and provides handouts/information on other late night programming.

Hours Spent

Planning: 1; Promoting: 2; Producing: 1

Publicity Methods

The library's programming committee, nicknamed "NYPL at Nite" because most of the programs take place in the evening, has several social networking outlets set up. Facebook and Twitter pages were set up for the express purpose of advertising and promoting programs, and Anime Night has had a presence on these websites since it began. The library's website has information on each individual screening, as well as a blog that was produced after a few screenings took place. Events on Yelp and MySpace have also been infrequently produced to attract a broader audience. Original flyers, designed by another committee member, are also used and displayed.

Accompanying Library Resources

(types of books, videos, etc., used to create displays)
Manga displays have accompanied most anime nights; if the library owns a manga equivalent of the anime being shown, this is of course highlighted. It is usually communicated to patrons that the library has an extensive collection of manga books and anime DVDs and where these materials are outside of the programming space.

Equipment and Technology Used

A DVD player, digital projector, and projection screen are used. Before a DVD player was purchased, we used a laptop with DVD playing capability instead. This equipment is used for other film screenings and programs that take place in the library at night.

Refreshments Served?

No

Average Attendance

18

Audience Evaluations/Reactions to Program

It has been generally favorable. At least ten of the individuals have been to more than one screening. There is always an influx of new people, and many older patrons who are unfamiliar with anime will sit and watch at least one episode to see if they like it. There are about five patrons who come to every single screening and have developed a camaraderie and friendship as a result.

WomanLore: Performing Women in History
Lake Bluff (Illinois) Public Library

Description of Program
WomanLore brings to life powerful women of bygone eras through a complete theatrical experience with authentic costumes that accurately evoke the era in which each woman lived. Betsey Means is a professional actress dedicated to portraying women whose contributions have been forgotten or overlooked: Alicia Appleman-Jurman, Gertrude Bell, Agatha Christie, Mother Jones, Mary Kingsley, Juliette Kinzie, and Elizabeth Cady Stanton.

Target Audience
Teens and adults with an interest in women, history, live performances, and entertainment

Partner Organizations
None

Cost
$290

Number of Staff Persons Needed
Plan the Program: One—Program Coordinator

Promote the Program: One—Program Coordinator e-mails the information to all of the area newspapers in print and online and to local schools and village websites. She also creates flyers to display in the library and nearby public buildings.

Produce the Program (set up the room, introduce the speaker, distribute and collect evaluations, create displays in meeting room, etc.): The performer, Betsey Means, sets up the room and introduces herself while in character. One staff member greets patrons at the program room door and helps with seating.

Hours Spent
Planning: 1; Promoting: 4; Producing: 1.5

Publicity Methods
Information sent to newspapers and local websites, flyers displayed in library and community

Accompanying Library Resources

(types of books, videos, etc., used to create displays)

Biographies, memoirs, and autobiographies of women are displayed near the circulation desk to promote the program and the nonfiction books.

Equipment and Technology Used

None. Performer brings everything she needs. Chairs are set up for attendees and a small table holds refreshments.

Refreshments Served?

Yes (bottled water, prepackaged cookies/crackers)

Average Attendance

20 (We are a small library in a town of 6,000 with a collection of about 50,000 materials.)

Audience Evaluations/Reactions to Program

At the end of the program, attendees enthusiastically ask questions of the performer about her character and herself. She now has a following at our library and before they leave, patrons want to know when she will be returning to portray another character. Attendees comment to the hostess as they leave the program room.

Estate Planning
Arapahoe (Colorado) Library District

Description of Program

It's never too early to begin estate planning. This informative session gives an overview of what you need to know. Distribute your estate according to *your* wishes. This program is led by Natalie Decker, an attorney with more than thirteen years' experience in this field.

Target Audience

Adults and seniors

Partner Organizations

A local law office that handles estate issues

Cost

Free

Number of Staff Persons Needed

Plan the Program: One—Adult Program Specialist

Promote the Program: A minimum of three people. The program specialist wrote the description, the Communications Department staffer entered all the program descriptions on the print material, and the Web Librarian highlighted the program on the district's website. Then staff at each of the three libraries where this program was held talked it up with their patrons.

Produce the Program (set up the room, introduce the speaker, distribute and collect evaluations, create displays in meeting room, etc.): One person at each library acted as host for the program, and as such, had the responsibility for this part. Hosts called the presenter two weeks prior to the program to check on any needs or issues, created a display, pulled books for patrons to check out, and so on.

Hours Spent

Planning: 4; Promoting: about 3; Producing: 2

Publicity Methods

Our district monthly newsletter, our web page, and web calendar. Also, the Publicity Coordinator sent press releases to local newspapers, both city and smaller community papers.

Accompanying Library Resources

(types of books, videos, etc. used to create displays)

A list of books/DVDs and a list of display ideas (including pictures) were sent out to the libraries for their use, focusing on books about wills, trusts, estate and financial matters. The program host pulled the books for display in the meeting room. The hosts could expand on the display suggestions that were sent out, or create their own based on local interest.

Equipment and Technology Used

The attorney used her laptop for a PowerPoint presentation. The rooms have pull-down screens and projectors. Chairs and a few tables were used.

Refreshments Served?

No

Average Attendance

25

Audience Evaluations/Reactions to Program

"Great"; "Informative"; "The presenter did an excellent job." Attendees thought that it was very timely and well-presented and that the speaker really knew her topic. They want more like this, and maybe a bit longer with more time for Q&A.

Lifescapes: Senior Writing Program
Northwest Reno (Nevada) Library

Description of Program

Lifescapes is an ongoing systemwide program created eleven years ago. It encourages seniors to come together, read selected literature, talk about the related subjects, and spend time writing and then sharing their stories aloud.

Lifescapes was originally established in 2000 by Washoe County Librarian Julie Machado and Dr. Stephen Tchudi, dean of the University of Nevada, Reno (UNR) English Department, Dr. Monica Grecu, professor of English at UNR, and Marc Johnson, an intern of Dr. Grecu's at the time. The program runs from September to May of each year with one or two locations offering summer classes. When the program started there was a designated staff person or volunteer at each branch who received training and resources in order to facilitate the programs, our Lifescapes Leaders! Under the guidance of the Lifescapes Leader, the participants first read a short story or memoir, or learned other tips of memoir writing, then discussed the writing and any memories that it inspired. The participants then spent thirty minutes writing memories that were triggered by the discussion, and then read them aloud during the class, if they felt like sharing. Participants also published their own books with collected memoirs and photos. These were edited by Dr. Tchudi or Julie Machado and published at the UNR Copy Center with a grant from the Nevada Humanities Committee. Each year participants were offered a chance to publish by submitting a short story on a different topic. Each participating member received a free copy. Each library branch also received a copy to catalog in the 920s. When participants publish their own book they get five free copies, and extra copies can be ordered for $5 each.

Several years ago, when budgets began to tighten up and staff members were taking on more duties because of the leaving of other staff, the program was transitioned fully to volunteers to run. The volunteers have done a great job with keeping the same feel and same outcome of the program.

In early May, Lifescapes hosts a free program to the public called Spring Swing Fling. We work together with the City of Reno Parks and Recreation Department, Washoe County Parks and Recreation Department, Osher Lifelong Learning Institute, and other area Senior Coalition members in promoting this event. This event includes a dance to music from a local big band, an ice cream social with donated ice cream from our local dairy, Model Dairy, and the launching of the Lifescapes anthologies. May is Older Americans Month, and at the beginning of this event there are proclamations read by representatives from the Senators' and Governor's offices.

For information and a Lifescapes Handbook with full instructions on creating this program see www.lifescapesmemoirs.net or go to www.washoecountylibrary.us and it is under the Seniors section of the web page.

Target Audience

Seniors 55+

Partner Organizations

University of Nevada, Reno English Department, Osher Lifelong Learning Institute (OLLI, formerly Elder College), Nevada Humanities Committee, and the Washoe County Library System

Cost

None

Number of Staff Persons Needed

Plan the Program: One, with help from volunteer facilitator

Promote the Program: One from each branch presenting a program

Produce the Program (set up the room, introduce the speaker, distribute and collect evaluations, create displays in meeting room, etc.): One to set up the room, and so forth. The volunteer facilitator does all the rest.

Hours Spent

Planning: 6–8 hours per year; Promoting: 6–8 hours per year; Producing: 2 hours per class, 2 classes per month/ site

Publicity Methods

Collateral such as flyers and handouts, small articles in the newspapers (in their calendar of events), mentioned on the library website in events and also on a link to a PDF file of monthly branch calendars. Also has its own website at www.lifescapesmemoirs.net.

Accompanying Library Resources

(types of books, videos, etc., used to create displays)

Sometimes we pull books on memoirs and how to write memoirs, and also display Lifescapes anthologies from years past.

Equipment and Technology Used

Pens and paper; eventually the participants need access to computers to put their story in electronic files to submit to the facilitators for publication in either a group anthology story or a personal story.

Refreshments Served?

Library supplies coffee and tea, members bring treats

Average Attendance

6–12 twice a month

Audience Evaluations/Reactions to Program

Very positive response. This program brings seniors out of the house and into a group that for the most part shares their same point of reference in their personal histories. They bond together as a unit. They laugh, they cry, and through listening to others' stories, they validate all of their lives. These programs create tight-knit groups, although they are always overjoyed welcoming new participants.

Classic Conversations

Laramie County (Wyoming) Library System

Description of Program

Patrons are encouraged to bring a bag lunch to the library on the Friday before every Cheyenne Symphony Orchestra (CSO) performance to listen to a preview of the concert that follows on Saturday. The Conductor of the CSO plays passages from the music chosen from the concert and talks about the composers, their experiences, and the history of the pieces. The CSO also brings its current visiting soloist to the program to play and discuss what his or her life is like as a professional musician.

Target Audience

Adults

Partner Organizations

The Cheyenne Symphony Orchestra

Cost

Staff time setting up and taking down the program, creating displays and publicity, plus a selection of limited beverages at the program

Number of Staff Persons Needed

Plan the Program: One—Adult Programming Specialist works with the CSO for every program to make sure that the visiting artist's needs are met.

Promote the Program: Three—Adult Programming Specialist, Design and Humanities Coordinator, and Webmaster work together to promote the program, which has been ongoing since 2008.

Produce the Program (set up the room, introduce the speaker, distribute and collect evaluations, create displays in meeting room, etc.): One—Adult Programming Specialist (and an occasional volunteer).

Hours Spent

7 per month—Planning: 1; Promoting: 2; Producing: 4

Publicity Methods

Classic Conversations is promoted through the local newspapers, the library calendar, website, and Facebook. We no longer send out single press releases for the program, as it has a consistent audience. The Cheyenne Symphony Orchestra occasionally does additional promotion as well.

Accompanying Library Resources

(types of books, videos, etc., used to create displays)
The book display changes each session to reflect the current selection of music/composers for the symphony as well as the instruments being used by the visiting soloist.

Equipment and Technology Used

The meeting room has built-in speakers that we hook up to the conductor's iPod, as well as microphones for the performer and the conductor. Most of these programs utilize at least one of the library's two pianos as well.

Refreshments Served?

Patrons generally bring their own lunches, but we provide coffee, tea, and hot chocolate during the winter, and cold drinks in the summer.

Average Attendance

78

Audience Evaluations/Reactions to Program

This program has been very well received since its beginning in 2008. We've never had fewer than 50 people attend, even when winter weather was severe. We don't have formal audience evaluations, but our patrons are always extremely complimentary about this program series. One of our first-time volunteers for the program promptly bought symphony tickets for the next day after his shift.

Ames Free Library Foodie Group
Ames (Massachusetts) Free Library

Description of Program
A monthly gathering of food aficionados who organize programs related to food and nutrition, food safety, ethical agriculture, cooking, specialized ingredients, baking, regional and ethnic cuisines, beverages, and more. Programs have ranged from chocolate and cheese tastings to Dutch oven cooking and foraging. This year the agenda has expanded to include an additional monthly food-related movie night. The movies so far have been of the social conscience–raising genre (e.g., *Food, Inc.* and *Two Angry Moms*), rather than more general entertainment films about food.

Target Audience
Adults primarily, but sessions sometimes attract teenagers

Partner Organizations
Community organizations such as local farms often contribute but the organizing spirit that initiated the Foodie Group came from several library patrons who are passionate about the subject. This is a true grassroots organization now in its fourth year at the Ames Free Library.

Cost
The library budgets $50 per program for speaker honoraria. Cost of materials is absorbed by the speaker or covered by small fund-raisers conducted by the Foodie members (e.g., raffles).

Number of Staff Persons Needed
Plan the Program: This is done by the group's members but coordinated by the library's Assistant Director who may spend 2–4 hours a year with the program planners.

Promote the Program: Library staff design and print flyers, maintain an e-mail list, and include all events in our website events calendar. Foodie Group organizers are in charge of press publicity and are the primary contributors to the group blog.

Produce the Program (set up the room, introduce the speaker, distribute and collect evaluations, create displays in meeting room, etc.): Foodie Group members

Hours Spent
Planning: 2–4; Promoting: 2–4; Producing: 1–2

Publicity Methods

All possible outlets are used: local media, area newspaper event calendars, flyers and save-the-date postcards, e-newsletter, website, blog, announcements at other library programs, direct e-mail reminders

Accompanying Library Resources

(types of books, videos, etc., used to create displays)
Displays are often pulled together from the library's collection for the night of the program.

Equipment and Technology Used

Video display output from computer to large-screen monitor; DVDs; filming equipment for local cable replays

Refreshments Served?

Most programs include liberal sampling of the food being discussed, or sniffs of spices, bread dipped in flavored olive oils, and the like. No special refreshments are planned unless they are part of the program topic.

Average Attendance

30–60

Audience Evaluations/Reactions to Program

This is a very popular program with excellent audience participation and feedback. It has also been replicated by other libraries in the area.

Apple Harvest Social

Manross (Connecticut) Memorial Library

Description of Program

In celebration of National Apple Month in October, we planned our monthly Senior Social around an apple theme. Local apple orchard owners did a presentation on the history of their family-owned orchard, Roberts Orchard. They highlighted the growing process and the different varieties of apples they grow. They demonstrated a manual apple peeler and slicer machine that they use for preparing apples for pies and other baked goods. A variety of apples were brought for the audience to sample. As patrons entered the library auditorium, they were given a slip of paper with the name of an apple variety on it. When it was time for refreshments, each variety was called out one at a time to come up for refreshments. This method helps eliminate everyone coming to the tables at the same time causing long lines. Patrons were asked when they registered for the program to bring their favorite apple recipe for the refreshment table. If they cared to share the written recipe they could bring that for inclusion in an apple cookbook that we compiled after the program. Participants' names and recipes were included, and the final cookbook was made available at the circulation desk for free.

Target Audience

Seniors

Partner Organizations

None

Cost

$30 for coffee, tea, paper goods, and so on. The apple orchard owners charged nothing. Apple cookbook was printed in-house using Print Shop Deluxe.

Number of Staff Persons Needed

Plan the Program: One staff person in charge of adult programming did all planning, including contacting the owners of the orchard, researching the special month, and so on.

Promote the Program: Two staff people were responsible for publicity.

Produce the Program (set up the room, introduce the speaker, distribute and collect evaluations, create displays in meeting room, etc.): Three staff members were involved in producing the program. Custodial staff was responsible for the actual room setup. The adult programming staff person introduced the special guests and acted as MC for the event and as hostess at the refreshment tables. One staff member compiled all the apple recipes and labeled dishes as they were put out.

Hours Spent

Planning: 3.5; Promoting: 4; Producing: 3

Publicity Methods

One staff person handled press releases for the local newspapers, radio stations, flyers, and generating e-mail alerts citywide. The adult programming staff person was responsible for updating the library website, including the program details on the adult activities blog and on the library Facebook page.

Accompanying Library Resources

(types of books, videos, etc., used to create displays)
Book displays of food-themed fiction titles and cookbooks

Equipment and Technology Used

Chairs for audience seating, two tables for refreshments, coffee makers, PA system for speakers, digital camera for pictures of the program

Refreshments Served?

Yes (coffee, tea, apple cider [made and donated by the Roberts Orchard], variety of apple dishes prepared by the audience)

Average Attendance

55

Audience Evaluations/Reactions to Program

The audience reaction was very positive. They especially enjoyed sampling each other's apple recipes and in many cases came back for seconds! Since the owners of the orchard were local, they knew many in the audience, which made it easier for them to speak to the group since they don't do this very often. Their presentation was very well received because of this. The other surprise hit of the event was the apple peeler and slicer machine. We had to track down where patrons could purchase them, so that generated some local sales also.

Adult Summer Reading Program
Southwest (Florida) Regional Library

Description of Program

An eight-week program to encourage adults to visit the library and register for a summer reading program. The goal is to promote reading and offer special programming and other activities tied into weekly themes.

Target Audience

Ages 18 and over

Partner Organizations

Broward County Library Foundation, Library Friends

Cost

Friends group funded $500 this year

Number of Staff Persons Needed

Plan the Program: Three

Promote the Program: At least five

Produce the Program (set up the room, introduce the speaker, distribute and collect evaluations, create displays in meeting room, etc.): Depends on the number of programs and activities offered since we have limited funds to hire outside speakers or performers. At least five staff members are needed to run the program.

Hours Spent

Planning: 40; Promoting: 20; Producing: 20

Publicity Methods

Facebook page for Southwest cluster, online catalog, in-house flyers, and letting people know from public service desk

Accompanying Library Resources

(types of books, videos, etc. used to create displays)
Weekly displays of books, music CDs, DVDs, and audiobooks that tie in with weekly theme

Equipment and Technology Used

Wii games, projector to show movies, PowerPoint presentations, computer center to conduct classes

Refreshments Served?

Yes (free popcorn, soft drinks at film presentations)

Average Attendance

Depends on program, but averages 20

Audience Evaluations/Reactions to Program

Great response. People say it's fun, they like the prizes, and they like the fact that it gives them something to do during the summer.

Prairie Bayou Cajun Band

Middleton (Wisconsin) Public Library

Description of Program

The Madison area's only all-female Cajun band—one hour of music interspersed with commentary and history about Cajun music and culture.

Target Audience

Adults 25 and older

Partner Organizations

None

Cost

$250 for the band; $15 for popcorn, soft drinks, bottled water, and so on

Number of Staff Persons Needed

Plan the Program: One
Promote the Program: One
Produce the Program (set up the room, introduce the speaker, distribute and collect evaluations, create
  displays in meeting room, etc.): One

Hours Spent

Planning: 1 (hearing the band at a Farmer's Market, making contact and communicating in a few e-mail
  exchanges)
Promoting: 2 (planning the flyer, sending out promotional information to different venues, recopying flyer,
  putting the info on library website and in a PowerPoint lobby program advertisement)
Producing: 2.5 (setting up, introducing band, enjoying band, cleaning up)

Publicity Methods

Local paper, city electronic mailing list, flyers, book display on Cajun music, PowerPoint display in library
lobby, local alternative newspaper (includes online version)

Accompanying Library Resources

(types of books, videos, etc., used to create displays)
Display included books on Cajun music, as well as American music in general; display included a poster of a
Thomas Benton painting titled "Sources of Country Music"

Equipment and Technology Used

None

Refreshments Served?

Yes (popcorn, various beverages)

Average Attendance

64 (pretty good for a cold, wintry night in Wisconsin!)

Audience Evaluations/Reactions to Program

Loved them! I've already invited them back for 2012. Lots of positive comments and thank-yous after the program.

Novel Talk: Smart Conversations for Serious Readers
Tulsa (Oklahoma) City-County Library

Description of Program
Novel Talk is a series of thrice-annual programs that the Readers' Library Department of the Tulsa City-County Library inaugurated in January of 2008.

Designed to bridge the worlds of nonfiction and fiction and solidly supporting the view that "literature is the lie that tells the truth," Novel Talk aspires to explore serious cultural and real-world issues—mental illness, gender relations, and war, to name a few topics we've tackled in the past—through the prism of a variety of award-winning novels. Most Novel Talks feature a moderator and a panel of distinguished experts related to the topic at hand. Spring Novel Talks are generally a bit different and explore offbeat topics (vampires in literature) or employ different formats (half-day seminar, series of four weekly presentations).

Target Audience
Adults in Tulsa and Tulsa County, particularly those who consider themselves serious readers or wish to discuss social and cultural issues at depth

Partner Organizations
We have had various sponsors who provide publicity and door prizes, including local restaurants in the downtown area (where our Central Library is), gift shops, and even a bar. The Friends of the Tulsa City-County Library has also been a partner.

Cost
Varies. Most often, just staff time and publicity materials because speakers do not charge, but we have paid for an out-of-town author's airfare and hotel and a $50 speaking fee for a moderator once. Additionally, we have had one program with refreshments at a cost of $75, but that cost was covered by the Friends of the Library.

Number of Staff Persons Needed
Plan the Program: One coordinator and two additional staff members as support. We either begin with a novel and brainstorm related themes and possible speakers, or with a theme and try to find a novel to fit.

Promote the Program: Three—Coordinator writes the description and promotional copy and then works with a graphic designer and public relations specialist (in library's PR office) to create posters, flyers or bookmarks, and press release. The PR specialist works with area TV stations and publications for additional publicity.

Produce the Program (set up the room, introduce the speaker, distribute and collect evaluations, create displays in meeting room, etc.): Coordinator and support staff members work together to get the room ready and introduce speakers.

Hours Spent
Planning: 5–10; Promoting: 5; Producing: 1.5

Publicity Methods
Library's monthly event guide, posters at all libraries and other neighborhood locations, flyers or bookmarks at library desks, a series of e-mails to electronic distribution list developed since 2008 at Novel Talk events (usually an initial e-mail two months beforehand, then one e-mail per week the month before the program)

Accompanying Library Resources
(types of books, videos, etc., used to create displays)
We usually decorate the room itself (an auditorium) with interesting quotes and photos or other artwork relevant to the topic, and we always begin the program with a five- to ten-minute "book talk" to summarize the novel. Additionally, we often include video clips from movies or TV shows that either relate to the topic or the novel itself, which the moderator then uses as a springboard for further discussion.

Equipment and Technology Used
Laptop and overhead projector

Refreshments Served?
Usually not. There are exceptions, as when we asked the Friends to partner with us and they provided both money and volunteers.

Average Attendance
100

Audience Evaluations/Reactions to Program
Generally very positive. We have a "diehard" cohort of people who eagerly look forward to the programs and often get new audience members based on the topic or novel. As one person wrote in an e-mail after a program: "Thanks for all you do to get this Novel Talk together—it is a real pleasure to be so intellectually stimulated. This last one was particularly resonant for me, as I'm sure for all of us in one way or another."

Additionally, we were honored with the 2011 Community Leadership Award from the Oklahoma Humanities Council for creating and implementing the Novel Talk program.

Literature with Bite: Vampires in Books, Film, and Pop Culture
(part of the Novel Talk series of programs)

Tulsa (Oklahoma) City-County Library

Description of Program

A two-hour symposium (with three presentations) exploring vampires in literature, movies, and popular culture. We began with a talk from an English professor with a background and interest in gothic literature explaining "How to Read Bram Stoker's *Dracula*," continued with a presentation on "17 Reasons Why Vampires Are Popular Today" from a library staff member, and ended with a Q&A with *Vampire a Go-Go* novelist (and Marvel Comics' "vampire expert") Victor Gischler.

Target Audience

Tulsa and Tulsa County area adults, particularly younger adults (ages 20 to 35)

Partner Organizations

Friends of the Tulsa City-County Library provided volunteers and money for refreshments. They also advertised the program to their members through e-mail and flyers.

Cost

Staff and volunteer time, $75 for refreshments (provided by Friends of the Library), $500 for airfare and hotel for out-of-town author

Number of Staff Persons Needed

Plan the Program: Two—Coordinator and second staff member as support

Promote the Program: Three—Coordinator wrote description and promotional copy. The library's graphic designer created logo, poster, and half-page flyers. The library's PR specialist sent out a press release and worked with local newspapers for articles (see Publicity Methods).

Produce the Program (set up the room, introduce the speaker, distribute and collect evaluations, create displays in meeting room, etc.): Coordinator and support staff members work together to get the room ready and introduce speakers.

Hours Spent

Planning: 10; Promoting: 5; Producing: 2

Publicity Methods

Library's monthly event guide; half-page flyers at library desks; posters at all libraries; e-mails to Novel Talk distribution list (about five total); press release which resulted in two lengthy articles, one in the largest local newspaper (*Tulsa World*) and one in the independent newspaper (*Urban Tulsa Weekly*)

Accompanying Library Resources

(types of books, videos, etc., used to create displays)
We decorated the room with photos of famous vampires (from Dracula to Count Chocula) and quotations about vampires.

Equipment and Technology Used

Laptop and overhead projector for first two presentations; SurveyMonkey to solicit and organize registrations

Refreshments Served?

Yes (punch, cookies, cupcakes, decorated to go with vampire theme—cookies had smiley faces with fangs, and cupcakes had two puncture "wounds" with red gel frosting to simulate vampire bites)

Average Attendance

This was a one-time event; 85 people attended (on a Saturday morning!).

Audience Evaluations/Reactions to Program

Very positive! Many people stayed afterward to talk to the speakers (and each other).

Not So Quiet! Concert Series
St. Louis (Missouri) Public Library

Description of Program

A summer concert series, featuring a variety of music, held outside of Central Express Branch in downtown St. Louis.

Target Audience

Downtown workers and residents

Partner Organizations

Partnership for Downtown St. Louis, KDHX 88.1 Radio

Cost

$7,000 (band fees and poster printing)

Number of Staff Persons Needed

Plan the Program: One

Promote the Program: Four

Produce the Program (set up the room, introduce the speaker, distribute and collect evaluations, create displays in meeting room, etc.): Three

Hours Spent

Planning: 16; Promoting: 8; Producing: 4

Publicity Methods

Press release to various media outlets; posting to several cultural activity websites (including library's website); library newsletter (reaches 75,000+ people); posters in downtown restaurants, cafés, and other businesses and area schools; Facebook, Twitter, FourSquare; and radio announcements

Accompanying Library Resources

(types of books, videos, etc., used to create displays)

The library sets up a table to display CDs and books about similar music being performed that particular day. We also sign up patrons for summer reading club.

Equipment and Technology Used

PA system for bands (microphone, speakers, soundboard)

Refreshments Served?

No. There are several restaurants and food stands in the area.

Average Attendance

Approximately 100 per show (800–1,000 total) for a two-month series of weekly concerts

Audience Evaluations/Reactions to Program

Downtown workers love that they can sit outside during their lunch breaks and enjoy a great variety of music for an hour. The only complaint we've received was about the heat in June and July. This is our fourth year doing the series, and every year, several people ask, "Are you doing this again next year? I hope so."

Know Dirt

Deschutes (Oregon) Public Library

Description of Program

Know Dirt was a series of ten programs hosted throughout Deschutes Public Library branches during the month of March. The series featured programs highlighting all things dirty. For example, we had local nursery owners deliver programs on deer resistant gardening, edible landscaping, and cold climate gardening. A local expert on worms offered two programs on how to raise worms for composting, and Sarahlee Lawrence, author of *Riverhouse* and local farmer, added two readings to the schedule.

Target Audience

Adults

Partner Organizations

Local nursery owners, local author

Cost

$800 (honorariums, posters, bibliographies, event guides)

Number of Staff Persons Needed

Plan the Program: Two
Promote the Program: Two
Produce the Program (set up the room, introduce the speaker, distribute and collect evaluations, create displays in meeting room, etc.): Four

Hours Spent

Planning: 10; Promoting: 6; Producing: 35

Publicity Methods

Press releases for the series and for individual programs, posters, bibliographies, counter displays, library event guide, library website

Accompanying Library Resources

(types of books, videos, etc., used to create displays)
Bibliographies, gardening books

Equipment and Technology Used

PowerPoint slideshows, laptops, projectors

Refreshments Served?

No

Average Attendance

25

Audience Evaluations/Reactions to Program

Programs that provide residents of Deschutes County the opportunity to learn a new skill are popular programs at the library. We had good attendance at the majority of the series programs, and the audience was engaged, entertained, and educated.

Coming Together in Skokie

Skokie (Illinois) Public Library

Description of Program

Skokie is one of the most diverse towns in Illinois. We have a population of approximately 65,000 residents, and nearly 100 languages are spoken in households in our Village. More than 40 percent of the population is foreign-born, and immigrants continue to settle here in Skokie, most recently coming from Iraq and Pakistan.

Coming Together in Skokie seeks to explore in-depth a different culture each year through reading and discussing a common book, complemented by a variety of educational and cultural programming. The program serves to promote cross-cultural awareness and understanding and support community-building. The program launched in late January 2010 with a focus on the Indian American community. More than 3,000 people attended thirty-two events held over a period of six weeks. The events included: book discussions at the library, high schools, and the local community college; meeting Vineeta Vijayaraghavan, author of *Motherland*, the chosen book for the first program; and a variety of cooking, dance, and educational programs. In 2011 the Filipino community was highlighted, and more than 3,200 people attended thirty-six events that took place throughout the winter. In addition to the primary adult book, selected books included elementary, junior-high, and teenage materials that were incorporated into local school curricula and activities.

Target Audience

Adults

Partner Organizations

Village of Skokie, School District 219 (Skokie high schools), English Language Learners Center of Niles Township, Skokie Park District, Oakton Community College, Skokie Hospital, Indian Community of Niles Township, Filipino Community of Skokie, Skokie elementary schools, and various local businesses and organizations

Cost

Each organization pays for its own costs. There is no separate budget for the overall project.

Number of Staff Persons Needed

Plan the Program: Fifteen to twenty—includes representatives from all the different partner organizations

Promote the Program: Five—Communications leaders from different partner organizations

Produce the Program (set up the room, introduce the speaker, distribute and collect evaluations, create displays in meeting room, etc.): Varied event to event

Hours Spent

Due to the number of venues and partners, this has not been tracked thus far.

Publicity Methods

Website, press conference, informational video, local newspapers and newsletters. Additionally, a color, 20-plus-page booklet is created and distributed that includes: Welcome letter from the Mayor of Skokie, listing of events and featured books, questions for book discussions for the featured books and suggested readings, historical information and summary of traditions of the featured community, list of notable members of the community, and common phrases in native languages.

Accompanying Library Resources

(types of books, videos, etc., used to create displays)

Adult fiction displays with books written by the celebrated community were maintained each year. The library's book discussion groups read the featured adult book, and a book discussion kit was created for area book groups to check out. Last, art from the Filipino community was displayed in the library's exhibit space throughout this past year's program.

Equipment and Technology Used

Varied event to event

Refreshments Served?

Varied event to event

Average Attendance

3,100/year

Audience Evaluations/Reactions to Program

The program has been tremendously successful and has received positive feedback from participants and media outlets both years. Additionally, in 2011 our featured author, Cecilia Brainard, was so impressed with the program that after her three-day visit with our library and high schools, she sent us one hundred books by Filipino and Filipina authors, some of which were signed first editions, to be added to our collection.

Job Seeker Series

Arlington Heights (Illinois) Memorial Library

Description of Program

When tough economic times set in and unemployment began to rise, the library responded with a series of forty-two workshops and presentations that were conducted over an eight-month period to help job seekers in Arlington Heights attain the skills and knowledge needed to find employment.

A sampling of program topics included: Using Social Networking in Your Job Search, Hidden Interview Skills, LinkedIn workshops, Uncommon Sources of Job Opportunities, and Finding a Job after 50. Program presenters included individuals from local businesses, human resources consultants, authors, the local community college's career center, and so on.

Funding for the series was made possible by vocational grants totaling $5,000 from the Rotary Club of Arlington Heights. Because of the series' success, these programs are continuing to be funded by successive vocational grants currently totaling $8,000. The partnership has garnered attention both locally and nationally, including a mention on the front page of the *New York Times*. The Rotary Club was recently honored with a "vocational service of the year" award for its commitment to the series.

Target Audience

Adults seeking a variety of up-to-date information to attain the skills and knowledge needed today to find employment

Partner Organizations

Rotary Club of Arlington Heights

Cost

Rotary Club paid for the program presenters. The library paid for the printing of the Job Seekers brochure ($2,400 for 2,000 copies).

Number of Staff Persons Needed

Plan the Program: Two—Adult Programmer and Business Librarian collaborated on local resources
Promote the Program: Three—Communications and Marketing staff members promoted through library newsletter, brochure, posters, local media outlets, and library e-newsletters
Produce the Program (set up the room, introduce the speaker, distribute and collect evaluations, create displays in meeting room, etc.): One—Adult Programmer or Business Librarian

Hours Spent

Planning: 15; Promoting: 10; Producing: 14

Publicity Methods

Bimonthly newsletter, local media outlets, website, special brochure given out at community career centers and job support groups, and a photo and feature in the local newspaper

Accompanying Library Resources

(types of books, videos, etc., used to create displays)

Handouts provided by the individual presenters, list of library resources available, résumé workbook, job networking and support group guide, and a program survey so that we could follow up with attendees after each series of programs

Equipment and Technology Used

Tables, chairs, microphone, computer projector and screen

Refreshments Served?

No

Average Attendance

About 40. It ranged from 15 to 80 depending on the type of program. Some were workshops geared toward a limited number of attendees. Some were lecture-oriented geared toward a larger audience.

Audience Evaluations/Reactions to Program

More than 1,570 people attended the first series for job seekers. In a survey of attendees, 78 percent of those who responded found the programs valuable to their job search.

Here are two excerpts from the evaluations:

"My husband and I went to [a program] with Karen Evertson. I aced an interview using her techniques a few days later. The company was so impressed they hired me right away . . . My husband also found a job using her information. We are now both employed and able to support our family. Thanks for making a difference in a tough economy!"

"Great speaker, good information and motivational! I have been in the search for a long time, so I struggle to learn something new—most sessions like this are merely review for me, but there were so many ideas that had not occurred to me. I totally enjoyed the presentation, and gained a wealth of knowledge and resources for my career search."

Here are comments made by Arlington Heights Mayor Arlene Mulder:

"The library's partnership with the Rotary Club of Arlington Heights to provide the successful 'Job Seekers' series the past 18 months demonstrates the library's relevance in the most challenging labor market in decades . . . Arlington Heights is now regarded as a leader in providing people with the resources they need when looking for work, which we know contributes to the economic vitality of our village."

Bad Art Night at the Library!

Emmet O'Neal (Alabama) Library

Description of Program

Bad Art Night is a chance to roll up your sleeves and get your hands dirty in a relaxing and fun atmosphere. Our patrons gather in the library's meeting room where we have tables and chairs set up facing the large screen at the front of the room. Audience members are shown a brief slide presentation of images from the Museum of Bad Art in Boston and asked to create some Bad Art of their own! We turn on some jazz and introduce participants to the four areas of the room where the different types of art are represented (painting, drawing, collage, and mixed media or sculpture) and explain that they can play in any of the areas, but they can only enter one piece of bad art into the contest for worst art. We give away prizes ($25 gift cards to local shops and restaurants) in each category: worst painting, worst collage, worst drawing, and worst sculpture (or sometimes mixed media). The audience votes on the all-around worst art of the night as well.

We give participants about forty-five minutes to create their masterpiece, have snacks, and sip some of their favorite beverage. As they finish their art, participants are asked to take their finished work to the proper section (painting, drawing, etc). After all the bad art is lined up around the room, we give each person five colored tickets. Each type of artwork has a corresponding colored ticket. Each participant is able to vote once in each of the four categories and use the last ticket to vote for worst art of the night. The Worst Art winner receives a $25 gift card (so someone could win twice!). We have had several patrons take their bad art home and frame it. Mixed Media and Collage are *always* great sources of amusement as patrons take the opportunity to comment on popular culture through bad art since most magazines are library discards of *People, Vogue, Rolling Stone, Time*, and the like. There have been some interesting discussions over the mixed media and collage areas through the years!

Target Audience

For our library, we do this program specifically for the Adult Summer Reading program, but I am sure teens would have fun as well!

Partner Organizations

None for this program

Cost

Since the program consists of arts and crafts, this can be a pretty cheap program. We usually raid our Children's Department for construction paper, crayons, glue sticks, sequins, glitter, and anything else we can come up with. Over the years we have collected chalks, heavier and better quality drawing paper, paints and paintbrushes, cardboard boxes, pipe cleaners, macaroni noodles of all shapes and sizes, and more! This would be a really great way to incorporate upcycling or recycling into your programming. It usually costs us approximately $100 to purchase some supplies or refill areas used from the previous year. We do not always spend $100, because some years we find we have enough materials.

Number of Staff Persons Needed

Plan the Program: One or two

Promote the Program: When we prepare for Bad Art Night it's always part of Adult Summer Reading, so we all promote it when we talk up the summer reading program. Really, though, you could promote this with just one person.

Produce the Program (set up the room, introduce the speaker, distribute and collect evaluations, create displays in meeting room, etc.): Two to three, because of the amount of art supplies required and setup of food and tables.

Hours Spent

Planning: 1–2; Promoting: 4; Producing: 4

Publicity Methods

Adult Summer Reading calendar (if applicable), flyers, library calendar and website, e-mail alerts, blog, Facebook, announcements at regular programming events, local newspapers, and online calendars. We were asked to be on our local NPR affiliate one year to talk about Bad Art Night—the word spreads quickly! We also invite local art teachers to join us.

Accompanying Library Resources

(types of books, videos, etc., used to create displays)

We show a slide presentation of collections from the Museum of Bad Art (Boston; www.museumofbadart.org/collection) to get everyone in the mood. We also create a display of art books, DVDs, and magazines . . . but we make sure to remind participants that the goal is to make *Bad* art!

Equipment and Technology Used

We set up four tables in the meeting room. One corner has supplies for painting, one corner has supplies for drawing (pencils, chalks, and crayons), one corner has materials for collage (everything from magazines to macaroni noodles to bits of tissue paper and glitter), and the last corner we set aside for sculpture where we put pipe cleaners and any other objects and items we collect through the year that lend themselves to sculpture. Some years this corner becomes mixed media because patrons will take items from both sculpture and collage. We also make sure to have water so people can rinse paintbrushes, wipe up glue and glitter spills, and such.

Refreshments Served?

Yes! We usually serve heavy appetizers or pizza and wine along with soft drinks and dessert.

Average Attendance

30–40

Audience Evaluations/Reactions to Program

This year will be the fifth year to produce Bad Art Night, and it's now an annual favorite. Our adult patrons love being able to get their hands dirty and enjoy the company of new and old friends. It's a fun way to laugh and be a little silly. We have also found it a great way to meet new people and chat about what our patrons are reading, because the librarians sit down at the tables and create bad art as well!

Pros and Cons of the Iraq War

Carroll County (Maryland) Public Library

Description of Program

No matter what your views are on the Iraq War, you will learn something new. Please join us for this informative discussion program with Mark Croatti, MA, Instructor of Comparative Politics at The George Washington University, and Martin K. Gordon, PhD, adjunct Professor of History, University of Maryland University College, and adjunct member of the graduate faculty at American Military University. They are both guest speakers from the Johns Hopkins University Odyssey Program.

Target Audience

Adults interested in politics, history, the Middle East, and terrorism

Partner Organizations

Johns Hopkins University Odyssey Program of Non-Credit Liberal Arts Courses

Cost

$600 ($300 per speaker)

Number of Staff Persons Needed

Plan the Program: One

Promote the Program: One as primary promoter, via announcements and flyer distribution at community meetings she attended, but circulation and information staff in six libraries and outreach helped promote it to library customers, too.

Produce the Program (set up the room, introduce the speaker, distribute and collect evaluations, create displays in meeting room, etc.): One

Hours Spent

Planning: 1.5; Promoting: no extra time, already attending meetings; Producing: 1 for setup and cleanup, 2 for program

Publicity Methods

Library website, newsletter, flyers, and announced program and distributed flyers at community meetings

Accompanying Library Resources

(types of books, videos, etc. used to create displays)
History books, books on the Middle East, and the like

Equipment and Technology Used

Presenters requested blackboard/whiteboard

Refreshments Served?

Yes (pretzels, cookies, water)

Average Attendance

26

Audience Evaluations/Reactions to Program

Several audience members asked the speakers questions. The questions and comments from the audience were thoughtful. The speakers encouraged lively discussion.

Mile in My Shoes: The Human Library

Multnomah County (Oregon) Library

Description of Program

Duplicating a program started by a group of activists in Denmark, we invited three people with unique experiences to give insight into their lives. The speakers became "living books" and allowed the audience to ask questions and see life from another perspective. The speakers included a Muslim woman, a homeless man, and a woman who was a victim of sex trafficking. We engaged a local radio interviewer from Oregon Public Broadcasting to act as a moderator. The programs were also made available through podcast on our website.

Target Audience

Teens and adults

Partner Organizations

Oregon Public Broadcasting

Cost

Speaker costs: $200 for each speaker, and $200 for a moderator for each session, for a total of $1,200; refreshment costs of $60 for each session, for a total of $180

Number of Staff Persons Needed

Plan the Program: Two

Promote the Program: Two

Produce the Program (set up the room, introduce the speaker, distribute and collect evaluations, create displays in meeting room, etc.): One

Hours Spent

Planning: 12; Promoting: 4; Producing: 5

Publicity Methods

Announcements on website, Twitter, Facebook; press releases to media outlets; flyer distribution; in-house promotion. An article on the program was published in the local *Street Roots* newspaper.

Accompanying Library Resources

(types of books, videos, etc. used to create displays)
None

Equipment and Technology Used

Sound system, podcasting equipment

Refreshments Served?

Yes (light snacks with coffee, tea, water)

Average Attendance

50

Audience Evaluations/Reactions to Program

We received profuse thanks from audience members for hosting these programs, especially in reaction to the Muslim woman's presentation. Many interested community members stayed after the session on homelessness to hear more about how they could help with the problem. In the question periods, people asked thoughtful and interesting questions.

The Mind

Appleton (Wisconsin) Public Library

Description of Program
A video/discussion series based on the nine-part PBS series *The Mind*. After each film, a health-care professional answered questions.

Target Audience
General public

Partner Organizations
None

Cost
$525 for *The Mind*

Number of Staff Persons Needed
Plan the Program: Two
Promote the Program: Three
Produce the Program (set up the room, introduce the speaker, distribute and collect evaluations, create displays in meeting room, etc.): One

Hours Spent
Planning: 5; Promoting: 7; Producing: 20

Publicity Methods
Bookmarks, posters, newspaper press releases and ads, letter openers

Accompanying Library Resources
(types of books, videos, etc., used to create displays)
Health topics

Equipment and Technology Used
Video projector/screen

Refreshments Served?

Yes (hot beverages)

Average Attendance

50

Audience Evaluations/Reactions to Program

Uniformly positive. Participants appreciated having the health-care professional provide current information.

Antiques and Collectibles Appraisal Fair

Rocky River (Ohio) Public Library

Description of Program

Our "Antiques and Collectibles Appraisal Fair" invited people to bring their treasures to our auditorium from 1:00 p.m. to 3:00 p.m. on a Saturday afternoon. We hired five appraisers, each of whom had expertise with such items as china, silver, and art.

As people came through the doors, we matched them up, by item, to the most appropriate appraiser and gave each person a number. We color-coded the numbered slips of paper with each individual appraiser's sign so people knew exactly where to go when we announced, for instance, "Blue 5 through 10 can join the line." We called them up in groups to keep the line moving. Even though people were allowed to bring two items, they met with only one appraiser because of time constraints. But because each appraiser had a minimum of thirty years in the business, even if that second item wasn't in his or her area of expertise, the appraiser was almost always able to impart some information.

As numbers were called, people approached their appraiser seated at a table and had their items appraised.

Target Audience

Adults

Partner Organizations

None

Cost

$100 per appraiser

Number of Staff Persons Needed

Plan the Program: One

Promote the Program: One

Produce the Program (set up the room, introduce the speaker, distribute and collect evaluations, create displays in meeting room, etc.): Four—two to distribute and call the numbers; two to set up the room

Hours Spent

Planning: 8; Promoting: 2; Producing: 5

Publicity Methods

Signage and flyers throughout the library, press releases to local newspapers, flyers to area antique shops

Accompanying Library Resources

(types of books, videos, etc., used to create displays)
Books on antiques were displayed on units throughout the library.

Equipment and Technology Used

One 8-by-12-foot table per appraiser

Refreshments Served?

No

Average Attendance

300 patrons attended our first fair; 200 came to our second.

Audience Evaluations/Reactions to Program

People commented on how much they appreciated this opportunity and were pleased that they weren't charged for it. Many simply were thankful to learn more about their possessions from the knowledgeable appraisers we found at area antique shops.

One Book, One Vancouver—Vogon Poetry Slam and Vog-Off

Vancouver (British Columbia) Public Library

Description of Program

The Vogon Poetry Slam and Vog-Off was part of the Library's One Book, One Vancouver, a citywide book program (www.vpl.ca/obov). During this successful program we hosted eight outrageous programs created to bring alive the featured book, *The Hitchhiker's Guide to the Galaxy* by Douglas Adams. The Vogon Poetry Slam and Vog-Off was one of the most popular programs by far, garnering rave reviews from attendees and calls for a repeat of the program in 2011.

Participants were invited to come to the "Restaurant at the End of the Universe" to "enjoy" the work of twelve brave contestants who presented the universe's *worst* poems "slam style" for the audience's and judges' pleasure (or not) in an effort to win a spiffy grand prize of $100!

The evening's activities started with complimentary barf bags with careful instruction on their proper use and ubiquitous Don't Panic towels for any intergalactic emergencies. The enthusiastic crowd then made the Vogon Poetry Pledge, promising, among other things, to "wholeheartedly agree to encourage the contestants to do their worst," and to "promise not to vomit on the floor or die." This somber moment was then followed by the head judge of the contest and library staffer serenading the crowd with two recorders played through his nose, a feat that was wildly appreciated by the slightly nauseated audience.

With that the contest began, and the costumed contestants of all ages, carefully chosen from numerous entries, began their fight to be the worst Vogon Poet in Vancouver. The judges' panel, also carefully selected from the audience, were subjected to a wide variety of horrible poetry, giving bonus points to those who included made-up words, references to the library, and interstellar subject matters.

For a list of complete rules and regulations, go to www.vpl.ca/obov/vogonpoetry.html.

Target Audience

Aimed at teens through adults; however, audience ages ranged from children to senior citizens

Partner Organizations

The Friends of the Vancouver Public Library, H. B. Fenn & Company, HR Macmillan Space Centre, White Dwarf Books, The Word on the Street Festival, and the *Vancouver Sun*

Cost

$539 (MC's honorarium: $200; judges' honorariums [Bookmark gift certificates]: $45; prizes [1st—$100, 2nd—$50, 3rd—$25]: $175; decorations, barf bags, and door prizes [not complete]: $119; door prizes: in kind)

Number of Staff Persons Needed

Plan the Program: A subcommittee of about five people from the One Book, One Vancouver working group came together to plan the event. Each committee member took on a few of the tasks required to bring the event together, such as vetting contestants' poetry, coordinating participants, and booking the MC, creating speaking notes and fictional contestant bios, purchasing set décor materials, making alien balloon sculpture table settings and flower bouquets for the winners, and so on.

Promote the Program: The Library's Marketing and Communications team (one Manager, one Coordinator, one Programming Librarian, and one Graphics Tech) created and distributed the publicity for the program.

Produce the Program (set up the room, introduce the speaker, distribute and collect evaluations, create displays in meeting room, etc.): Six

Hours Spent
Planning: 4; Promoting: 12; Producing: 20 (includes shopping and day of production)

Publicity Methods
Media releases; One Book, One Vancouver Guide; announcements on Twitter and Facebook; strong web presence on Library's website and the One Book, One Vancouver site; posters; interviews on radio; sent out to targeted electronic mailing lists; in-house event calendars; out-of-house event calendars; Craigslist; word of mouth; promotion at other related events; and the like.

Accompanying Library Resources
(types of books, videos, etc., used to create displays)
Please see the One Book, One Vancouver Guide for examples of other resources used to promote this program: www.vpl.ca/obov/pdfs/OBOV_2010_ReadersGuide_revOCT04.pdf.

Equipment and Technology Used
Tables, chairs, microphones, 2 projectors and screen, 2 laptops, stereo for background music, sci-fi-inspired decorations, prizes, balloon sculptures, crowns and bouquets, lava lamps, confetti guns, refreshment serving equipment, nose recorders, personalized vomit bags, Don't Panic towels, prizes, various costume bits, point cards for judges, a podium at door for both ambience and checking in contestants, and many decorative towels

Refreshments Served?
Yes (juice, tea, coffee)

Average Attendance
130 (full house)

Audience Evaluations/Reactions to Program
An overwhelming success. Many audience members and contestants stopped to tell staff how much they enjoyed the event. Several e-mailed to share their compliments and request that the event become an annual program at the Library.

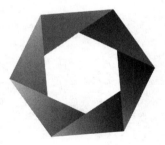

Well, there you have it. Now it's time to take one of these great programs out for a test drive. Or create your own itinerary. The journey ahead should be an exciting one. Best of luck!

Resource Directory

The following resources complement the information that is included within this book. The directory is arranged to coincide with the chapters that you have just read. These sources were selected because they provide valuable information in a coherent manner. I have used many of these resources many times over the years. I hope they will serve you as well as they have served me.

GETTING STARTED

ALA Public Programs Office. Public Programs Office of the American Library Association. www.ala.org/offices/ppo.

This site presents various resources for libraries engaged or interested in programming, from professional development opportunities to information about grants and awards. The Public Programs Office produces *Programming Librarian*, "an online community and resource center for librarians who plan and present cultural, community programs," complete with feature stories and videos highlighting library program successes, an active blog, an event calendar for planning tie-ins, and a forum for professional sharing.

Brown, Barbara J. *Programming for Librarians: A How-to-Do-It Manual.* New York: Neal-Schuman, 1992.

A good, concise guide to library programming, this book also contains information on programming for children and young adults. The information provided on community analysis is particularly helpful.

McGovern, Gail, Amy Bernath, Kenna Forsyth, Laura Kimberly, and Kathleen Stacey. *Program Planning: Tips for Librarians.* Chicago: Continuing Library Education Network Exchange Round Table, American Library Association, 1997.

This publication is very brief—25 pages plus appendixes—and is geared primarily toward libraries that are planning an in-house staff development or training activity. The authors offer tips on how to conduct a needs assessment, design the program content, and set up a room (both seating and equipment). This is a good resource for librarians who intend to create and present the content themselves.

O'Donnell, Peggy, and Patsy Read. *Planning Library Programs.* Chicago: Public Library Association, 1979.

This title is no longer in print, but copies are available via interlibrary loan. It is another slim publication (49 pages). Although the authors encourage the reader to host humanities programs sponsored by the National Endowment for the Humanities (NEH), this work offers some great nuggets of information. Highlights include a community survey worksheet and a chart that helps the reader select the best program format.

Painter, Chris, and Maureen Crocker. *Rated "A" for Adult: A Guide to Library Programming.* Pinecliff, CO: Colorado Library Association, 1991.

No longer in print, this brief, 51-page manual contains good, basic information, including how to get program ideas and what programs will work in your community, and a programming checklist. Beware: the 16-page programming resource list contains organizations that are predominantly located in Colorado.

Ranier, Raymond. *Programming for Adults: A Guide for Small- and Medium-Sized Libraries.* Lanham, MD: Scarecrow Press, 2005.

In this book, an adult services librarian describes his experiences developing library programs for adults from scratch. Ranier covers educational programs, cultural programs, craft programs, and book groups. He also discusses ways to target your marketing toward specific audiences.

Robertson, Deborah A. *Humanities Programming for Libraries: Linking Libraries, Communities, and Culture.* Chicago: American Library Association, 2005.

The director of ALA's Public Programs Office provides a broad view of how and why to offer adult programs in your library, beginning with making the case for programming through establishing goals and objectives that tie into your library's mission. She shares reasons that people attend library programs and then discusses strategies for targeting certain audiences and effectively engaging underserved populations. In addition to providing worksheets for developing goals and objectives, a planning calendar, and a budget worksheet, Robertson offers several examples of successful collaborations and library program series. The book offers a wealth of possible program types to inspire creativity, including series, themes, formats, and tie-ins to calendar events.

Robotham, John S., and Lydia LaFleur. *Library Programs: How to Select, Plan, and Produce Them.* 2nd ed. Metuchen, NJ: Scarecrow Press, 1981.

This book is no longer in print, but it is a wonderful resource. The first part of the book is organized by program formats. This is the book's greatest strength. The authors lead you through what you need to know if you intend to host a discussion group, film series, workshop, and so forth. For each format, the authors discuss staffing needs, equipment needs, space requirements, suggestions for topics, and more. The second part of the book explains how to select and find programs. The third part offers advice on how to produce the program.

Rubin, Rhea Joyce. *Humanities Programming: A How-to-Do-It Manual*. New York: Neal-Schuman, 1997.

Here is another strong title from Neal-Schuman. Although geared toward humanities programs, this book offers good advice on planning, funding, budgeting, publicizing, and evaluating programs that can be used for any type of adult programming.

RUSA-SUPS Services to Adults Committee. *Adult Programming: A Manual for Libraries*. Chicago: Reference and User Services Association, American Library Association, 1997.

Confession: I served on the committee that wrote this manual, so I am quite fond of it. Yet another slender publication (57 pages), the manual leads you through the adult programming process from beginning to end. It contains a set of appendixes with examples of a programming policy, a program planning worksheet, a program planning checklist, a press release, a PSA, and program evaluation forms.

DEMOGRAPHICS

De Rosa, Cathy, Joanne Cantrell, Matthew Carlson, Margaret Gallagher, Janet Hawk, and Charlotte Sturtz. *Perceptions of Libraries, 2010: Context and Community; A Report to the OCLC Membership*. Dublin, OH: OCLC, 2011. www.oclc.org/reports/2010perceptions/2010perceptions_all.pdf.

OCLC published this report based on a survey of more than 2,000 Americans to share "the online practices and perceptions of the 2010 information consumer." Here you can find statistics about which technologies are growing in use and by how much, ways that the recession has affected our communities, and how all these factors affect library use. In addition to reporting practices, this document gives advice from patrons for ways in which libraries can improve services by becoming more responsive and user-driven. Use this report as the national context for your own process of getting to know your community!

Public Library Association. *Statistical Report 2010: Public Library Data Service*. Chicago: Public Library Association, 2010.

This annual report gives statistical information on the populations and library use—including number of programs and program attendance—for nearly 1,000 public library systems in the United States and Canada. Data tables will let you quickly compare your own library to others of its size. Latest editions also include a chapter on technology in public libraries.

The State of America's Libraries: A Report from the American Library Association. Chicago: American Library Association, 2011. www.ala.org/news/sites/ala.org.news/files/content/mediapresscenter/americaslibraries/state_of_americas_libraries_report_2011.pdf.

This annual report provides insight into trends in library use as well as insight into Americans' beliefs and values as they pertain to libraries. The data are based on a phone survey of about a thousand Americans. It also highlights major issues, challenges, and campaigns within U.S. libraries and provides information on initiatives and institutions that support the library community.

Tuggle, Ann Montgomery, and Dawn Hansen Heller. *Grand Schemes and Nitty-Gritty Details: Library PR That Works*. Littleton, CO: Libraries Unlimited, 1987.

Although no longer in print, this title is worth a look if you can locate a copy. The purpose of this book is to ensure that your library runs a successful public relations program. The book stresses the importance of making connections with your community. One section called "Fact-Finding and Research" gives some excellent tips on conducting surveys.

U.S. Census Bureau. *American FactFinder*. Washington, DC: U.S. Dept. of Commerce, Economics and Statistics Administration, U.S. Census Bureau. factfinder2.census.gov.

The Census Bureau has recently launched a new version of *American FactFinder*, allowing you to search by city, zip code, metro area, or county. You can spend a week gathering data from this source—unemployment rates, percentage of the population that speak a language other than English, information on race, number of people who work from home, and much more. Just browsing this source will give you programming ideas.

BUDGETING AND FUNDING

American Library Association and the Taft Group Staff. *The Big Book of Library Grant Money: 1998 to 1999*. Chicago: American Library Association, 1998.

This source includes thousands of philanthropic programs that have either given grants to libraries in recent years or list libraries as potential recipients. A new 8th edition was published in 2012.

Annual Register of Grant Support. New Providence, NJ: R. R. Bowker, published annually.

This massive piece of work contains more than 3,000 grant support programs. Fortunately, *libraries* is one of the words indexed, so you can zero in on funding sources for libraries. The volume also contains a section on proposal writing.

Barber, Peggy, and Linda D. Crowe. *Getting Your Grant: A How-to-Do-It Manual for Librarians*. New York: Neal-Schuman, 1993.

Although this title is getting older, the step-by-step approach, geared specifically toward libraries, is very helpful. The authors take you from the idea stage, through the grant-writing process, and into the follow-through stage, which includes publicizing your newly funded project. The book also includes many checklists and sample grant applications.

Dolnick, Sandy, ed. *Friends of Libraries Sourcebook*. 3rd ed. Chicago: American Library Association, 1996.

This title is written as a guide to be used by Friends organizations. It does include a chapter on programming, which is useful as it gives you ideas about the types of programs that are attractive to Friends groups. Another chapter on fund-raising includes programming ideas that can raise funds, such as meet-the-author events. This book should help you identify program ideas that your Friends group will be interested in sponsoring.

Farmer, Lesley S. J. *When Your Library Budget Is Almost Zero*. Englewood, CO: Libraries Unlimited, 1993.

This book contains a section on offering library programs and includes good advice on how to ask funders for money and what to do after you get your money.

The Foundation Directory. New York: Foundation Center, published annually.

Each of the more than 10,000 foundations listed here possesses at least $2 million in assets or gives at least $200,000 a year. *Libraries* is an indexed term.

Miner, Jeremy T., and Lynn E. Miner. *Proposal Planning and Writing*. 4th ed. Westport, CT: Greenwood Press, 2008.

This source offers a clear introduction to grant seeking, followed by chapters on how to find both public and private funding. The authors provide detailed information on every step of the process, from preproposal tasks to examples and instructions for each section of your proposal. The book also lists resources to use when searching for funds, with updated web sources.

Prentice, Ann E. *Financial Planning for Libraries*. 2nd ed. Lanham, MD: Scarecrow Press, 1996.

This in-depth guide to financial planning provides a thorough chapter on sources of library funding (taxes, state funding, federal funding, private funding, and fee-based services).

Reed, Sally Gardner. *Even More Great Ideas for Libraries and Friends*. New York: Neal-Schuman, 2008.

Written by two executives from Friends of Libraries U.S.A., this book gives a great number of real programs sponsored by Friends groups both to raise the profile of the library in the community and to raise funds. Almost every example includes an image of publicity used. Check this out (and also its predecessor, *101+ Great Ideas for Libraries and Friends*) and you'll definitely come up with ideas for developing programs alongside funders and supporters. Friends groups actually planned and produced the bulk of the programs included in the book.

Rounds, Richard S. *Basic Budgeting Practices for Librarians*. 2nd ed. Chicago: American Library Association, 1994.

Although geared toward an administrator who is developing the overall library budget, this is a good source that leads you step-by-step through the budgeting process. The author covers community profiling, presenting your budget to the decision makers, and managing the budget.

Warner, Alice S. *Budgeting: A How-to-Do-It Manual for Librarians*. New York: Neal-Schuman, 1998.

Written for librarians, this title offers detailed assistance in establishing budgets. It also offers guidance on how to manage funding that is achieved through grants, endowments, and fundraising events.

SELECTING A TOPIC

Chase's Calendar of Events. Chicago: Contemporary Books, published annually.

This is such an amazing resource. You can really use it a couple of ways. You can browse through the months to find festivals, anniversaries, and celebrity birthdays and then plan a program around one of these events. Or, you might already have a program idea in mind, such as a cooking program on making desserts. When should you have the program? Check *Chase's*. It'll tell you that October is National Dessert Month!

YOUR TARGET AUDIENCE

Alire, Camila, and Orlando Archibeque. *Serving Latino Communities: A How-to-Do-It Manual for Librarians*. New York: Neal-Schuman, 1998.

I love this book. I've read it cover-to-cover at least twice. A great book to read if you are just beginning to serve a Latino population, it offers demographic information on Latinos, provides in-depth information on how to conduct a needs assessment, includes programming ideas and resources, offers information on effective outreach, includes funding tips, and much, much more!

Jones, Patrick. *Connecting Young Adults and Libraries*. New York: Neal-Schuman, 1992.

A chapter titled "Programming" includes information on planning, promoting, and producing YA programs. This chapter also contains detailed information about how to produce specific programs for YAs, such as book discussion groups, and includes strategies, such as listening and "keeping your cool," that library staff can use to better communicate with YAs.

Roberts, Ann, and Richard J. Smith. *Crash Course in Library Services to People with Disabilities*. Santa Barbara, CA: Libraries Unlimited, 2010.

This book is a good general resource for recognizing and addressing issues that affect access to library services for people with disabilities, including programming. In addition to presenting issues related to library facilities, demographics, marketing, and outreach, the authors provide several specific program ideas for including and targeting people with disabilities in your program offerings. Ideas include technology-rich programs such as gaming events, as well as traditional book discussions, and opportunities for raising community awareness and inclusion, such as observation of Deaf Awareness Week. A section titled "Library Services to Baby Boomers and Older Adults" touches on programming ideas to improve the physical and mental health of boomers and seniors and points to additional resources for further programming ideas.

Rothstein, Pauline, and Diantha Dow Schull. *Boomers and Beyond: Reconsidering the Role of Libraries*. Chicago: American Library Association, 2010.

This book brings together chapters written by professionals in a variety of fields, from anthropology to gerontology, in order to explore the aspects and implications of longer life spans and the changing ways that older people are living. Articles in part 1 address various ways in which aging people may experience issues such as health, work, and spirituality. Part 2 discusses how various institutions including libraries can support an older population effectively. Part 3 brings the focus squarely onto library services, sharing librarians' perspectives on ways to engage midlifers and older adults as library users. Stephen Abram's chapter in particular includes a great collection of sample programming ideas.

Rubin, Rhea Joyce. *Intergenerational Programming: A How-to-Do-It Manual for Librarians*. New York: Neal-Schuman, 1993.

The author offers detailed information on providing intergenerational programs and partnering with other agencies in your community. The book includes detailed examples of successful programs from around the United States along with program-planning worksheets on specific types of intergenerational programs, such as family literacy projects and history programs.

Trotta, Marcia. *Managing Library Outreach Programs: A How-to-Do-It Manual for Librarians*. New York: Neal-Schuman, 1993.

Although it focuses on outreach services for children and young adults, this title is a good resource to consult if you are just getting started with outreach services. It reviews the history of outreach services in libraries, provides information on conducting a community needs assessment, and offers insight into the importance of forging community partnerships. The author includes examples of actual outreach programs and explains how to develop outreach staff.

IDENTIFYING PERFORMERS

Encyclopedia of Associations: Regional, State, and Local Organizations. Detroit, MI: Gale Research, published annually.

I use this resource constantly. It lists more than 22,000 associations, and just about any topic—diabetes, dance, or darts—will have one to several associations that dedicate themselves to that topic. Many of these associations will have local chapters. Give them a call. They might be happy to supply a speaker or performer.

The Whole Person Catalog No. 4: The Librarian's Source for Information about Cultural Programming for Adults. Chicago: American Library Association, Public Programs Office, 1998.

Here you will find many discussion and literary programs developed by libraries, state humanities councils, historical societies, and other groups. Contact information is included. If you come across a program that looks interesting, find out more about it. It might be funded by an agency, such as the NEH or your state humanities council, that will present the program at your library and provide you with a scholar to lead the discussion series.

BOOK DISCUSSIONS

Balcom, Ted. *Book Discussions for Adults: A Leader's Guide.* Chicago: American Library Association, 1992.

Although out of print, this book is a great place to start when planning a discussion group at your library. The author does a great job of articulating the value that book discussions can bring to those who attend. Balcom gives good advice on conducting a community needs assessment, selecting titles,

and preparing for and leading a book discussion. He also provides information on how to evaluate the success of your book discussions.

John, Lauren Zina. *Running Book Discussion Groups: A How-to-Do-It Manual.* New York: Neal-Schuman, 2006.

This book provides clear and complete guidance to every part of the process of presenting a successful book discussion program. The author begins with the elements of getting started, including participant recruitment, book choices and the many creative ways to approach selection, logistical details for holding your group, and methods for generating effective publicity. Part 2 of the book focuses on practices for maintaining healthy discussion, with tips for group facilitation—from icebreakers to the development of supplemental materials—as well as ideas for hosting an author event and developing an online book discussion group. A large selection of very thorough sample book discussion plans makes up part 3 of the book, followed by a thoughtfully annotated list of print and online resources for book discussion groups.

Libraries for the Future, Americans for Libraries Council, and MetLife Foundation. *The Reading America Toolkit: How to Plan and Implement an Intergenerational and Intercultural Reading and Discussion Program at Your Library.* New York: Libraries for the Future, Americans for Libraries Council, 2005. www.aging.unc.edu/programs/nccolle/lff/ReadingAmericaToolkit.pdf.

This publication gives you the nuts-and-bolts information you'll need to start your own intergenerational or intercultural reading and discussion program. The toolkit stresses the importance of forming community partners to help you develop your reading programs and attract participants from throughout your community. It includes sections on finding a partner, planning the program, conducting outreach to build awareness of your program, and marketing.

TECHNOLOGY

Lietzau, Zeth, and Jamie Helgren. *U.S. Public Libraries and the Use of Web Technologies, 2010.* Denver, CO: Colorado State Library, Library Research Service, 2011. www.lrs.org/documents/web20/WebTech2010_CloserLookReport_Final.pdf.

Check out this study for a "snapshot in time" that details which technologies libraries are using and with what levels of success. The report describes how many libraries are adopting web technologies such as social media, RSS, blogging, and websites optimized for users of mobile devices. The study found that libraries that were early adopters of technology saw greater increases in library visits, circulation, and program attendance than those libraries that had not been active in adopting new web technology.

OCLC Online Computer Library Center. *WebJunction.* Dublin, OH: Author, continuously updated. www.webjunction.org/explore-topics.html.

Here you'll find "a place for you to learn and share ideas about how to successfully integrate technology in your library." Articles provide basic overviews of subjects like mobile devices and social networking, and members post lengthy reports to this site. Spend some time here if you'd like to get some great ideas for using Web 2.0 to market or produce programs.

Peters, Thomas A. *Library Programs Online: Possibilities and Practicalities of Web Conferencing.* Santa Barbara, CA: Libraries Unlimited, 2009.

Author Thomas Peters developed a collaborative online programming initiative called OPAL (Online Programs for All), and in this book he shares the expertise he developed through years of experience with web conferencing. He assumes little in the way of prior knowledge, experience, or resources on the part of the reader, starting with some basic definitions and presenting the rationale and purpose for offering programs online. Peters then delves into the types of programs that could be presented online, giving real-life examples. If you're looking for ways to expand your programming audience by reaching folks who don't come into your building, this is a great book to get you started.

PUBLICITY

Dowd, Nancy, Mary Evangeliste, and Jonathan Silberman. *Bite-Sized Marketing: Realistic Solutions for the Overworked Librarian.* Chicago: American Library Association, 2010.

This book provides an array of new marketing ideas, from an in-depth exploration of WOMM (Word-Of-Mouth-Marketing) to an overview of Web 2.0 tools. The authors make the case that such user-driven marketing techniques require a commitment to seeking active audience participation. This intimacy with your audience will enhance your ability to plan programs that focus on the interests of your library users. Short chapters deliver ideas in a clear and concise style while including the specific details needed to make your press releases and podcasts as professional and effective as possible. Throughout the book, you'll find ideas to spark creative programming and help you build buzz around your programs.

Field, Selma G., and Edwin M. Field. *Publicity Manual for Libraries: A Comprehensive Professional Guide to Communications . . . A Book That No Library Should Be Without.* 1st ed. Monticello, NY: Knowledge Network Press, 1993.

This great, step-by-step resource will help you write news releases and news stories, target your story to radio, and evaluate the success of your publicity efforts. It includes many sample press releases.

Gould, Mark R. *The Library PR Handbook: High-Impact Communications.* Chicago: American Library Association, 2009.

The authors included in this collection come from various specialty areas in addition to libraries, such as communications and the hospitality industry. Chapters cover topics such as effective multicultural communication, partnerships, and special events. Specific chapters on Web 2.0, podcasts, and gaming in the library provide ideas for programming, as well as resource lists for more sites to learn about incorporating technology into your offerings.

Leerburger, Benedict A. *Promoting and Marketing the Library.* Rev. ed. Boston: G. K. Hall, 1989.

This title contains good information on publicity techniques and a 36-page chapter called "Special Programs and Events."

Walters, Suzanne. *Marketing: A How-to-Do-It Manual for Librarians.* New York: Neal-Schuman, 1992.

The author leads you through the marketing process, which involves talking to our customers and developing services that meet their needs. The process also involves strategies (public relations, advertising, direct mailings, etc.) that your library can use to ensure that patrons are aware of the services you offer. Sample marketing plans are included.

Wolfe, Lisa A. *Library Public Relations, Promotions, and Communications.* New York: Neal-Schuman, 2005.

This is an excellent resource to consult if your library is new to the public relations/communications process. It will lead you through the development, implementation, and evaluation of a public relations/communications plan. The author also includes outlines and checklists that will help you create effective newsletters and brochures, and offers tips on working with the media and conducting outreach activities. The book has a chapter titled "Programs and Special Events as Communications Tools."

EXAMPLES OF SUCCESSFUL ADULT PROGRAMS

Public Library Association, Small and Medium-Sized Libraries, 1986 Conference Program Committee. *Adults Only: Program Ideas of Interest to Your Adult Patrons.* Chicago: Public Library Association, 1986.

This out-of-print title contains ten detailed examples of programs for adults, including descriptions of the programs, equipment and staff needed, publicity used, and so forth. Some of the examples are a "Chef of the Month" program and a series of programs on antiques. The book includes guidelines to consider when planning programs, a program planning worksheet, and staff and patron evaluation forms.

Smallwood, Carol. *Librarians as Community Partners: An Outreach Handbook.* Chicago: American Library Association, 2010.

Through sixty-six brief articles written by thirty-four different librarians, this densely packed volume offers a rich array of great sample library programs and strategies for success. Including as many programs offered inside libraries as outside them, the book features the creative ways librarians have brought resources to community members despite tough economic times. Chapter topics include senior outreach, diversity outreach, book festivals, and how to work with local media and collaborate with local organizations to promote programs.

Index